© 2007 by SCALA Group, S.p.A., Firenze, su licenza E-ducation.it, Firenze

This 2007 edition published by Barnes & Noble, Inc. by arrangement with
SCALA Group, S.p.A.

Texts: Cristina Bucci, Susanna Buricchi
Project director: Cinzia Caiazzo
Editor-in-chief: Filippo Melli
Design: Gruppo Bandello Comunicazione
Graphics: Puntoeacapo srl
Translation: Heather Mackay Roberts

ISBN-13: 978-0-7607-8886-8
ISBN-10: 0-7607-8886-3

Printed and bound in China

1 3 5 7 9 10 8 6 4 2

RENAISSANCE ART

Cristina Bucci
Susanna Buricchi

BARNES & NOBLE

NEW YORK

TABLE OF CONTENTS

1. THE STUDY OF ANTIQUITY

Introduction 15

Ancient words in a new language 16
The architecture of Brunelleschi 18
Brunelleschi: the study of classical monuments
and the dome of Florence cathedral 20
Masterpieces *Filippo Brunelleschi, Pazzi Chapel* 22
The competition of 1401: Brunelleschi and Ghiberti 24

Love of antiquity and expressive tension:
Andrea Mantegna 26
Masterpieces *Mantegna, Dead Christ* 28
Leon Battista Alberti, theorist and architect 32
Masterpieces *Leon Battista Alberti, Tempio malatestiano* 34
Florentine Palaces 46

The rediscovery of sculpture in the round
and of movement 38
Donatello and bronze casting
with the *cire perdue* method 41
Masterpieces *Donatello, Judith and Holofernes* 42
Luca della Robbia and the glazed terracotta 46
The *Cantorie* of Luca della Robbia and Donatello 49

2. THE DISCOVERY OF PERSPECTIVE

Introduction 53

The innovators 54
The perspective panels of Brunelleschi 55
Masaccio: ethical tension and formal renewal 56
Masterpieces *Masaccio, Trinity* 58
The frescoes in the Brancacci Chapel: the representation
of man and of urban space 60
Donatello and "stiacciato" relief 62
The Baptismal font in Siena 63

Transition and Experimentation 64
Lorenzo Ghiberti and the baptistery doors in Florence 65
Fra Angelico: a new sense of the sacred in painting 68
Masterpieces *Fra Angelico, Annunciation* 72
The Journey of the Magi. The Benozzo Gozzoli Chapel 76

	Mino da Fiesole, Desiderio da Settignano and Rossellino	78
	Paolo Uccello and experimentation with perspective	80
Masterpieces	*Paolo Uccello, Battle of San Romano*	82
	Piero della Francesca: artist and theorist	84
	The *Legend of the True Cross* in San Francesco in Arezzo	87
Masterpieces	*Piero della Francesca, Flagellation*	90
Masterpieces	*Piero della Francesca, Sacra conversazione*	94
	The Sant' Apollonia Last Supper by Andrea del Castagno	98

3. THE DETAILED DEPICTION OF REALITY

	Introduction	*101*
	Light in Flemish painting	**103**
	Jan Van Eyck and Flemish realism	104
Masterpieces	*Jan Van Eyck, The Virgin of Chancellor Rolin*	*106*
	Hugo Van del Goes: monumentality and minute description	111
	Human emotion in the work of Rogier Van der Weyden	112
Masterpieces	*Rogier Van der Weyden, Deposition*	*114*
	Portrait painting in Northern Europe	**118**
	The *Arnolfini Wedding* by Jan Van Eyck	119
	Daily Life in Sacred Flemish Painting	**120**
	Robert Campin or the Master of Flémalle	121
	Flemish Interiors in the *Annunciation* by Master of Flémalle	122
	Flemish Interiors in the *Annunciation* by Rogier Van der Weyden	123
	Landscape in Flemish Painting	**124**
	The *Adoration of the Mystical Lamb* by Jan Van Eyck	126
	Commercial exchange and artistic relations between Northern and Southern Europe	**130**
	The *Portinari Altarpiece* by Hugo Van der Goes in Florence	132
	Devotion and realism	**134**
	Painting and Sculpture:	

TABLE OF CONTENTS

the great German altarpieces   134
Wolfang Altarpiece by Michael Pacher   135
The expressionism of Veit Stoss   136
Enguerrand Quarton and Provencal Art   137
Catalan retables   138

4. MAN AT THE CENTER OF THE UNIVERSE
Introduction   141

The portrait   **142**
Fifteenth-Century portrait busts   143

Equestrian and Funerary Monuments   **144**
Funerary Monuments. The Humanist tomb   146

Men, saints and heroes   **148**
The Sacra conversazione   150
Cycles of "Famous Men"   152
The *Triumphs* of Mantegna   153
The Bridal Chamber in Mantua   154
Masterpieces   *Andrea Mantegna, Oculus of the Bridal Chamber* 156
The Medici Family depicted in the *Adoration
of the Magi* by Botticelli   160
Antonello da Messina   162
Masterpieces   *Antonello da Messina, Pietà*   164
Pietro Perugino: a cultured
and productive artist   168
The *Cycle of the Months* in Palazzo Schifanoia   171

Art and Science   **174**
Leonardo da Vinci's manuscripts   176

5. THE VENETIAN SCENE
Introduction   179

Giovanni Bellini and Venetian classicism   **180**
Masterpieces   *Giovanni Bellini, Presentation in the Temple*   182
The Young Bellini: his relationship with Mantegna,
nature and the antique   184
Color, light, and opening onto landscape   185
Masterpieces   *Giovanni Bellini, Pietà*   186
Bellini's encounter with Antonello da Messina   188

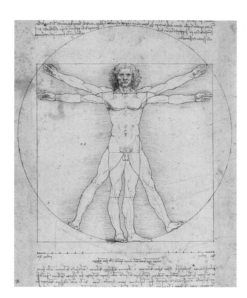

6. LORENZO THE MAGNIFICENT

Introduction   193

Artists at the time of Lorenzo the Magnificent   **194**

Sandro Botticelli and ideal beauty   196

Masterpieces   *Sandro Botticelli, The allegory of Spring*   198

Masterpieces   *Sandro Botticelli, Birth of Venus*   202

The Republic of Savanarola and Botticelli's late works   204

The inventiveness of Filippino Lippi   206

Art in Rome at the time of Sixtus IV
and Alexander VI   **210**

The fifteenth-century decoration of the Sistine Chapel   211

The early years of Leonardo and Michelangelo
in Florence   **212**

Naturalism in the art of Verrocchio   214

Masterpieces   *The Baptism of Christ by Verrocchio*   216

Masterpieces   *The narrative flair of Domenico Ghirlandaio*   217

Michelangelo in Ghirlandaio's workshop:
drawings by the great masters   219

Bramante and Leonardo in Milan   **220**

Leonardo and sfumato: *The Virgin of the Rocks*   221

Masterpieces   *Leonardo, Last Supper*   222

Michelangelo: The early years   **226**

The Madonna of the Stairs
and the *Battle of the Centaurs*   226

The statues on the *Arca di San Domenico* in Bologna   228

The Vatican *Pietà*   230

Masterpieces   *Michelangelo, Bacchus*   234

7. FLORENCE AND THE BIRTH
OF THE "MODERN MANNER"

Introduction   239

Leonardo in Florence   **240**

Sacred subjects: the depiction of feeling   241

Life flowing into portraiture: the *Mona Lisa*   243

The exploration of nature   244

The *treatise on painting* by Leonardo   245

TABLE OF CONTENTS

	The presence of Michelangelo	**246**
	David: Republican ideals	*247*
	Michelangelo and Leonardo	*248*
	The St Matthew	*249*
Masterpieces	*Michelangelo, Holy Family, The Doni Tondo*	*250*
	Palazzo Vecchio, the "school of the world"	*254*
	The *Battle of Anghiari* by Leonardo	*255*
	The *Battle of Cascina* by Michelangelo	*257*
	Raphael in Florence	**258**
	The Virgin and Child: variations on a theme	*259*
Masterpieces	*Raphael, Madonna of the goldfinch*	*260*
	The psychological portrait	*262*
	Michelangelo's last years in Florence	**264**
	The facade of San Lorenzo	*264*
	The New Sacristy in San Lorenzo	*265*
	The Laurentian Library	*270*
	Michelangelo's aesthetics:	
	"unfinished works"	*271*
Masterpieces	*Self-portraits of painters*	*273*
	8. THE ARTISTIC SUPREMACY OF ROME	
	Introduction	*277*
	The architecture of Bramante	**278**
Masterpieces	Rules and proportions	*279*
	The Belvedere and the architecture of antiquity	*280*
	The project for St Peter's	**282**
Special focus	*Centrally-planned buildings*	*284*
	Michelangelo in the service of Julius II	**286**
	The tomb of Julius II	*287*
Masterpieces	*Michelangelo Buonarroti, Dying slave and Rebel slave*	*288*
	The ceiling of the Sistine Chapel	*290*
	Raphael for Julius II	**293**
	La Stanza della Segnatura and the celebration	
	of Humanist culture	*294*
Masterpieces	*Raphael, School of Athens*	*295*

TABLE OF CONTENTS

Masterpieces | The Stanza di Eliodoro and the celebration of Catholic Doctrine | 300
| Portraits and altarpieces | 303
| *Raphael, Madonna della seggiola* | *306*

Raphael and Leo X: the rebirth of antiquity | **308**
The Stanza dell'Incendio di Borgo | 309
The cartoons for the tapestries in the Sistine Chapel | 312
Raphael and antiquity: the letter to Leo X | 313

Grotesque decoration in the school of Raphael | **314**

Raphael the architect in the service of Agostino Chigi | **315**
The decoration of the Villa Farnesina | 317
The Chigi Chapel in Santa Maria del Popolo | 319
The model villa: villa Madama | 320

Rome at the time of Bramante, Raphael and Michelangelo | **321**
Baldassarre Peruzzi and Antonio da Sangallo the Younger | 322
The architects of St Peter's | 323
The paintings of Sebastiano del Piombo | 324
The training of Jacopo Sansovino in Rome and Florence | 325

9. VENICE AND THE BIRTH OF TONAL PAINTING
Introduction | 327

The revolutionary work of Giorgione | **328**
Giorgione in the *Lives* of Vasari: the painter who did away with drawing | 329
The *sacra conversazione* in a landscape | 331
The classical style of the Fondaco dei Tedeschi | 332
Hidden meaning in paintings for a select few | 332
Masterpieces | *Giorgione, The Tempesta* | *334*

The late works of Giovanni Bellini | **338**
Light and color in the Venetian tradition | 339
Mythological subjects | 340

TABLE OF CONTENTS

Early Titian: naturalism and classical restraint   **341**

Early work: the Fondaco dei Tedeschi   342

Allegorical subjects   343

Masterpieces   *Titian, Sacred and profane Love*   *344*

The renewal of religious subjects   346

The mythological paintings   348

Masterpieces   *Titian, Venus of Urbino*   *350*

The portraits   354

The contributions of Giorgione and Titian   **356**

Sebastiano del Piombo and the monumental style   357

Contact with the north: Albrecht Dürer in Venice   **358**

Masterpieces   *Albrecht Dürer, Adoration of the Magi*   *360*

Dürer and Italian Art   364

Dürer and the spread of northern prints   366

10. THE RENAISSANCE IN CRISIS : THE EMERGENCE OF MANNERISM

Introduction   369

Jacopo Pontormo, an unstable genius   370

Art in Europe from the Renaissance to Mannerism   **374**

The Renaissance in Germany   375

Hieronymus Bosch and
the Flemish Renaissance   377

Masterpieces   *Hieronymus Bosch, Garden of Earthly delights*   *378*

The school of Fontainbleau   382

The court of Rudolph II of Prague   383

**Rome in the mid-sixteenth century:
the papacy of Paul III Farnese**   **384**

Michelangelo the painter: the *Last Judgement*
and the Pauline Chapel   385

Michelangelo the architect   386

Michelangelo: the late sculptures   387

Masterpieces   *Michelangelo, Pietà Rondinini*   *388*

Painting during the pontificate of Paul III Farnese   390

TABLE OF CONTENTS

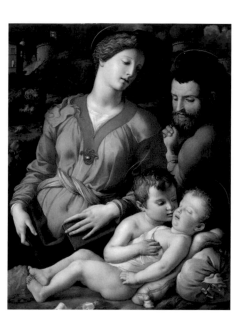

**11. VENICE IN THE SECOND HALF OF THE SIXTEENTH
CENTURY**
Introduction   393

Titian's late works: the free handling of paint   **394**
Space and light in the Farnese *Danae*   395
Titian: the dramatic intensity of the late works   396

Mannerism in Venice   **397**

**The chief painters after Titian: Tintoretto,
Veronese and Jacopo Bassano**   **398**
Tintoretto: theatrical effects   400
Masterpieces   *Tintoretto, Miracle of St Mark*   404
Paolo Veronese: opulence and color   406
Masterpieces   *Veronese, Wedding feast at Cana*   408
Jacopo Bassano and rustic genre painting   410

The architecture of Andrea Palladio   **412**
Palladio in Vicenza   413

Special focus   **Theaters**   414
The Venetian churches: San Giorgio Maggiore
and the Redentore   415
The villas in the Veneto   418
Masterpieces   *Andrea Palladio, La Rotonda*   420

CRONOLOGY   **422**
INDEX OF ARTISTS   **430**

1. The study of Antiquity

The cultural life of the Renaissance was characterized by the rediscovery of the classical world. The humanist concept of "rebirth", which is what the word Renaissance means, implies a reawakening of both the spirit and the art of antiquity. The theory of a return to the values of antiquity set down by Petrarch in the fourteenth century influenced artists well into the fifteenth century. Even masters who still worked in the late-gothic style found themselves drawn to classical art, but it was in early fifteenth-century Florence that the study of Antiquity became a really dominant force. Through history and literature the classical world was both explored and repossessed, and became the source of a startling new creativity. For the leading figures of the Florentine Renaissance – Brunelleschi, Donatello and Masaccio – classicism represented not only a source of inspiration in their creative lives but also the key to rediscovering nature, to the representation of the human body, and to understanding the workings of the body and the spirit.

2

3

1. Facing page: Andrea Mantegna, *St Sebastian*, detail, about 1480. Paris, Louvre.

2. Pantheon, 118-125 A.D. Rome.

3. Boy taking a thorn out of his foot, Roman copy of a 2nd-century B.C. original. Florence, Uffizi.

ANCIENT WORDS IN A NEW LANGUAGE

Throughout the Middle Ages references to classical models in the subject matter, figures and composition of art had never disappeared completely.

But at the beginning of the fifteenth century, as a result of the investigations and research carried out by three Florentine artists, the architect Brunelleschi, the sculptor Donatello and the painter Masaccio, classicism became a means of renewing form, giving it realism, but also a means of exploring reality. The Florentine experience was unique, well in advance of the rest of Italy

4

5

4. Andrea Mantegna,
St George, detail, about
1460. Venice, Accademia.

5. *Sarcophagus
of Bellicus*, detail.
Pisa, Camposanto.

and Europe, but soon spread to other Italian centers. After Florence the city most excited by the new movement was Padua, with its ancient university, where the humanists played a decisive role. It was Donatello who brought the Florentine advances to that northern city where he stayed for some ten years from 1443. His presence excited a new interest in the search for clas- sical models and was of fundamental importance to the development of Mantegna, one of the most passionate interpreters of antiquity in the north of Italy. In nearly the whole of Lombardy, on the other hand, the archeologi- cal discoveries led to the creation of a rich and complex ornamental reper- tory, never going beyond a superficial interpretation of the antique.

6

7

8

6. Donatello, detail from the High Altar, 1446-50. Padua, Basilica of Sant'Antonio.

7. Antique *torso of a satyr*, 2nd century B.C. Florence, Uffizi.

8. Masaccio, *St Peter baptizing the neophytes*, detail, 1424-27. Florence, Santa Maria del Carmine, Brancacci Chapel.

THE ARCHITECTURE OF BRUNELLESCHI

Buildings designed by Filippo Brunelleschi are distinctive for the harmonious proportions of their form and component parts as well as for their relationship to their surroundings. The loggia of the Ospedale degli Innocenti in Florence, begun in 1419, and built on one side of Piazza della Santissima Annunziata, serves to unite the building to the whole square. The structure is based on the modular repetition of a square bay with a cross vault; the nine arches are supported by classically inspired Corinthian capitals. The churches of San Lorenzo and of Santo Spirito, also designed by Brunelleschi in Florence, adopt the same scheme as used for the loggia of the Ospedale, developing it symmetrically on both sides of the interior. San Lorenzo, with side aisles and chapels, is remarkable for the perfect proportions of each part to the whole, creating an extraordinarily unified effect. In the church of Santo Spirito the space is more articulated, due to the curvilinear treatment of the chapels and the wider area of the presbytery. In his other buildings, such as the Old Sacristy in San Lorenzo, the Pazzi Chapel, and the rotunda of Santa Maria degli Angeli, Brunelleschi experimented with other centrally-planned solutions, with a strong classical resonance.

9

10

11

9. Filippo Brunelleschi, San Lorenzo, view of the interior, 1421-60. Florence.

10. Filippo Brunelleschi, Ospedale degli Innocenti, detail, 1419-44. Florence.

11. Filippo Brunelleschi, Ospedale degli Innocenti, 1419-44. Florence.

**12. Filippo Brunelleschi,
Santo Spirito, view of the
interior, 1440-65. Florence.**

BRUNELLESCHI: THE STUDY OF CLASSICAL MONUMENTS AND THE DOME OF FLORENCE CATHEDRAL

In the mid-fourteenth century the building of Florence cathedral, begun in 1296, had reached the point just above the octagonal drum designed to support a giant dome but it was not until 1418 that a competition was announced for plans to complete it. Brunelleschi and Ghiberti were joint winners, but Brunelleschi's superior technical ability eventually weighed in his favor and he was given sole charge of the project. The problem to be solved was essentially a technical one: the disappearance of specialized workers and the shortage of any carpenters capable of constructing the huge scaffolding required to support the dome while it was undergoing construction. Brunelleschi's direct study of ancient monuments such as the Pantheon, where all the problems related to supporting the weight of the dome had been dealt with internally, gave him the confidence to adopt a revolutionary solution. He would construct the dome without wooden supports but with mobile scaffolding. He could dispense with the more cumbersome support by building with bricks laid in herring-bone fashion as used in Roman construction, giving solidity to the walls without overburdening them. The weight was evenly distributed with the construction of a double shell which also meant that the inner and stronger dome bore the weight of the outer one. Brunelleschi not only devised a remarkable technical solution but completed a building begun more than a hundred years earlier in a breathtakingly new way, dramatically altering the panorama of Florence.

13

14

13. Filippo Brunelleschi, Wooden model for the lantern for the cupola of Santa Maria del Fiore. Florence, Opera del Duomo Museum.

14. Filippo Brunelleschi, Santa Maria del Fiore, lantern on the cupola, 1420-36. Florence.

**15. Filippo Brunelleschi,
Santa Maria del Fiore,
cupola, 1420-36. Florence.**

PAZZI CHAPEL
Filippo Brunelleschi, from 1430, Florence, Santa Croce

EXTERIOR
The noble Florentine family of the Pazzi commissioned Brunelleschi to build the chapel and their coat of arms appears four times in the spandrels below the dome.

The portico outside gains movement and grace from the contrast of shaded openings below with the projecting solids of the surfaces above.
The rigid, square geometry of the facade is broken by the large, central, barrel arch,
derived from Roman triumphal models.

The building is built on a square plan, covered by an umbrella dome. There are two, small, barrel-vaulted side wings.

The interior is charged with a dynamic conception of architecture which exploits the expressive potential of color. The simple white plastered walls are broken by architectural elements in grey pietra serena, by the blue and white glazed terracotta roundels of the Apostles by Luca della Robbia, and by the painted frieze on the architrave.

The brightly colored roundels in the spandrels of the dome of the Evangelists are the work of Andrea della Robbia.

INTERIOR

The chapel is the first renaissance building in which both the exterior and interior are of monumental scale and character. The distribution of space is very complex, based on the geometrical relationship between straight and curved lines.

The square ground plan meets the circular dome above it through the play of arches and spandrels, creating the cubic and circular space typical of a chapel.

The lower half of the chapel has a static arrangement with vertical lines and a series of pilasters at regular intervals along the walls, surmounted by a striking horizontal architrave.

On the upper level the dynamic structural interplay of arches and circles terminates in the ribs of the dome and its central oculus.

In 1401 a competition was announced in Florence to make a new bronze door for the baptistery. The competitors were to cast a quadrilobe panel depicting the *Sacrifice of Isaac*, of the same shape and size as those on the fourteenth-century door made by Andrea Pisano. The panels by Ghiberti, who won the competition, and by Brunelleschi have survived, and a comparison between the two is worth making. Ghiberti's composition is perfectly contained within the frame: the scene takes place in a unified space and the

16

17

**16-17. Lorenzo Ghiberti,
Sacrifice of Isaac and
detail, 1401. Florence,
Bargello.**

beautiful torso of Isaac is a clear reference to the classical world. Brunelleschi's panel adopts a number of innovatory solutions. The figures in the foreground are not confined by the frame with the donkey occupying the dominant position almost by way of a challenge.

The scene is fragmented into a series of independent episodes that highlight the dramatic impact of the main event: the arrival of the angel to stay Abraham's hand. Brunelleschi also pays direct homage to antiquity in the figure in the left foreground adopted from a Hellenistic sculpture of a boy removing a thorn from his foot.

18

19

20

18-20. Filippo Brunelleschi, *Sacrifice of Isaac* **and details, 1401. Florence, Bargello.**

LOVE OF ANTIQUITY AND EXPRESSIVE TENSION: ANDREA MANTEGNA

Andrea Mantegna trained in Padua between 1441 and 1448, under Francesco Squarcione, an eccentric artist and antiquarian, also a collector of curios, whose workshop was a popular meeting place with artists. From the Tuscans active in Padua Mantegna acquired his skill in sculptural, linear drawing and the capacity to represent space according to the laws of perspective, while his contact with Venetian antiquarians gave him the opportunity to deepen his understanding of the classical world. His archeological approach to antiquity is evident in his fascination with classical lettering, seen in the *Episodes*

from the lives of St James and St Christopher in the Ovetari Chapel in the Paduan church of the Eremitani.

Even in his early works it is clear that classicism was more to Mantegna than a means of rediscovering reality and man but also served as an elaborate stage design for his figures that were depicted with statuesque solidity and expressive power. The idea of the antique, as indispensable to the civilized artist, is demonstrated in the *Agony in the Garden* in the National Gallery of London, where a city reminiscent of Rome rises against a barren, expressionistic and symbolic background. In a late work, the *Dead Christ* in the Brera, Mantegna translates his interest in antique art into his own realistic and harsh language.

21

26

21. Andrea Mantegna, *Agony in the garden*, about 1460. London, National Gallery.

22. Facing page: Andrea Mantegna, *Martyrdom of St Christopher*, detail, 1457-59. Padua, church of the Eremitani.

DEAD CHRIST
Andrea Mantegna, about 1480, Milan, Brera

SUBJECT

Mantegna draws on classical sculpture in high relief: the tragedy of the scene is accentuated by the violent foreshortening of the reclining figure and the emphatic treatment of the damaged body, the swollen chest in particular.

The painting represents the body of the dead Christ, stretched out on a marble table and mourned over by the Virgin and St John.

The supine body of Christ is viewed by the spectator from only a slightly higher point than his feet torn by the nail wounds in the foreground, imparting a strong emotional tension to the scene.

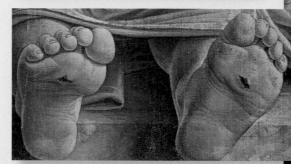

The dramatic impact is highlighted by the livid coloring of the body and the crisp treatment of the drapery which has all the appearance of marble.

The pathos is further increased by the grieving faces to the left, observed with unflinching attention to all their physical traits.

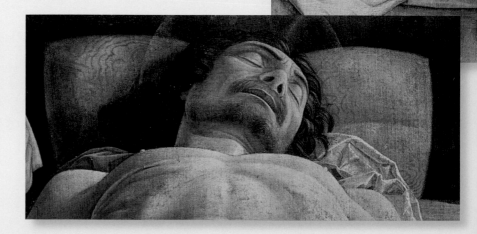

A cushion, supporting the lifeless head of Christ, closes in the scene as it rest vertically against the back wall.

COMPOSITION

The whole scene is all arranged around the rectangular slab of marble bearing the sharply foreshortened body of Christ devoid of all sense of harmony and proportion. The near edge of the marble is seen at close range together with the feet of Christ projected forwards.

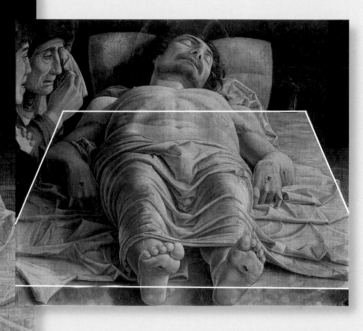

The central axis lies half way through the body of Christ running from his head to the triangular folds of cloth between the legs.

The simplicity and arrangement of the composition reveal Mantegna's understanding of classical art, but his artistic language is innovatory in its searing expressive realism.

LEON BATTISTA ALBERTI, THEORIST AND ARCHITECT

Leon Battista Alberti, architect, architectural theorist, author of philosophical, political, literary and theatrical texts is a problematical figure in the Italian Renaissance.

His interest in discovering rules capable of regulating artistic activity led him to codify in his treatise on architecture the principles he himself adopted in his work.

The various kinds of buildings are discussed in relation to their purpose and to their urban context.

Gothic architecture with its wealth of ornamentation is contrasted to the disciplined classical style. The treatise became the basis of the modern interpretation of antiquity, inaugurated by Brunelleschi. Albert's first important building was the Tempio Malatestiano in Rimini, which transformed the original church of San Francesco into a "Christian" temple built to the glory of the patron, Sigismondo Pandolfo Malatesta, and his family.

In Florence Alberti worked mainly for the Rucellai, an important family of merchants.

Palazzo Rucellai is an example of Renaissance classicism and geometrical discipline while the facade of the church of Santa Maria Novella, commissioned by the same family, reflects Alberti's tendency to repeat simple modules in the creation of a harmonious unity. Alberti's treatment of the facade shows him at his most

23

24

23. Leon Battista Alberti, Sant'Andrea, facade, from 1470. Mantua.

24. Leon Battista Alberti, Temple of the Holy Sepulchre. Florence, San Pancrazio.

brilliant and inventive as he had to incorporate his additions with pre-existing elements: the arches of the lower order and the side doors. His use of marble inlay serves to unify the upper and lower orders; the green and white romanesque stone is rearranged to meet Alberti's classical demands for rationalism and proportion evident in the triumphal arch of the main door and the triangular pediment crowning the facade.

In later works, and in particular in his plans for the churches of San Sebastiano and Sant'Andrea in Mantua, where he moved in 1460 to the court of Ludovico Gonzaga, the artist experimented with less orthodox classical models and interpreted them with increasing freedom.

25

26

25. Leon Battista Alberti, Rucellai Loggia, 1463-66. Florence.

26. Leon Battista Alberti, Santa Maria Novella, facade, about 1456. Florence.

TEMPIO MALATESTIANO
Leon Battista Alberti, from 1450
Rimini

EXTERIOR

In 1450 Sigismondo Pandolfo Malatesta, lord of Rimini, decided to renovate the church of San Francesco, the family mausoleum.

The commission was entrusted to Leon Battista Alberti who maintained the existing structure but transformed it completely by enclosing it in a marble surround.

Sigismondo's death left the work incomplete, but a medal commemorating the foundation of the temple by Matteo de' Pasti, shows that the long nave with its side chapels was originally intended to receive the addition of a large tribune inspired by the Pantheon and covered by a dome.

The upper part of the facade was also left unfinished as was the left side of the church. Despite this the Tempio Malatestiano is one of the most important buildings of the Italian Renaissance.

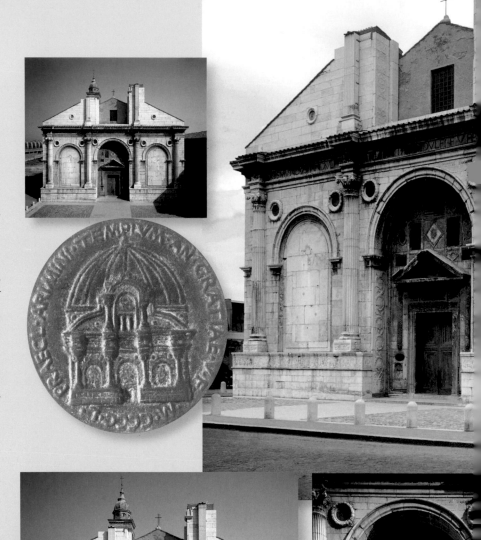

For the first time the structure of Roman architecture was adapted by Alberti according to the principles he himself devised in his architectural treatise, completed in 1452.

INTERIOR

The facade revived the model of the Roman triumphal arch with three openings. The central arch, directly inspired by the arch to Augustus in Rimini, frames the main doorway, set back on the level of the original facade. The two side arches were intended to house the tombs of Sigismondo and his wife Isotta degli Atti.

On the right side (the only one to be completed) a succession of deep arches supported by piers recalls the architecture of Roman aqueducts. A high base, as used in classical temples, underlines the continuity between the facade and the sides.

Sigismondo Malatesta was excommunicated by Pope Pius II, who considered the building more suited to pagan worship than Christian ritual. In fact, apart from the blatant references to classical and therefore pagan architecture on the exterior, and in the interior decoration, the Tempio Malatestiano was built to the glorification of Malatesta and his court.

The name of Sigismondo appears in capital letters on the frieze of the facade, usually reserved for a dedication to God or the Virgin, and recurs throughout the building, together with the Malatesta coat of arms, heraldic devices and the initials of Sigismondo and Isotta degli Atti are incorporated into the decoration of the interior carried out by Matteo de' Pasti and Agostino di Duccio.

FLORENTINE PALACES

In Florence throughout the fifteenth century new models of building appeared. Important families commissioned the great artists of the Renaissance to build palaces to reflect their social prestige and power.

These new buildings transformed the city's urban structure, as they were erected in the heart of the medieval city near the cathedral and town hall.

Filippo Brunelleschi was influential in the development of these grand new private residences and designed the original plan for Palazzo Pitti, later considerably enlarged and altered. But the real prototype for an urban Renaissance palace was the Palazzo Medici, built by Michelozzo from 1444.

The building is of a simple square plan, with rows of windows underlined by horizontal elements dividing the floors.

The division is given further emphasis by the treatment of the stone, heavily rusticated on the ground floor and progressively smoother as the building rises with a completely even and plastered surface on the top floor.

The interior has a courtyard with a loggia, inspired by the monastic cloister, with elegant arches supported by columns. A double order of windows above the courtyard repeats the arrangement on the exterior. Palazzo Rucellai, designed by Leon Battista Alberti and be-

27

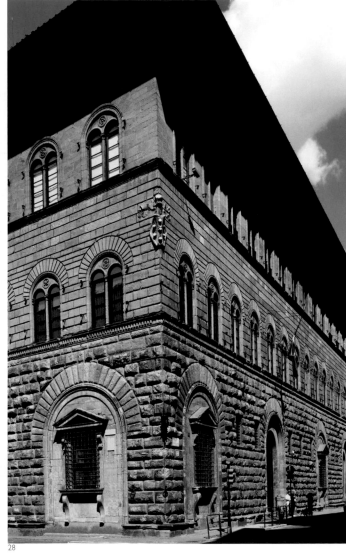

28

27. Leon Battista Alberti, Palazzo Rucellai, 1450-60. Florence.

28. Michelozzo di Bartolomeo, Palazzo Medici Riccardi, 1444-64. Florence.

gun a few years later, was extraordinarily influential above all in the sixteenth century. Alberti's adherence to classical form is evident in his use of the orders, in the architraves above the doors, and in his application of *opus reticolatum*, the lozenge pattern at the base of the ground floor, typical of Roman building.

Palazzo Strozzi, built between 1489 and 1502 for Filippo Strozzi, draws inspiration form all these buildings.

It was the combined work of Benedetto da Maiano, Giuliano da Sangallo and Simone Del Pollaiolo known as Cronaca, and stands isolated from the surrounding buildings. The internal space is remarkable for the practical arrangement of the rooms around the central courtyard.

29

30

31

29. Palazzo Pitti, facade. Florence.

30. Palazzo Strozzi, 1489-1502. Florence.

31. *'Catena' map*, detail of Palazzo Pitti in 1470, 19th-century copy. Florence, Museo di Firenze com'era.

THE REDISCOVERY OF SCULPTURE IN THE ROUND AND OF MOVEMENT

The study of antiquity stirred the leading artists of the early Florentine Renaissance to renew form with heightening realism.

Antique art was rich with models of extraordinary realism worked in the round. Hellenistic art too had produced supreme example of figures in movement.

Through his study of such models Donatello discovered and then reinvented the representation of the human body with particular regard to expressing movement, but also inner animation. These concerns were shared by Brunelleschi and find expression in the crucifixes carved by both artists at about the same time in Florence. In his *Crucifix* for the church of Santa Maria Novella, Brunelleschi strove to adhere to the classical rules of proportion which Donatello, by contrast, totally ignores in his *Crucifix* for the church of Santa Croce. He was determined to underline the drama of the subject.

The ability to look at classical works with curiosity and an open mind led to the revival of forgotten techniques such as the casting of bronze with the *cire perdue*, used for representing figures in the round, freed of their architectural setting and independent of the surrounding space.

This necessarily involved a return to the portrait bust and equestrian monument.

32

33

32. Filippo Brunelleschi, *Crucifix*, about 1420. Florence, Santa Maria Novella.

33. Donatello, *Crucifix*, 1412-15. Florence, Santa Croce.

34

35

36

34. Donatello, *Cupid or Attis*, 1430-40. Florence, Bargello.

35. Greek art, Vase. Pisa, Camposanto.

36. Donatello, *Cantoria*, detail with dancing putti, 1433-38. Florence, Opera del Duomo Museum.

37

39

38

37-39. Donatello, *David*
and details, about 1434.
Florence, Bargello.

DONATELLO AND BRONZE CASTING WITH THE *CIRE PERDUE* METHOD

In about 1434 Donatello made the bronze David, now in the Bargello in Florence, for the Medici. This was the first statue since antiquity to be made in the round and of life size. It revived the classical technique of casting using the *cire perdue* method.

The artist makes a reinforced model in clay that is then coated in perfectly-finished wax. This model is then covered with an additional mold attached to the model with metal nails and fitted with a series of channels to allow the wax to flow out as the model is heated.

The molten bronze is poured in to fill the space left by the melted wax. Donatello is credited with the revival of this technique, which had all but disappeared during the Middle Ages, and used it for some of his finest creations such as the equestrian statue to Gattamelata and his Judith and Holofernes.

In the David in the Bargello there are further references to Antiquity: the pose is taken from Hellenistic models although Donatello's interpretation is quite original.

The reflections of the light on the surface of the bronze confer a restlessness on the figure and his face bears a faint, slightly disconcerting, smile.

40

40. Donatello,
Equestrian monument
to Gattamelata, **1445-50.**
Padua, Piazza del Santo.

JUDITH AND HOLOFERNES
Donatello, 1455-60
Florence, Palazzo Vecchio, Sala dei Gigli

SUBJECT

This bronze group represents the biblical heroine Judith decapitating Holofernes. He was the commander of the enemy army and she went to his tent as if to seduce him, but then cut off his head after making him drunk.

The base has scenes of putti harvesting grapes in reference to the drunken state of Holofernes.

The group may have been a fountain for wine; there are four round holes at the corners of the cushion.

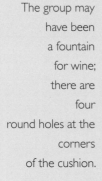

The statue originally stood in the garden of the Medici palace in Via Larga and was perhaps commissioned by Lorenzo the Magnificent's father, Piero the Gouty, in memory of Cosimo the Elder. In 1495 it was moved outside Palazzo Vecchio, on a new base especially designed to commemorate the defeat of the enemies of the republic of Savonarola.

It is signed *Opus Donatelli Flo* on the cushion. It was cast in eleven pieces using the *cire perdue* method. Judith's robe was modeled separately on a piece of cloth impregnated with wax, a segment of which can be seen in the veil above her forehead.

COMPOSITION

The dramatic treatment of the event is well suited to the multiple viewpoints of the sculpture. The group is enclosed within a pyramid culminating in the intense expression on Judith's face and in the blade of the sword about to strike the mortal blow.

The diagonals cross over the central point of focus, the head of Holofernes, heavy with drink.

The forearm holding up the sword forms a right angle to match that formed by the veil resting on Judith's shoulder.

41

LUCA DELLA ROBBIA AND THE GLAZED TERRACOTTA

Although all of the same generation, Donatello, Nanni di Banco and Luca della Robbia, in their work bear witness to the different interpretations given to classical art in Florence in the first half of the fifteenth century. Donatello concentrated on its dramatic power, Nanni di Banco accentuated the monumental character of the figures and Ghiberti's work recalls the elegance of Hellenistic sculpture. Luca della Robbia 's interpretation was essentially serene, characterized by harmonious rhythm and forms. His fame as an artist is primarily associated with the production of painted and glazed terracotta, adopting a technique already used sporadically in Florence but one which he perfected and made popular. In his work

42

41. Luca della Robbia,
St John the Evangelist.
Florence, Pazzi Chapel.

42. Luca della Robbia,
Ascension, 1442-45.
Florence, Cathedral.

the terracotta is imbued with the chromatic and luminous quality typical of painting, which exalts the decorative effect of the whole In general these pieces were used for tabernacles, altarpieces or as reliefs such as the lunettes of the *Resurrection* and the *Ascension* above the entrances to the sacristies in Florence cathedral. In the *Visitation* in the church of San Giovanni Fuorcivitas in Pistoia however Luca applied the technique to a life-size sculptural group in the round, achieving a profoundly moving effect. Luca usually only used white for his figures and blue for the background while other colors were reserved for the decorative elements.

After his death the della Robbia work was carried on by his nephews and grand-nephews and was so successful that production became "industrialized" with molds used to reproduce the most popular pieces and segments.

43

44

43. Luca della Robbia, *Fortitude*, 1461-66. Florence, San Miniato al Monte.

44. Luca della Robbia, *Resurrection*, 1442-45. Florence, Cathedral.

45

45. Luca della Robbia,
Visitation, about 1445.
Pistoia, San Giovanni
Fuorcivitas.

THE *CANTORIE* OF LUCA DELLA ROBBIA AND DONATELLO

The *Cantoria*, or singing gallery, made by Luca della Robbia for the cathedral of Florence between 1431 and 1435, is a magnificent example of the emerging Florentine classicism. The artist, in his first important commission, appears already to have developed an individual and mature style although clearly indebted to the work of Lorenzo Ghiberti and Nanni di Banco.

The architectural arrangement of the choir loft, with double pilasters dividing the upper scenes and corbels the lower ones, frames reliefs depicting singing and dancing.

The scenes serve as a commentary on the Psalm 150 by David: the text appears in capitals on the cornices.

The work has always been compared to the companion *Cantoria*

by Donatello, finished a few years later between 1433 and 1438. Certainly Luca's *Cantoria* is not as innovatory as Donatello's but his singers are depicted with lively realism and a variety of expressions and gestures.

Donatello had the advantage of seeing Luca della Robbia's gallery completed and proposed an alternative treatment which was both more unified and more dynamic.

He created a continuous space with paired columns in the foreground and mosaic decoration covering the back wall.

The whole scene is animated by dancing putti of distinctly pagan vitality quite unsuited to a Christian setting.

With a remarkable historical instinct Donatello combines Hellenistic elements, aspects of late-Roman and early-Christian art and cosmatesque decoration as though demonstrating the uninterrupted and irrepressible fervor of classical art.

46

46. Donatello, *Cantoria*, 1433-38. Florence, Opera del Duomo Museum.

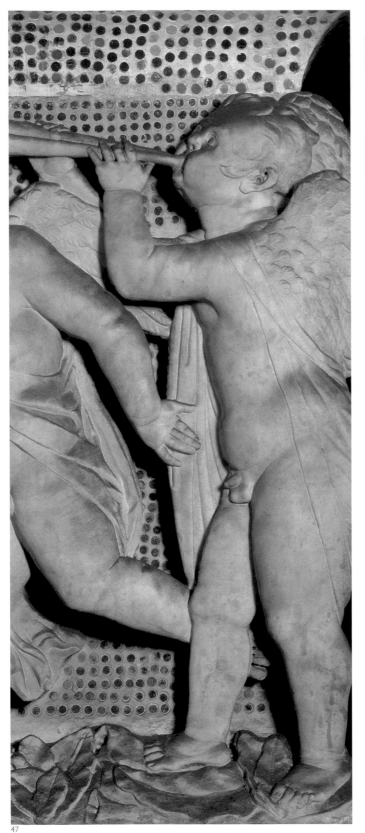

47

48

47. Donatello, *Cantoria*,
detail with putti, 1433-38.
Florence, Opera del
Duomo Museum.

48. Luca della Robbia,
Cantoria, detail of flute
player, 1431-35. Florence,
Opera del Duomo
Museum.

49

50

51

49. Luca della Robbia, *Cantoria*, detail of boys playing the trumpet, 1431-35. Florence, Opera del Duomo Museum.

50. Luca della Robbia, *Cantoria*, detail of boys playing drums and the flute, 1431-35. Florence, Opera del Duomo Museum.

51. Luca della Robbia, *Cantoria*, 1431-35. Florence, Opera del Duomo Museum.

2. The discovery of perspective

I n Florence in the first two decades of the fifteenth century Filippo Brunelleschi worked out a scientific method of representing three-dimensional objects on a flat surface. This fundamental discovery marks the division between medieval and renaissance art. For the first time the problem of spatial representation was resolved through the application of geometrical rules rather than by trial and error. Linear perspective with a single vanishing point amounted to more than a combination of mathematical laws: it was instrumental to the expansion of scientific knowledge and to our understanding of reality. The fragmented vision of the international gothic was unified and, although not exactly reflective of the vision of the human eye, gave rational order to the section of the world to be represented. It placed objects in a codifiable space, defined by the precise rules of perspective.

2

3

1. Facing page: Paolo Uccello, *Story of Noah. Sacrifice and drunkenness of Noah*, detail, 1446-48. Florence, Santa Maria Novella, Green Cloister.

2. Perugino, *Christ consigns the keys to St Peter*, 1481-82. Rome, Sistine Chapel.

3. Pisanello, *Study with figures in a vaulted space*. Paris, Louvre, Cabinet des Dessins.

THE INNOVATORS

In early-fifteenth century Florence there were an extraordinary number of artists of genius who created a new form of art and gave a new dimension to the figure of the artist. Similar periods of history are rare (there was Athens in the fifth century at the time of Pericles) when the whole city became caught up in the flowering of talent.

Filippo Brunelleschi was the pioneer of this movement and the invention of the rules of perspective and the single vanishing point marked its foundation. This Florentine architect was the first to elaborate mathematical rules and to use them in the architectural construction of space and in figurative representation. At the same time Masaccio translated Brunelleschi's rational and classically inspired

language into painting and in his short career changed the course of Western painting. Masaccio portrayed Man as a distinct individual, capable of feeling and possessing a rounded and solid body: he depicted his figures by directly studying nature and antique models. Human beings were portrayed in a rational pictorial space and their humanity was given expressive power. Natural reality and antique forms were reappropriated in the sculpture of Donatello and it was his innovatory spirit, together with Brunelleschi and Masaccio, which broke with the late-gothic world.

But in the work of Donatello, although scientific laws and the study of nature facilitated his representation of reality, his expressive intensity penetrated still further into the exploration of the psychology of the individual.

4

5

54

4. Masaccio, *Resurrection of the son of Theophilus and St Peter*, detail with Masaccio's self-portrait and portrait of Brunelleschi, 1424-27.

Florence, Santa Maria del Carmine, Brancacci Chapel.

5. *"Catena" map*, view of Florence in 1470, detail, 19th-century copy. Florence, Museo di Firenze com'era.

THE PERSPECTIVE PANELS OF BRUNELLESCHI

Brunelleschi's research into the scientific rules governing the representation of space on a flat surface centered on the geometry of Euclid and on antiquity.

Classical architecture, with its modular structure, represented an example of the possibility of measuring architectural space and of subjecting it to rigorous mathematical formulae. Brunelleschi's progress from measuring real space to its representation to scale was set down on two panels (lost, but described in the sources) depicting two key monuments in Florence: the baptistery of San Giovanni and the Palazzo Vecchio, the town hall. The choice of these two buildings was linked to their geometrical elements: the marble inlay work in the case of the baptistery, and the network of *pietra serena* lines in the red paving outside the town hall.

The panels were not viewed directly but from behind, though a hole, in their reflection in a mirror. In that way the spectator's eye was in direct relationship to the vanishing point and at the right distance from the picture. This made it possible to illustrate the points on which Brunelleschi's method was founded: the convergence of orthogonal lines towards a vanishing point and the proportional diminution of objects in space determined though geometrical theorems.

6

7

6. *Burning of Savanarola,* detail. Florence, San Marco Museum. Notice the old terracotta paving in Piazza della Signoria.

7. Baptistery of San Giovanni. Florence.

MASACCIO: ETHICAL TENSION AND FORMAL RENEWAL

Tommaso di ser Giovanni Cassai known as Masaccio, was active for a very short period between 1422 and 1428, when he died in Rome. His first known work, the *St Juvenal triptych*, dated 1422, reveals his adherence to the new principles of perspective. The traditional arrangement of the painting, divided into three panels, is in contrast to his use of a single vanishing point, while the gold ground, far from flattening the background, throws the monumentality of the figures into relief. The innovatory aspects of his art were therefore evident from the first. His relationship with Masolino da Panicale, the painter who took Masaccio as his assistant, was not one of disciple to master but more one of partnership between two mature artists, even though Masaccio was very much his junior. It was, in fact, Masolino

who adapted to Masaccio's style in the frescoes in the Brancacci chapel and in his other independent works. The *Sant'Anna Metterza* in the Uffizi of 1424, documents how far the masters had diverged since their collaboration began.

The traditional composition, devised by Masolino, is jolted into a new mode with the powerful three-dimensional treatment of the Madonna and Child which interrupts the unity of the whole. Immediately afterwards the two artists began working together of the frescoes relating to *Episodes in the life of St Peter* in the Brancacci Chapel in the Florentine church of the Carmine. The decoration was done in stages between 1424 and 1428 and was unfinished at the time of Masaccio's death. It was not until 1481-83 that the cycle was finally completed by Filippino Lippi. In 1426 Masaccio alone painted the dismembered polyptych for the Carmelite church . In the *Crucifixion* the plasticity of the figures gives spatiality to the scene, while the viewpoint from

8

8. Masaccio, *St Juvenal tryptych*, 1422. Cascia di Reggello, Church of St Juvenal.

below enhances the dramatic quality of the event. Christ is depicted with his head sunk between his shoulders with his body modeled by contrasting use of light and shade. Poignant gestures convey the suffering of the onlookers. Among these the kneeling Magdalen with her red cloak and long fair hair and arms raised in desperation, only finds a precedent in the *Lamentation* by Giotto in the Scrovegni Chapel in Padua. Between 1426 and 1427 Masaccio painted the fresco of the *Trinity* in the church of Santa Maria Novella in Florence, according to Brunelleschi's rules of centralized perspective. Immediately afterwards he moved to Rome where he again worked with Masolino on the triptych for Santa Maria Maggiore. He died there shortly afterwards.

10

9

11

9. Masolino and Masaccio, *Sant'Anna Metterza*, about 1424. Florence, Uffizi.

10. Masaccio, *Crucifixion*, from the polyptych once in the church of the Carmine in Pisa, 1426. Naples, Capodimonte.

11. Giotto, *Lamentation*, 1303-05. Padua, Scrovegni Chapel.

TRINITY
Masaccio, 1426-27
Florence, Santa Maria Novella

The fresco articulates the doctrine of the Trinity, depicted with tender and human connotations as the mystery revealed to man through Christ's suffering.

The scene is set within a renaissance church inspired by the Roman triumphal arch: witness the coffered ceiling, the Ionic columns and the barrel vault.

In addition to the figures of the Trinity, Mary the Mother of Christ and St John the Evangelist are depicted at the foot of the Cross.

Lower still are the figures of the two donors kneeling before the sacred scene but otherwise detached.

An illusionistic marble altar serves as a base, with a skeleton below it in an allusion to death.

The concept of Man as the center of the universe is expressed in the figure of Christ, also at the focal point of the composition, and above all at the dramatic heart of the narration.

The painting serves as a kind of visual manifesto of the basic principles of the Renaissance: Man, the measure of all things, moves in a space that can be accurately depicted. Masaccio faithfully represents the spatial relationship between man and architecture, including for the first time the figures of the donors drawn to scale.

COMPOSITION

Masaccio's command of perspective is assured and provides a totally convincing rendition of space and volume. He also uses perspective to clarify the hierarchical relationship between the figures.

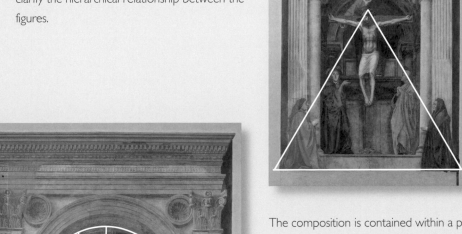

The composition is contained within a pyramid and the symbolic importance of the triangle and of the number three is underlined in the composition.
The first triangle linking the figures has the two donors at its base with Christ at the apex.

Two other equilateral triangles can be traced, serving to unite the saints with the Divinity. The first, its base being the wooden elevation, links the Virgin, St John the Evangelist and Christ. The second encompassing Christ, the dove of the Holy Spirit and God the Father, is upside down, with its base running from the two capitals at the level of the head of God the Father.

THE FRESCOES IN THE BRANCACCI CHAPEL: THE REPRESENTATION OF MAN AND OF URBAN SPACE

Between 1424 and 1427 Masaccio and Masolino worked together on the decoration of the Brancacci Chapel in the Florentine church of the Carmine. The cycle, commissioned by the Florentine merchant Felice Brancacci, depicts *Original Sin*, the *Expulsion of Adam and Eve from Paradise* and *Episodes from the life of St Peter*. In these frescoes Masaccio provides his most accomplished meditation of the dignity of humanity. In his *Expulsion of Adam and Eve from Paradise*, the vulnerability of the figures is expressed in their naked-ness, depicted with great naturalism. The miraculous events in the *Episodes from the life of St Peter* take place in a recognizable urban setting: the miracle of St Peter healing the sick is set in a narrow street like many still visible in Florence with a house faced in rusticated stone and others with projecting upper floors. The scene showing the *Resurrection of Tabitha and the healing of the lame man*, by Masolino, is also depicted against a realistic and detailed urban background.

The choice of a familiar urban setting for the depiction of biblical events confers dignity on everyday reality in all its manifestations, even the most humble.

12

13

12. Masaccio, *The expulsion from Paradise*, 1424-25. Florence, Santa Maria del Carmine, Brancacci Chapel.

13. Masaccio, *Story of St Peter, St Peter heals the sick*, 1424-27. Florence, Santa Maria del Carmine, Brancacci Chapel.

14

15

16

14-15. Masolino,
Resurrection of Tabitha
and healing the lame man
and detail, 1424-25.
Florence, Santa Maria del
Carmine, Brancacci
Chapel.

16. Masaccio, ***The tribute***
money, **detail, 1427.**
Florence, Santa Maria del
Carmine, Brancacci
Chapel.

DONATELLO AND "STIACCIATO" RELIEF

Donatello's invention of "stiacciato", literally "squashed" relief, that is with the minimum of variation in the height of the relief with respect to the background, is his response in sculpture to Brunelleschi's advances in the study of perspective. In 1417, on the low relief designed for the base of the statue of *St George* in the church of Orsanmichele in Florence, Donatello achieved an extraordinary sense of depth with the subtlest variations in carving. The receding loggia behind the princess and the grotto on the extreme left focus our attention on the central event - St George' combat with the dragon. The play of light and shadow on the scene creates a pictorial and atmospheric effect which greatly enhances the drama. Donatello's reference to Roman models, most evident in the pose of the princess, hints at the possibility of representing figures in movement. This same very low relief was used by Donatello elsewhere and in other mediums. In the bronze reliefs for the high altar in the basilica of Sant'Antonio in Padua, in 1447, years after the St George, he created views of landscapes and grandiose architectural scenes. In the *Miracle of the Repentent Son*, the scene takes place in the open air against a complex and theatrical setting. The saint is the focal point of each panel with figures crowded around him, a compact group but depicted as individuals, serving to unite the action.

17

18

17. Donatello, *St George and the dragon*, 1417. Florence, Bargello.

18. Donatello, *Story of St Anthony, Healing the possessed boy*, 1447. Padua, Basilica of Sant Antonio, High Altar.

THE BAPTISMAL FONT IN SIENA

The reliefs on the font in the baptistery of Siena are a clear example of the creative potential of Donatello's "stiacciato" or very low relief. This is clear when we compare them to the other reliefs by his contemporaries. The panels begun in 1416, were entrusted to Ghiberti, but by 1417 Jacopo della Quercia became involved and from 1427 took charge of the whole project.

The font is an harmonious combination of reliefs, statues and statuettes, in marble and bronze realized by a number of different artists. In Ghiberti's relief on the *Baptism of Christ*, the elegant but still gothic figures, stand out clearly from the background. The panel by Donatello of *Herod's feast*, 1425 to 1427, conveys an extraordinary sense of depth: the main scene, set in space with the diminishing area of the floor projecting the viewer into a series of arched spaces behind, shows the horror of the onlookers at the sight of the decapitated head of the Baptist.

The succession of arched spaces is conveyed with minimal relief. The Sienese artist Jacopo della Quercia, on the other hand, while applying the rules of perspective to his representation of the temple, placed the figures in front of the architecture, upsetting the ratio but giving them an heroic quality.

19

21

20

19. Lorenzo Ghiberti, *Baptism of Christ*, 1417-27. Siena, Baptistery, Font.

20. Font. Siena, Baptistery.

21. Donatello, *Herod's banquet*, detail, 1425-27. Siena, Baptistery, Font.

TRANSITION AND EXPERIMENTATION

The invention of a new artistic language in the Renaissance was not thoroughly adopted by all the artists of the day and in fact remained limited initially to a restricted circle working in Florence.

The great innovations required a certain intellectual preparation and were open to a variety of interpretations, traditional elements sometimes surviving alongside adaptation to the more advanced artistic language.

Among those artists who accepted some of the revolutionary aspects of the Renaissance while retaining elements of late gothic art were Lorenzo Ghiberti and Fra Angelico. Ghiberti was given some of the most important commissions in Florence in the first half of the fifteenth century.

His workshop was for years engaged on making the bronze doors for the baptistery in Florence and served as the training ground for nearly all the artists who later played a leading role in Florence. Among all the painters of fifteenth century, Fra Angelico succeeded in reconciling many of Masaccio's innovations with devotional art, rejecting Masaccio's tendency to interpret sacred subjects in a more secular context.

22

23

64

22. Lorenzo Ghiberti,
St Matthew, 1419-22.
Florence, Orsanmichele.

23. Fra Angelico,
Coronation of the Virgin,
1434-35. Paris, Louvre.

LORENZO GHIBERTI AND THE BAPTISTERY DOORS IN FLORENCE

Between 1403 and 1424 Lorenzo Ghiberti worked on the north door for the baptistery of Florence. The door adopts the same scheme as used in the earlier south door by Andrea Pisano: there are twenty-eight quadilobe panels, arranged in seven rows. Ghiberti's upper panels depict *Episodes from the life of Christ* while the lower ones show the *Fathers of the Church* and the *Evangelists*.

The panels reflect a range of style from the most naturalistic treatment of the *Nativity*, to the spare calligraphic *Crucifixion*, still in adherence to the international gothic, while the scene depicting the *Flagellation* is charged with the spirit of the Renaissance. Between 1425 and 1452 Ghiberti worked on the third pair of baptistery doors known as the Doors of Paradise.

By contrasting these panels with the ones on the earlier doors it is fully apparent how far the artist has absorbed the modern conception of space and the innovations of Donatello. The Doors of Paradise have only ten panels but each one relates a number of episodes from the Old Testament. In the *Story of Joseph*, Ghiberti achieves a unified effect by setting the scene against a convincingly rendered architectural background.

24

24. Lorenzo Ghiberti, *Story of Joseph*, 1425-52. Florence, Opera del Duomo Museum (Doors of Paradise).

25

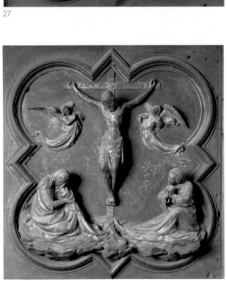

27

28

26

25. Lorenzo Ghiberti,
Nativity, **1403-24.**
Florence, Baptistery,
North door.

26. Lorenzo Ghiberti,
North door, 1403-24.
Florence, Baptistery.

27. Lorenzo Ghiberti,
Flagellation, **1403-24.**
Florence, Baptistery,
North door.

28. Lorenzo Ghiberti,
Crucifixion, **1403-24.**
Florence, Baptistery,
North door.

**29. Lorenzo Ghiberti,
Doors of Paradise,
1425-52. Florence,
Baptistery.**

**30. Lorenzo Ghiberti,
Doors of Paradise, detail
of the frame,1425-52.
Florence, Baptistery.**

FRA ANGELICO: A NEW SENSE OF THE SACRED IN PAINTING

For a number of years art historians considered Fra Angelico as a traditional and even a reactionary painter in comparison with the more progressive Masaccio. The truth is that he was one of the first artists to study and absorb Masaccio's innovatory style. His conception of the world was however quite different and he chose to interpret Masaccio's advances in a profoundly religious mode.

His earliest works, witness the *Last Judgement* in the San Marco museum in Florence, demonstrate his lingering attachment to the late-gothic manner of Lorenzo Monaco although his interest in contemporary

31

32

33

31-33. Fra Angelico, *Last Judgment and details*, about 1430-33. Florence, San Marco Museum.

34. Fra Angelico,
Annalena altarpiece,
1436. Florence, San
Marco Museum.

35. Fra Angelico,
San Marco altarpiece,
about 1440. Florence,
San Marco Museum.

experimentation in conveying spatial depth is already apparent. In his later works his acceptance of the new language becomes more clearly defined but although he embraced the morally uplifting aspects of the new realism he adopted them only in so far as they enhanced the sacred quality of his work. In the *Annalena altarpiece* of 1436 for the very first time the gothic arrangement of the figures in separate panels is rejected and the Madonna, Child and Saints are depicted in a unified space, creating the "sacra conversazione". This term is used to describe a theological discussion among saints in the presence of the Virgin, which Fra Angelico developed further in his *San Marco altarpiece*. The most striking element in Fra Angelico's painting is the very clear light, which both revives its medieval symbolism and adds solidity to the figures and exalts the coloring. His mature development

can be seen in the series of frescoes painted between 1438 and 1446 in the convent of San Marco, rebuilt by Michelozzo for Cosimo the Elder. The paintings in the cells were destined as meditational works: the language is simple and essential and concentrates on the symbolic importance of the sacred narratives. But Fra Angelico was always conscious of the power of recent artistic developments, reflected in his measured compositional arrangements and in the solidity of his figures. His last masterpiece was the decoration of the chapel for Nicholas V in the Vatican with episodes from the lives of St Stephen and of St Lawrence. The magnificence of Roman architecture clearly inspired the classical buildings in the background while the slow and measured gestures of the dignified figures sustain the courtly tone in these narrative scenes.

36

37

36. Fra Angelico, *Story of St Stephan and St Lawrence, St Lawrence distributing alms to the poor*, 1446. Rome, Vatican Palaces, Chapel of Nicholas V.

37. Fra Angelico, *The mocking of Christ*, 1439-45. Florence, San Marco Museum.

ANNUNCIATION
Fra Angelico, 1438-46
Florence, San Marco Museum

SUBJECT

The scene of the *Annunciation* is painted on the wall facing the top of the stairs on the first floor of the convent, at the entrance to the dormitory. The modesty and simplicity of the scene, with the Virgin seated on a stool, is in perfect accord with the Dominican rule.

Mary and the archangel Gabriel exchange greetings with arms crossed according to ancient Byzantine ceremonial.

The scene appears both intimate and domestic. The Virgin's garments are plain and unadorned while the angel is clothed in a fine pink robe embroidered with gold.

Fra Angelico sets the sacred scene in a portico reminiscent of a cloister, the arches supported by beautifully carved Corinthian and Ionic columns. This serves to create the illusion that the miraculous event is taking place right inside the convent.

To the left we can glimpse an enclosed garden with a wood rising up beyond the fence.

This painting is typical of Fra Angelico's close observation of the world – witness the iron bars reinforcing the architecture between the columns.

COMPOSITION

The scene is divided into parts by the central column of the portico under which the action takes place.

The rules of perspective are applied with a central vanishing point and a sense of depth is created primarily by the succession of receding arches.

The external arches are rounded, while the ones in the background resting on corbels are slightly pointed in the gothic manner.

The figures of the Virgin and the archangel Gabriel are arranged along a slight diagonal line with Mary seated further inside the portico.

THE JOURNEY OF THE MAGI. THE BENOZZO GOZZOLI CHAPEL

In 1459 Benozzo Gozzoli was commissioned to decorate the chapel in the Palazzo Medici in Florence recently completed by Michelozzo. Piero de' Medici chose Gozzoli on account of his familiarity with the latest advances in Florentine painting which he incorporated into this celebratory and highly decorative work. As a pupil of Ghiberti and of Fra Angelico, Gozzoli admired formal elegance and adopted it as his medium to demonstrate his paramount skill as a story-teller. The simple architectural structure of the chapel is enhanced by the addition of classical elements. Michelozzo was also responsible for the design of the pavement decorated with marble and porphyry inlay, the carved and gilded ceiling, and the furnishings.

The walls are completely covered in Gozzoli's frescoes depicting the *Journey of the Magi* which culminates in the painting of the *Adoration*

38

**38. Michelozzo di
Bartolomeo, Chapel
of the Magi, 1444-59.
Florence, Palazzo Medici
Riccardi.**

of the Christ Child by Filippo Lippi. The narrative tone is distinctly secular and a Tuscan landscape provides the setting.

The richly dressed procession is described with minute attention as it wends its way through the countryside. Gozzoli included portraits of the Medici family among those traveling with the Magi. Lorenzo in fact appears dressed as a king behind his father Piero who leads the procession, while his brother Giuliano is on the opposite wall in the guise of a young knight accompanied by two leopards. Gozzoli himself is among the throng, his name appears in gold letters on his red hat. The first Magi is a portrait of the patriarch of Constantinople, while the second is the Byzantine Emperor John VIII Paleologus: they were both in Florence for the Council of 1439 between the Eastern and Western churches.

The Medici, by depicting themselves in the company of such illustrious figures, underlined their importance to the political and cultural life of the city.

39

39. Benozzo Gozzoli,
***Journey of the Magi,* detail**
with Lorenzo and Pietro
de' Medici, 1459-60.
Florence, Palazzo Medici
Riccardi.

MINO DA FIESOLE, DESIDERIO DA SETTIGNANO AND ROSSELLINO

The sculptors in the generation after Donatello were important in spreading the Renaissance language although they operated in a less innovatory and experimental style than their master.

The activity of Mino da Fiesole, Desiderio da Settignano and the Rossellino brothers was quite varied and they all developed a personal style despite sharing many of the same concerns. From the formal point of view, and deeply affected by the work of Ghiberti, they favored a controlled interpretation of classicism, often enriched with decorative detail.

Interpretation and artistic expression grew to be increasingly secular and sculpture became a means of glorifying man's terrestrial existence. Mino da Fiesole was most accomplished as a portraitist. His works are distinctive for their penetrating observation with

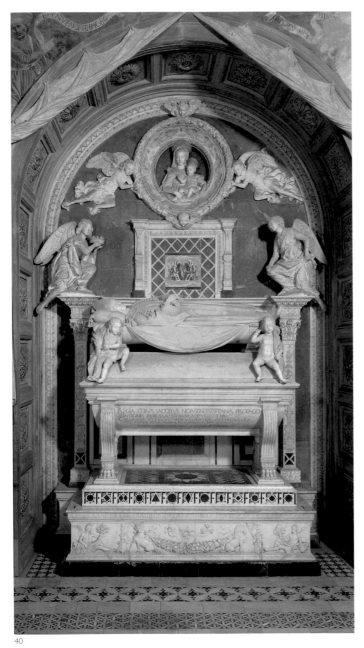

40

41

40. Antonio Rossellino,
Tomb of Cardinal of
Portugal, **1461-66.**
Florence, San Miniato
al Monte.

41. Bernardo Rossellino,
Tomb of Leonardo Bruni,
about 1446-50. Florence,
Santa Croce.

his clear reliance on Roman models, above all in his portraiture. Desiderio da Settignano had an extraordinary capacity to model marble as if it were wax, creating the illusion of the texture of skin, cloth and any other material to the finest detail.

Bernardo Rossellino, an architect as well as a sculptor, is most famous for his transformation of the small town of Corsignano into the city of Pienza. By uniting sculpture and architecture in the *Tomb of Leonardo Bruni* in the church of Santa Croce, he revitalized

the funerary monument and created a model much imitated by his contemporaries.

His brother Antonio Rossellino sculpted realistic portraits: in his *Bust of Giovanni Chellini* the face appears to have been taken from a cast. The *Tomb of the Cardinal of Portugal*, in the church of San Miniato al Monte in Florence, is striking for his confident use classical and therefore pagan decorative elements, attesting to the secularization of such works.

42

43

44

42. Benedetto da Maiano, *Bust of Pietro Mellini*, 1474. Florence, Bargello.

43. Desiderio da Settignano, *Bust of a boy*, 1450-54. Florence, Bargello.

44. Desiderio da Settignano, *Head of Christ Child*. St Petersburg, Hermitage.

PAOLO UCCELLO AND EXPERIMENTATION WITH PERSPECTIVE

Paolo Uccello, who trained between the first and second decades of the fifteenth century in Ghiberti's workshop learnt the rules of perspective shortly afterwards and applied them to his late gothic understanding of form. For Uccello therefore perspective was not always used as a unifying and rational principle but was adopted from time to time for a variety of expressive purposes. In his 1436 fresco of the *Equestrian monument to Sir John Hawkwood* in the cathedral

45

46

45. Paolo Uccello,
*Blessed Jacopone da
Todi.* Prato, Opera del
Duomo Museum.

46. Paolo Uccello,
*Equestrian monument to
Sir John Hawkwood,*
1436. Florence, Cathedral.

of Florence, the horse and knight are depicted at eye level while the tomb and supporting altar are seen from below.

The single view point as proposed by Brunelleschi was discarded in favor of multiple viewpoints designed to reflect the versatility of human vision. In the fresco of the *Flood in the Green Cloister* of Santa Maria Novella, there is a dramatic convergence of lines into a single vanishing point while in the *Battle of San Romano* in the Uffizi the lances on the ground indicate a vanishing point but any sense of depth is destroyed by the failure to make other distinctions of size between the fore and background.

47

48

47. Paolo Uccello,
Battle of San Romano,
Bernardino della Ciarda
Thrown Off His Horse,
about 1456.
Florence, Uffizi.

48. Paolo Uccello,
Story of Noah, The Flood,
1446-48. Florence,
Santa Maria Novella,
Green Cloister.

BATTLE OF SAN ROMANO
Paolo Uccello, about 1456
Paris, Louvre.

SUBJECT

The panel in the Louvre is the best preserved of the three painted in celebration of the Florentine victory over the Sienese in 1432. Painted in 1456, they illustrate three different moments in the Battle of San Romano and were all originally hung in the same room in the Palazzo Medici. They glorified both the Florentine victory and the role of the Medici in the city.

Uccello's almost obsessive passion for perspective gives an unreal and almost visionary quality to the scene. There is no sense of heroic exultation and the soldiers appears more like figures from some military roundabout.

The lively and abstract use of color recalls gothic painting, with fantastic effects

created by the use of gold and silver leaf on the horses' harnesses and trappings.

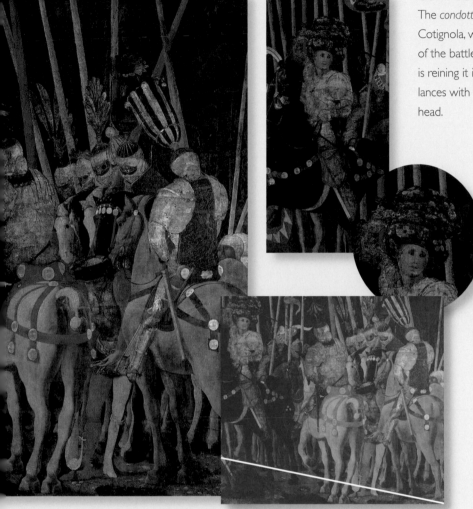

COMPOSITION

The *condottiere* Micheletto Attendolo da Cotignola, with his face uncovered in the center of the battle, is seated on his black horse and is reining it in. He is depicted against a forest of lances with the standards fluttering around his head.

His expression is both enigmatic and absent. His head is swathed in a huge turban, the material folded in circles high on his head.

To the right a group of soldiers, imprisoned in their fine armor, await the captain's orders. The two horses in the foreground, viewed at an angle, serve to convey an impression of depth.

Between them a bearded figure with a round hat is attending to his weapon.

The pictorial volume of the space is constructed of the men enclosed in their armor and of finely caparisoned horses.

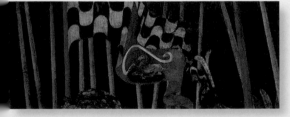

The figures are determined by the abstract geometry of their armor, while the colors form an elaborate interplay of flat and recessed surfaces bathed in light: the vertical and oblique lances form a complex network of lines.

To the left other horsemen appear ready to charge. There is a group in the right foreground of five knights, though the heads only appear to be four, with three feather crests, one of which is miraculously suspended in the air
The angle of the five lances is crossed by the red lance of the soldier adjusting his weapon.

Piero della Francesca, born in San Sepolcro near Arezzo, is one of the leading artists of the Renaissance, noted for the intellectual rigor and stylistic clarity of his works. These fundamental traits are evident in his earliest work, the *Misericordia Polyptych* in his native Sansepolcro. The *Crucifixion*, painted in about 1445, is indebted to the *Pisan Polyptych* by Masaccio, both in the plastic rendering of the figures and in the dramatic quality of the scene. But already in the *Madonna della Miseri-*

cordia, the central panel of the altarpiece, painted in about 1460 there is a rigorous rationalization of the composition which eliminates any dramatic content. The figures are geometrical, majestic but static, and are shaped by the light.

Although we have little information about Piero's training, his earliest works show the impact of his stay in Florence, documented from 1439. At that stage Piero was in contact with Domenico Veneziano and probably also with Fra Angelico. In 1450 he painted the *Baptism of Christ*, in which his individual style is used to shape his innovatory

49

49. Piero della Francesca,
Misericordia Polyptch,
1445-60. Sansepolcro,
Pinacoteca Comunale.

50. Piero della Francesca,
Resurrection, **about 1463.**
Sansepolcro, Pinacoteca
Comunale.

iconographic formula. The angels, standing on the left, instead of holding Christ's garments, have their hands linked in a gesture of friendship, which might possibly allude to the reconciliation between the Eastern and Western churches following the council of Florence of 1439. Christ occupies the central axis of the composition with the other elements in a perfectly balanced arrangement around him. Piero's understanding of geometry is employed to accentuate the sacred power of the image. He was highly praised by his contemporaries and worked at the Papal court in Rome, in Urbino for Federico da Montefeltro, at the Este court in Ferrara, and in Rimini for Sigismondo Pandolfo Malatesta.

While at the court of Urbino Piero della Francesca painted a number of works including the *Sacra conversazione*, now in the Brera in Milan, and wrote his treatise *De prospectiva pingendi*, a mathematical and humanist manifesto, which was received in triumph at the court of Federico da Montefeltro.

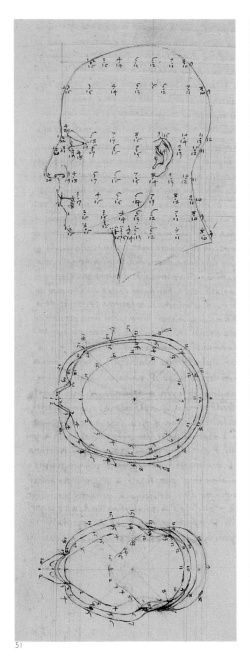

51

52

51. Piero della Francesca,
De prospectiva pingendi,
Studies of the human
head. **Parma, Palatina**
Library.

52. Piero della Francesca,
Senigallia Madonna,
about 1470. Urbino,
Galleria Nazionale
delle Marche.

THE LEGEND OF THE TRUE CROSS IN SAN FRANCESCO IN AREZZO

The fresco cycle of the *Legend of the True Cross* by Piero della Francesca in the church of San Francesco in Arezzo is the most complete documentation we have of Piero's artistic output. The subject, founded on a solid figurative tradition, is organized on three levels, with considerations of the compositional lay-out being more important than the interests of chronology. On the two long walls, at the top, are lunettes of the *Death of Adam* and of the *Entry of Heraclius*

53

54

53. Piero della Francesca,
Legend of the True Cross,
Dream of Constantine,
1452-66. Arezzo,
San Francesco.

54. San Francesco, view
of the choir. Arezzo,
San Francesco.

RENAISSANCE ART

into Jerusalem, the first and last episodes of the cycle, both set in open landscapes. In the next layer down, on one side are the *Adoration of the Holy wood and the meeting of Solomon and Sheba*, on the other the *Discovery of the three crosses and recognition of the True Cross*. The scenes here almost have a courtly tone, enhanced by the elaborate costumes, with the same measured pace as a liturgical ceremony. The forms are geometric, perfect and immobile, and confer nobility on even the simplest gestures. The lowest level contains two battle scenes:

55

56

55. Piero della Francesca, *Legend of the True Cross, Discovery of the three crosses and recognition of the True Cross*, 1452-66. Arezzo, San Francesco.

56. Piero della Francesca, *Legend of the True Cross, Adoration of the Holy Wood and the meeting between Solomon and Sheba*, 1452-66. Arezzo, San Francesco.

the *Victory of Constantine over Maxentius* and the *Battle of Heraclius and Chosroes*. Here the same stately rhythm prevails and the air of sacred ritual keeps the dramatic expression under constant check. More minor episodes are on the far wall of the choir, some of which were executed with the help of assistants. Piero, on the other hand, is totally responsible for the *Dream of Constantine* in which the darkness of the night is broken by a shaft of divine light falling into the Emperor's tent. This is the first night scene to be depicted in Italian painting.

57

58

59

60

57-58. Piero della Francesca, *Legend of the True Cross, Battle of Heraclius and Chosroes* and detail, 1452-66. Arezzo, San Francesco.

59. Piero della Francesca, *Legend of the True Cross, Adoration of the sacred wood and the meeting of Solomon and Sheba.*

60. Piero della Francesca, *Legend of the True Cross, Discovery of the three crosses and recognition of the True Cross*, 1452-66. Arezzo, San Francesco.

FLAGELLATION
**Piero della Francesca, about 1460.
Urbino, Galleria Nazionale delle Marche**

SUBJECT
The small panel depicts the flagellation of Christ. the figure of Christ is in the background and three enigmatic figures stand in the foreground. Various theories have been advanced about the identity of this prominent group: it is most likely that they were figures of importance at the court of Urbino in the years from 1440 -1460.

The flagellation takes place within an open space inspired by Greek architecture, with fluted columns, composite capitals, architraves and a flat coffered ceiling.

The body of Christ, echoes the shape of the column with but has softer contours, and appears almost as inanimate, with an expressionless face and listless body.

The rich clothing of the person on the extreme right is in contrast to the air of abstraction and clarity that otherwise pervades the composition. The pattern on the material is extremely elaborate, and the choice of colors, lapis lazuli and gold, suggests wealth and importance.

COMPOSITION

The perspective in this painting is the most elaborately devised of any in Piero's art. The figures are made to appear more imposing by setting them against a low horizon. The central axis of the painting divides it exactly in half and meets the end of the vanishing line created by the row of columns on the right.

The outside pavement is divided into a large square by broad white marble lines, with thinner subdivisions separating the area filled with terracotta tiles. A double framework is therefore created with the smaller one providing the exact measurements for the larger one. In the square where the flagellation takes place a perfect circle can be circumscribed with the cylindrical column at its center.

The whole composition is made up of elaborate and subtly balanced internal spatial relationships. There are calculated contrasts too: the closed area in the left background is counterposed by the open space in the right foreground and the figures drawn back from the figure of Christ are in contrast to those in the foreground gathered around the young man with blond hair. The spatial relationships are all calculated according to the "golden section" revived from antiquity and which finds its highest artistic expression in the painting of Piero della Francesca.

SACRA CONVERSAZIONE
Piero della Francesca, 1472-74
Milan, Brera.

SUBJECT

The hidden messages contained in this mysterious painting have still only been partially decoded. The Sacra conversazione takes place in a large Renaissance building, possibly a church, with rich decoration and marble panels.

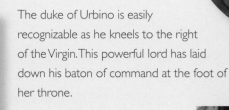

An ostrich egg is hung from a large shell at the back of the apse, a symbol invested with many meanings including allusions to the birth and resurrection of Christ. It might also be linked to the pregnancy of Battista Sforza, Duchess of Urbino who commissioned the altarpiece together with her husband Federico da Montefeltro.

The duke of Urbino is easily recognizable as he kneels to the right of the Virgin. This powerful lord has laid down his baton of command at the foot of her throne.

The whole composition is centered on the sleeping Christ Child whose figure in repose prefigures his death by crucifixion. In keeping with the iconography which gained ground in the Renaissance the Child is depicted naked and wears a coral necklace.

In the group of angels and saints closely gathered around the Madonna the head of St Bernardino of Siena is visible second from the left. The painting was destined for the Urbino church dedicated to the Sienese saint. Beside him stand St Jerome, who hold a stone to his chest as a sign of penitence, and St John the Baptist.

To the right of the Virgin are: St Francis, showing the signs of the stigmata, with behind him and showing the fatal wound of his martyrdom, the Dominican St Peter Martyr. An Evangelist stands to his left.

COMPOSITION

The perspective has a single vanishing point coinciding with the eyes of the Madonna.

The panel must originally have been larger with the center of the scene focused on the ostrich egg.

The Virgin is directly below the egg, its shape repeated in her oval face.

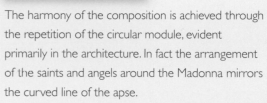

The harmony of the composition is achieved through the repetition of the circular module, evident primarily in the architecture. In fact the arrangement of the saints and angels around the Madonna mirrors the curved line of the apse.

THE SANT'APOLLONIA LAST SUPPER BY ANDREA DEL CASTAGNO

In 1447 Andrea del Castagno was given the commission to paint the refectory in the Benedictine convent of Sant'Apollonia, in Florence. On the north wall Andrea del Castagno created an extraor-dinarily complex pictorial cycle conceived on two levels.

On the upper one between the two windows he painted the *Crucifixion*, with the *Resurrection* to the left, and the *Entombment* to the right.

These scenes take place in an area "really" behind the building in which the *Last Supper*, occupying the lower wall, is depicted.

61

61. Andrea del Castagno,
Last Supper and episodes
from the *Passion*, 1447.
Florence, Refectory of
Sant'Apollonia.

The upper and lower halves are linked by the projecting roof and by the contrasting lighting effects of the external and internal scenes. The architectural area, constructed according to the rules of centralized perspective, appears almost as a continuation of the real space of the refectory. The dramatic nature of the event is highlighted by the various gestures of the Apostles, Christ turns towards his favorite, St John the Evangelist, to give him his blessing.

The perspective effect makes Christ appear to be slightly smaller than Judas, who is seated alone on this side of the table.

This bold arrangement is unimaginable outside the climate of the Florentine Renaissance and was never repeated.

62. **Andrea del Castagno,**
Last Supper, **detail, 1447.**
Florence, Refectory of
Sant'Apollonia.

3. The detailed depiction of reality

The exploration of the real world that took place in Florence in the first decades of the fifteenth century found a parallel in the activities of Flemish painters, and especially of Jan Van Eyck. But the results achieved by the northern painters were substantially different from those obtained in Italy and in Florence in particular. While Brunelleschi created the possibility of producing a unified vision in linear perspective Flemish art concentrated on the minute study of reality accompanied by a more empirical conception of space. Light provided the unifying element as it flooded and illuminated every detail. This lead to a remarkably accurate depiction of the visible universe in all its richness, in which the space allotted to man was neither central nor exclusive. Every element – whether a simple everyday object or a glimpsed landscape – is worthy of close attention and acquires symbolic significance.

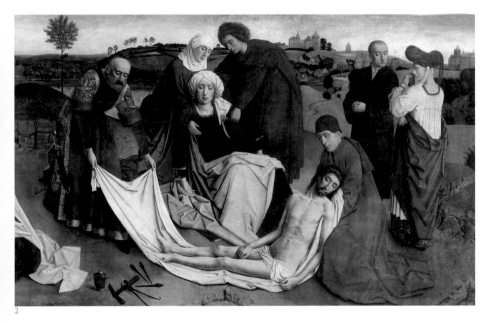

1. Facing page: Jan Van Eyck, *Ghent Polypytch, The Virgin*, detail, 1432. Ghent, Saint-Bavon.

2. Petrus Christus, *Pietà*, 1455-60. Brussels, Musées Royaux des Beaux-Arts.

3. Hans Memling, *Portrait of a man*, about 1480. The Hague, Mauritshuis.

4-5. Rogier Van der
Weyden, *Polypytch of the
Seven Sacraments,
Baptism, Confirmation,
Penitence*, and
Matrimony, Ordination,

Extreme Unction, 1445-50.
Antwerp, Musée des
Beaux-Arts.

LIGHT IN FLEMISH PAINTING

Peculiar to Flemish painting was the search for ways of depicting the effects of light, based on a close observation of natural light and optical phenomenona. In Flemish painting light appears as a fluid and unifying medium, identifying with the same attention the infinitely small and the infinitely vast, the near and the far. The integration of figures is achieved through this medium as it unifies space and at the same time delineates the single elements contained within it. The particular luminosity of Flemish painting is achieved with oils, applied in transparent layers, perfectly suited to conveying the endlessly varied surfaces and other precise details. The use of various sources of light tends to increase shadows and reflections, creating "lustre" effects, the specific reaction to luminous rays.

Examples of the expressive power of light and of luminous layers of color are identifiable in a number of monochrome compositions by Flemish artists in which the figures acquire volume and consistency through a skilful play of light and shade and by manipulating the internal and external lighting of the painting.

6. Jan Van Eyck,
St Francis receiving the stigmata, about 1425.
Turin, Galleria Sabauda.

7. Rogier Van der Weyden,
Three Pharisees. Madrid,
Prado.

JAN VAN EYCK AND FLEMISH REALISM

Jan Van Eyck founded the Flemish school and became one of the greatest painters of the fifteenth century. He began his artistic career by painting a number of illuminated pages for the *Book of Hours* which probably belonged to Duke William of Bavaria. His distinctive quality as a painter was clear from the first with his lively naturalistic interest in the depiction of delicate but vibrant landscapes. He established himself in Bruges and in 1432 painted the polyptych of the *Adoration of the Mystical Lamb* for the church of Saint Jean in Ghent. In this, his first known work and greatest masterpiece, the impressive spatial discipline and the atmospheric density of the color soften the perspective rigor to create a convincing sense of space and luminosity.

8-9. Jan Van Eyck,
Ghent Altarpiece
(outside), and detail of
St John the Evangelist,
1432. Ghent, Saint-
Bavon.

His method of presenting reality was analytical, using the numerous objects which our senses perceive as his point of departure.

Court artist to Philip the Good of Burgundy, for whom he also performed important diplomatic missions throughout Europe, Van Eyck also came into contact with the Florentine innovations. The Italian influence is reflected in the development of his personal style, one of the great artistic achievements and one of compelling emotional appeal.

10-11. Jan Van Eyck,
Ghent Altarpiece
(outside), Annunciation,
1432. Ghent, Saint-Bavon.

THE VIRGIN OF CHANCELLOR ROLIN
Jan Van Eyck, about 1435
Paris, Louvre

SUBJECT

The painting depicts the Virgin being crowned by an angel while showing the Christ Child to the Chancellor Nicholas Rolin, who commissioned the painting. He is dressed in a fine fur-lined coat and is praying on his knees before the sacred image which has the quality of an apparition.

In contrast to medieval tradition, which imposed a strict hierarchy of size in relation to the importance of the figures, the patron and the Virgin are the same size in this work by Van Eyck.

The architecture is enriched with carved capitals and stained glass, rather like a church.

The sacred theme is given a secular interpretation and is set in a sumptuous interior opening onto an airy landscape.

Van Eyck pays minute attention to the details of the rich cloth and jewelery

but also to the distant landscape, to the small figures crossing the bridge, to the peacocks, and to the vegetation.

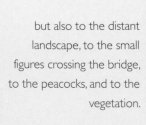

Quite possibly the city in the background is Autun, Chancellor Rolin's birthplace, where the painting was kept before it came to the Louvre.

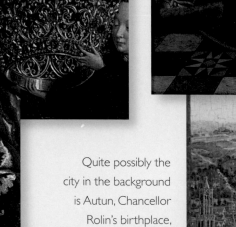

COMPOSITION

The composition is symmetrically arranged with the two figures on either side of the central space. The spectator's gaze is therefore drawn into the painting by the luminous landscape in the background and to the vanishing point of the perspective construction.

The space in which the event takes place seems to be raised with respect to the architecture painted in the background. A sense of depth is created by the row of arched columns at the sides.
The square tiles of the pavement reinforce the perspective, with a single row of tiles separating the celestial from the terrestrial sphere.

The distance of the mountains is suggested not only by their size but by the soft covering of mist.

12

12. Hugo Van der Goes,
Death of the Virgin, **about**
1480. Bruges,
Groeningemuseum.

HUGO VAN DER GOES: MONUMENTALITY AND MINUTE DESCRIPTION

Among Flemish painters, Hugo Van der Goes was unique in his ability to transpose into monumental form the minute attention to detail, interpreted with technical sophistication. He trained in his native city of Ghent, where he came into contact with Justus of Ghent, who worked at the court of Urbino for Federico da Montefeltro between 1472 and 1475. Hugo Van der Goes's knowledge of Renaissance art, essential to his stylistic maturity, might well have been acquired through Justus. In 1468 Hugo was called to Bruges to help in the decorative preparations for the wedding of Charles the Bold to Margaret of York. In these years he painted his first known works,

in which his religious sensibility is already apparent. This inspired his formation of dramatic groups of figures in somber compositions with a powerful narrative vein and very few incidental or background details. As he developed his monumental arrangement of the figures and the energetic modeling of form became increasingly confident and successful. He managed to combine this monumental aspect with the more traditional characteristics of the Flemish school, such as the rich treatment of textiles, analytical attention to detail, and the sophisticated rendering of reflected light, especially on metal. The overpowering religious tension and underlying melancholy in Van der Goes painting would appear to reflect the troubles of his personal life. In 1475 he entered a monastery where he spent his late years in mental anguish, and died following a breakdown in 1482.

13

14

13. Hugo Van der Goes,
Christ in blessing. **Genoa,**
Palazzo Bianco.

14. Hugo Van der Goes,
Deposition.
St Petersburg, Hermitage.

RENAISSANCE ART

111

HUMAN EMOTION IN THE WORK OF ROGIER VAN DER WEYDEN

Rogier Van der Weyden is thought to have trained in the workshop of Robert Campin, also known as the Master of Flémalle, for his work shows a similar concern for the human and emotional qualities of his personages.

To Van Eyck he was indebted for the luminous rendering of his scenes and of detail but his main interest concentrated on depicting man, on observing and describing his inner life in the variety and extremity of his emotions. He was fascinated by dramatic episodes, especially those charged with pathos that allowed him to explore a range of poses and expressions.

His compositions are nevertheless always organized with a strict regard for dignified composure, underlined by a choice of cold and brilliant colors. Van der Weyden was also able to introduce subtle changes into established religious iconography in his search for new and surprising forms.

He was in Rome for the Jubilee of 1450, and visited other important Italian cities where he came into contact with artists working in the most advanced style. His own work was greeted with enthusiasm at the courts he visited in Naples, Ferrara, Mantua and Milan and became more concentrated and monumental: witness the *Deposition* in the Uffizi, which adopts the compositional arrangement used by Fra Angelico but interprets it in a more pathetic and emotive vein.

15

16

15. Fra Angelico, *Deposition*, about 1440. Munich, Alte Pinakothek.

16. Rogier Van der Weyden, *Braque family triptych*, central panel with Christ, the Virgin and St John the Evangelist, about 1450. Paris, Louvre.

17. Rogier Van der
Weyden, *Deposition*,
about 1450. Florence,
Uffizi.

DEPOSITION
Rogier Van der Weyden, 1435
Madrid, Prado

SUBJECT

This work, painted for the chapel of the Confraternity of the Archers in the church of Notre-Dame hors les Murs in Louvain, dates from the middle period of the artist's activity. It depicts the moment when Christ's body was taken down from the Cross: the scene is contained within a boxlike space crowded with figures.

While the background suggests a room with bare wooden walls the ground is covered with plants and stones

The powerful dramatic impact is created by the number of figures crammed into such a small space together with the intense expressivity of their gestures and expressions. The sumptuous, glowing colors increase the theatrical effect.

The Virgin's body has collapsed in a faint: her limbs are in disarray and her pale face reflects her suffering.

Similarly the position of the Magdalene, on the right, with her curved body and hands wrung together conveys her desperation. These figures are modeled to give them round and palpable form.

In the upper corners are two carved decorative architectural elements.

COMPOSITION

Although the dramatic quality of the scene is immediately apparent the arrangement of the figures is carefully balanced and tuned, built on symmetrical relationships between the figures.

The position of the Virgin's body repeats the curve of Christ's, creating a compostional affinity but even more importantly a symbolic one. The others figures are grouped around these two narrative centers, Christ and the Madonna, in closed groups of three on either side of the painting.

The shape of the panel is unusual, for while uniting the narrative it is reminiscent of a medieval triptych with a taller central section given vertical emphasis by the Cross.

In the narrow confines of the room a sense of depth is conveyed by the angle of the ladder its base resting in the far background.

PORTRAIT PAINTING IN NORTHERN EUROPE

The lively characterization of the faces left to us by Jan Van Eyck explain why he is so often credited with being the founder of Flemish portraiture. With their close and accurate study of physiognomy, depth of psychological understanding, and the expressiveness of faces seen to full effect against neutral or dark backgrounds the portraits represent one of the highest achievements of the Flemish school. Subjects are often depicted within domestic interiors, with effects of light and color playing on the arrangement of the furniture and hangings. A number of motifs constantly reoccur such as the convex mirror in Van Eyck's painting which reflects elements concealed from the view of the onlooker or outside the composition completely. Most Flemish artist of the fifteenth century turned to portraiture and have left us a rich array of impressive works which had considerable impact on Italian renaissance painting of the same genre. Rogier Van der Weyden, Petrus Christus and Hans Memling were among the very best.

18

19

20

18. Petrus Christus, *Portrait of a young woman*, 1460-73. Berlin, Staatliche Museen.

19. Master of Flémalle (Robert Campin), *Portrait of Barthelemy Alatruye*. Tournai, Musée des Beaux-Arts.

20. Hans Memling, *Portrait of Giovanni da Candida*, about 1475-80. Antwerp, Musée des Beaux-Arts.

THE *ARNOLFINI WEDDING* BY JAN VAN EYCK

The painting was commissioned by Giovanni Arnolfini, a rich Tuscan merchant living in Bruges.

The patron is depicted together with his wife at the moment of making his solemn vow of fidelity.

The couple are shown within their comfortable and elegant home surrounded by familiar domestic objects.

The informality of the setting, the scene taking place in their bedroom, is in contrast to the formality of their pose and their rich and formal clothing. The symmetrical arrangement of the composition adds formality to the depiction of the event.

Despite the balance and apparent naturalism of the scene, the painting is charged with allusion and allegory.

There is the emphatic gesture of Arnolfini, and the presence of the dog and the candle, to symbolize matrimonial fidelity.

The painter's signature appears on the back wall, in elegant Latin script. The circular mirror reflects the room and includes reflections of two people entering the room one of whom, according to the inscription. is the painter Van Eyck.

21

22

23

21-23. Jan Van Eyck, *The Arnolfini Wedding* and details, 1434. London, National Gallery.

RENAISSANCE ART

DAILY LIFE IN SACRED FLEMISH PAINTING

In the late the fourteenth century people in northern Europe began to feel the need for a closer and more personal rapport with God.

It was articulated in painting which attempted to involve the faithful in religious art, so that they became active participants in the event depicted.

Private devotion was assisted by the proliferation of prayer books and devotional images. To aid this sense of participation images had to be concrete representations, full of minute and accurate details.

This gave birth to "Flemish realism", which set scenes from Holy Scripture in minutely described interiors and provides a near photographic documentation of the furnishings, and role of objects in domestic interiors of the fifteenth century.

24

24. Rogier Van der
Weyden, *St Luke painting
the Virgin*, 1435-37.
St Petersburg, Hermitage.

ROBERT CAMPIN OR THE MASTER OF FLÉMALLE

The works conventionally grouped as belonging to the Master of Flémalle are probably by Robert Campin, a Flemish painter active in Tournai, a small city in the south of Belgium, then part of France. His paintings are characterized, by motifs taken from Van Eyck, by the monumental treatment of the figures, by the search for dramatic effect and by clear and precise outlines. Form is also shaped by the use of light and shade, which in the drapery creates a marvelous decorative effect. Monumentality and plasticity are the key elements in his figures that have often been compared to Burgundian sculpture.

Campin combines his decorative late-gothic graphic mode, of French inspiration, with numerous and heterogeneous cultural references and adds fiber to a touching lyricism with his imaginative, fascinating, and original artistic vision.

25

25. Master of Flémalle (Robert Campin),
Betrothal of the Virgin,
about 1420. Madrid, Prado.

FLEMISH INTERIORS IN THE *ANNUNCIATION* BY THE MASTER OF FLÉMALLE

This panel is the central part of a triptych, dating from around 1430 and attributed to the Master of Flémalle. The comfortable interior, typical of the house of a prosperous merchant, is described in the minute detail in the manner of Flemish painting.

Particular care is given to the depiction of the open book with its pages flapping, the majolica jug holding the lilies, the brass candle holder and the snuffed candle. The sacred episode is interpreted as an everyday event. The perspective of the walls, ceiling and long narrow bench on the right do not create a convincing sense of spatial depth but convey the effect of an open box viewed at a distance by the onlooker. A number of elements are depicted with an intentionally distorted perspective, drawing the faithful closer to the scene.

Most obvious is the table top which is tipped towards the viewer and the position of the two figures that appear to be almost touching in the foreground but then diverge according to the constructive lines of the composition.

26

28

27

26-28. Master of Flémalle (Robert Campin),
Annunciation **and details, about 1430. Brussels, Musées Royaux des Beaux-Arts.**

FLEMISH INTERIORS IN THE *ANNUNCIATION* BY ROGIER VAN DER WEYDEN

In the *Annunciation* by Rogier Van der Weyden in the Louvre the sacred episode takes place in an interior typical of the house of a prosperous merchant, and is described in minute detail. Behind the Virgin there is a large four post bed, with heavy red hangings, used to conserve warmth and keep out drafts.

A votive medal hangs above the head of the bed. There are a few, essential pieces of furniture but they are solidly built. A chair to the left of the bed is carved with gothic motifs and there is a small cupboard beside it. A shiny metal ewer and basin rest on the top of the cupboard reflecting the light that pours in from the window. There is a bench covered with soft red cushions to the left in front of the fireplace. A branched bronze chandelier hangs from the ceiling. The floor is covered in blue and white tiles typical of northern Europe.

The artist's descriptive power is also demonstrated in the detailed rendering of the brocade cope, in the metal fittings of the shutters, and in the system of supports holding up the baldachin.

29

30

31

29-31. Rogier Van der Weyden, *Annunciation* and details, 1435. Paris, Louvre.

RENAISSANCE ART

LANDSCAPE IN FLEMISH PAINTING

The atmospheric treatment of background landscapes, first painted to exemplary effect by the Limbourg brothers, is together with portraiture one of the main achievements of Flemish painting.

Unlike Italian painting of the early fifteenth century, where the inclusion of a natural dimension is of secondary importance to the composition, paintings by Flemish masters soon achieved a sense of depth with landscape and included atmospheric and occasionally illusionistic effects.

32

33

34

32-34. Hans Memling,
Virgin and Child with two
***angels** and details, about*
1480. Florence, Uffizi.

The same analytical eye was eager to understand the workings of the human body, architectural construction, and the natural elements and gave them substance and realism in painting. Flemish painters invented the distant view in urban and country landscapes, often inserted as the background to religious paintings in order to relate episodes from the distant past spatially and geographically to the present.

Natural details in the foreground were also painstakingly described: blades of grass and a variety of flowers were depicted with almost scientific accuracy.

35-36. Rogier Van der Weyden, *Braque family triptych, St John the Baptist* and detail, about 1450 Paris, Louvre.

THE *ADORATION OF THE MYSTICAL LAMB* BY JAN VAN EYCK

The *Adoration of the Mystical Lamb* is the central panel of the *Ghent Polyptych* by Van Eyck, one of the most extraordinary masterpieces produced by the Flemish Renaissance. The scene is set in a luxuriant green landscape with gothic towers and pinnacles rising up in the background. The meticulous treatment of the natural elements in this painting makes the landscape a primary force in the composition. The central axis is clearly determined by the fountain in the foreground, which reaches up to the middle of the altar of the mystical Lamb.

The axis continues through the altar to the meet the luminous globe suspended in the sky. The landscape provides a sense of spatial development with the succession of meadows, woods and mountains in various shades of green.

The atmospheric distance is not constructed by following the rules of perspective The groups of figures, despite their different sizes, do not diminish in scale towards the background but appear more as if seen from above and as though superimposed. They are arranged in diagonal lines transporting us intuitively into the distance. This device maintains the internal harmony of the composition and gives it a particular fascination.

37

37. Jan Van Eyck, *Ghent altarpiece*, 1432. Ghent, Saint-Bavon.

38-39. Jan Van Eyck,
Ghent altarpiece, St John
the Baptist and the Virgin,
1432. Ghent, Saint-Bavon.

40. In the following pages:
Jan Van Eyck, *Ghent*
Altarpiece, Adoration of
***the Mystical Lamb,* 1432.**
Ghent, Saint-Bavon.

COMMERCIAL EXCHANGE AND ARTISTIC RELATIONS BETWEEN NORTHERN AND SOUTHERN EUROPE

The great innovations of the early Renaissance that took place in central Italy did not immediately affect painting in the rest of the peninsula where late-gothic tendencies continued. But gradually the influence first of French and Burgundian art was felt, to be overtaken and indeed supplanted by that of the Flemish artists. Their influence took hold in all the areas previously dominated by the International Gothic, in the wake of the political events of the period. From 1438 to 1442 René of Anjou, a lover of art and literature, ruled in Naples and did much to broadened the cultural outlook, introducing the southern court to the stylistic innovations of Van Eyck, Campin

41

43

42

41-43. Quentin Metsys,
Banker and his wife and
details, 1514. Paris,
Louvre.

and Sluter. From 1444 Alfonso of Aragon succeeded to the throne of Naples bringing the city in very close contact with his other territories. There arrived in Naples and Palermo paintings from outside Italy, but also artists from Spain and France trained in the new Flemish manner.

They offered a figurative language that mediated between the local culture and renaissance innovation. The importance of economic and commercial exchanges, conducted alongside international diplomatic relations, should not be undervalued. Bankers and merchants, intent on increasing their own social importance, made a substantial contribution to the importation and dissemination of the trends from the north of Europe so that works of art and painters also reached the courts of Florence, Urbino, Rome, Venice providing new stimulus to artistic development.

44

45

44. Sano di Pietro, *Statute of the Merchants' guild.* Siena, Archivio di Stato.

45. Filippino Lippi, *Nelli Altarpiece,* detail with the Porta di San Frediano. Florence, Santo Spirito.

46

47

THE *PORTINARI ALTARPIECE* BY HUGO VAN DER GOES IN FLORENCE

In 1475 Hugo Van der Goes was commissioned to paint a triptych for the church of Sant'Egidio in Florence by the agent for the Medici bankers in Bruges, Tommaso Portinari. The *Portinari altarpiece* is the only documented work by the painter and also the most ambitious in size. Such a large painting is unusual in Flemish painting, and was probably stipulated in the terms of the contract. The central panel represents the *Adoration of the shepherds*, while in the two side panels the Portinari family are presented by two pairs of saints. The side panels are also painted behind, with a monochrome *Annunciation*. The painting was immediately admired in Florence and sparked off a cultural dialogue and exchange of artistic ideas -witness the less rough group of shepherds included by Ghirlandaio in his *Adoration of the shepherds* in the Sassetti Chapel in the church

48

46. Domenico Ghirlandaio, *Adoration of the shepherds*, 1485. Florence, Santa Trinita.

47-48. Hugo Van der Goes, *Portinari Triptych* and detail, 1475-77. Florence, Uffizi.

of Santa Trinita. There is a striking contrast between the group of shepherds, depicted with brutal realism in their torn garments and with rough hands and faces, and the richness and nobility of the rest of the painting.

The angels and the Virgin are arranged around the Christ Child in an almost perfect circle on a steeply inclined plane, designed to accentuate the space. Van der Goes has constructed all the figures with exceptional plastic energy, combining minute attention to detail with an overall monumentality. Vases of flowers, one in a majolica jar in the foreground, provide an element of still-life, before such a genre existed, interesting for its introduction of elements of everyday objects into a religious subject.

49

49. Hugo Van der Goes,
Portinari Triptych,
Adoration of the
shepherds, 1475-77.
Florence, Uffizi.

RENAISSANCE ART

50

DEVOTION AND REALISM

The trends in Flemish painting, characterized by close attention to the real world and the setting of sacred scenes within it, were absorbed by Spanish and German artists. They however liked to take these rich and sumptuous compositions and integrate them into complex altars, combining painting and sculpture into theatrical arrangements that caught the attention of the faithful even when viewed down the length of a cathedral nave.

PAINTING AND SCULPTURE: THE GREAT GERMAN ALTARPIECES

In Germany painting and sculpture developed in a highly original way, even though they absorbed some of the advances made in Italy and Flanders. The forms are modeled through shading, colors react to natural light and not to an ideal one, space is defined in three dimensions even though advances in perspective are ignored. Michael Pacher, the greatest painter of the period, developed a violent realism built on Italian Renaissance concerns for balance and harmony. Veit Stoss, who transferred Pacher's advances in painting into sculpture, managed to organize extraordinarily expressive, crowded wooden "pictures" which are loaded with emphatic gestures and facial types.

51

50. Martin Schongauer,
Madonna of the rose
garden. **Bologna,**
Pinacoteca Nazionale.

51. Michael Pacher,
Fathers of the Church
Altarpiece, **about 1480.**
Munich, Alte Pinakothek.

ST WOLFANG ALTARPIECE BY MICHAEL PACHER

Artists in the Alpine regions also became aware of the figurative advances in the surrounding countries and produced a lively art that has only been assessed seriously in recent years. Realism and the taste for rich detail, distinctive features of German late gothic art, existed side by side with the volume and solidity associated with Burgundian art and the sophisticated treatment of light taken from Flemish painting. The leading Tyrolean artist was Michael Pacher, who confidently developed an eclectic style, which he often carried to extremes. The Italian Renaissance, and more specifically its development in Padua under Montello and Manteno, inspired his sharply defined and monumental forms, characterized by dramatic perspective angles. In his St Wolfgang altarpiece, dated to about 1480, expressivity and a dramatic dynamism appear triumphant in a composition combining intense colors and powerful chiaroscuro effects. The work was carved in perfect harmony with the interior of the sanctuary dedicated to St Wolfgang, its form and style reflecting that of the surrounding space. This explains the clear references to international gothic taste in its most sumptuous manifestations.

52

52. Michael Pacher,
Coronation of the Virgin,
about 1480. Sanctuary
of St Wolfgang.

53

The German painter, sculptor, and engraver, Veit Stoss, is one of the most important personalities marking the transition from the late-gothic to the Renaissance.

His early works are recognizable for their pronounced linearity and exaggerated expressionism, so typical of the German artistic tradition. After a long period in Krakow, where he worked for the most important churches in the city, Stoss returned to Nuremberg in 1496. His lyrical and dramatic outbursts were abandoned in favor of much calmer and more ordered compositions, clearly conditioned by his understanding of Italian innovations. The surface of the bodies, which had been contracted and bent, now appeared to expand into the space around them, the faces of the figures were no longer so exaggerated and the general impression is one of a serene artistic vision inspired by the artist's own inner peace.

54

53. Veit Stoss, *Altar of the Madonna*, detail. Bamberg, Cathedral.

54. Veit Stoss, *Group of Apostles*. Bamberg, Diözesanmuseum.

ENGUERRAND QUARTON AND PROVENCAL ART

The stylized rendering of volume accentuated by the use of a clear, crystalline light is the hallmark of the greatest Provencal painter, Enguerrand Quarton.

Quarton was born in Laon, one of the French-speaking provinces under the rule of the dukes of Burgundy, and had direct contact with the first generation of Flemish artists: Robert Campin, Jan Van Eyck, and Rogier Van der Weyden. He derived his luminous realism from them, interpreting it with all the elegance of the international gothic to create a fascinating style all his own. In the 1440s he moved to Avignon, where he encountered the lively Italian community focused on the Papal court, and from whom he gained his understanding of the Tuscan Renaissance.

In the Avignon *Pietà*, now in the Louvre, he displays his original and compact rendering of monumentality which he combined with a sensitive attention to detail.

The scene is pervaded with a sense of drama. The clear and limpid atmosphere exalts the chromatic range with its predominance of cold colors.

55

55. Enguerrand Quarton, Villeneuve-lès-Avignon *Pietà*, about 1455. Paris, Louvre.

CATALAN RETABLES

A retable is a large altarpiece divided into either painted or carved sections, with a highly decorative and elaborate architectural frame. Retables spread throughout Europe from the fourteenth century but were most popular in the Iberian peninsula.

Among the large number in the Museum of Catalan Art in Barcellona, the most outstanding is by Jaime Huguet and was painted for the altar of the confraternity of tanners between 1463 and 1485. Huguet used a large team of assistants to help him with this highly ambitious project. The main panel, depicting the *Consecration of St Augustine* to whom the church was dedicated, is certainly by the master's own

hand. The work is richly decorated, with gold applied lavishly and a floral background worked in stucco. The miters are encrusted with precious stones, depicted with extraordinary accuracy, and the sumptuous vestments are faithfully described in the rich variety of their patterns and ornamentation.

Most remarkable is St Augustine's stole hanging down over his red and gold cope. It is decorated with figures of the saints, which appear as real, if tiny, paintings within the larger one. In contrast to all this formal elegance the faces of the clergy are startling in their realism, and rare clearly portraits indebted to the Flemish tradition. The face on the extreme right looking out of the painting is thought to be a self-portrait by Jaime Huguet.

56

56. Luis Dalmau, *Madonna with the Counsellors of Barcellona*, 1445. Barcellona, Museu Nacional d'art de Catalunya.

57. Following page: Jaime Huguet, *Consacration of St Augustine*, 1463-85. Barcellona, Museu Nacional d'art de Catalunya.

4. Man at the center of the universe

Man as the centre of the universe was an idea fostered by the humanists which developed from their study of the classical authors. It is clearly reflected in renaissance art with the stylistic, expressive and iconographic transformation of figurative language. The new style appeared increasingly concerned with representing the human body and man's inner life. Iconographies were invented and others, such as the portrait bust and the equestrian statue, were revived from antiquity. Man was valued for his ability to shape his own destiny and his action as an individual was highly prized, so that men of letters and condottieri, or captains of war, became the heroes of secular art, while patrons and donors appeared as large as saints in religious paintings. In this climate artists were culturally enriched: their practical and technical knowledge, once confined to the workshop, increased, as did their theoretical understanding. This process led to the revaluation of the intellectual role of the artist and to his socio-cultural emancipation.

2

3

1. Facing page: Leonardo, *Proportions of the human body*, 1492. Venice, Accademia.

2. Agostino di Duccio, *Profile of Sigismondo Malatesta*, 1449-55. Rimini, Tempio Malatestiano.

3. *Master with his pupils*, codex 2167 c. 13 v. Milan, Biblioteca Trivulziana.

THE PORTRAIT

The portrait, the creation of the recognizable likeness of an individual, gained enormous popularity during the Renaissance as a result of the revived interest in antiquity and of the new approach to the real world and to ways of representing it.

In the early stages portraits were strictly in profile, according to a formula derived from medals, and were strongly associated with the classical revival. This trend was overtaken by one for independent portrait busts. The influence of Flemish painting, which was less bound to classical prototypes and more taken up with an analytical study of the contemporary world, led to the introduction in Italy of portraits, initially of a three-quarter view of the face and head, and later of the full face. In these years in Florence the fashion for sculpted portrait busts gained hold very rapidly and shaped the output of the next generation of great sculptors: Antonio Rossellino, Desiderio da Settignano and Mino da Fiesole.

Finally the desire felt by most patrons to have themselves celebrated and commemorated as individuals was provided for in the realism of the artistic language of the Renaissance. And so with Masaccio's work in Florence as a starting point, patrons became incorporated into the sacred scenes and were depicted on the same scale as the Madonna and saints, their faces and dress depicted with startling realism. Man became the measure of all things, at the top of any hierarchical scale of importance.

By the end of the century he was appearing in celebratory pictorial cycles, in which the sacred scenes were made topical through the introduction of portraits of contemporary figures.

4

5

4. Donatello, *Niccolò da Uzzano*, about 1430-32. Florence, Bargello.

5. *Portrait of John the Good,* about 1350. Paris, Louvre. One of the earliest French paintings and the first example of an individual portrait in profile in Europe.

FIFTEENTH-CENTURY PORTRAIT BUSTS

Donatello was the first to revive the sculptural portrait, from the models of Roman antiquity, in his 1424 *Reliquiary of St Rossore* in which the saint appears as a recognizable human being. In the *Bust of a young man* in the Bargello, of about 1440 he adopted the same prototype not for a reliquary but for an actual portrait, one however which is strongly idealized. This piece is in contrast to the works of the next generation of Florentine sculptors who softened the

dramatic treatment favored by Donatello in favor of a more graceful and approachable style. The portrait of *Piero de' Medici* by Mino da Fiesole carefully explores the physiognomy and expression of the subject, but also recreates the fine details of his clothing with considerable virtuosity, so conveying his elevated social standing.

In the same way, in the bust of the humanist *Matteo Palmieri*, by Antonio Rossellino, the characterization of the features offers more than an analytical facial study in order to convey his personality as an individual.

6. Mino da Fiesole, *Piero de' Medici*, 1453. Florence, Bargello.

7. Donatello, *Bust of a young man*, about 1440. Florence, Bargello.

EQUESTRIAN AND FUNERARY MONUMENTS

The glorification of man's terrestrial existence, of his standing at the centre of the humanist universe, found its maximum representation in the equestrian monument and in the new funerary monuments produced in the mid-Quattrocento. These monuments, in fact, celebrated man's active life, exalting his worth as an individual and his capacity to influence the course of history. These are secular works in which the religious aspects of death appears secondary. In the *Monument to Leonardo Bruni*, by Bernardo Rossellino, Bruni is depicted clutching a copy of his own *History of Florence*, rather than a sacred text. In this genre too Donatello provided the prototype: in the tombs of the anti-pope John XXIII in the baptistery of Florence and in that of Cardinal Brancacci in Naples, the fourteenth-century model arranged in layers is updated with the inclusion of classical elements and the creation of a more overtly architectural model. Then Donatello's *Equestrian statue to Gattamelata* in Padua in its turn became the point of reference for all such monuments erected in Europe from 1450 to the present.

8

9

8-9. Michelozzo di Bartolomeo, *Tomb of the anti-pope John XXIII* and detail of a *Virtue*, 1425-27. Florence, Baptistery.

10. Donatello, *Equestrian monument to Gattamelata*, 1445-50. Padua, Piazza del Santo.

11-12. Bernardo Rossellino, *Tomb of Leonardo Bruni* and detail, 1446-50. Florence, Santa Croce.

The humanist tomb, while retaining a degree of religious significance, tended to celebrate the terrestrial achievements and individuality of the subject. The new style of these monuments appeared in the mid-fifteenth century, with the tomb of the chancellor of the Florentine Republic, Leonardo Bruni, by Bernardo Rossellino in the church of Santa Croce in Florence. A rounded arch, decorated with classical motifs, frames a shallow opening, enclosing the tomb and the bier on which Bruni lies. The only religious reference is the *Madonna and Child* in the lunette. In the *Monument to Carlo Marsuppini* by Desiderio da Settignano, also in Santa Croce, the same scheme is adopted although it is given a less architectural and more decorative interpretation. The extraordinary virtuosity of the artist is evident in his modeling of the marble of the funeral drapes and in the shaping of the classical decoration of the tomb. Once defined, this model of the humanist tomb was repeated with infinite variations, as in the *Tomb of Cardinal Federighi* by Luca della Robbia, in which a border of festoons of fruit in glazed terracotta takes the place of the traditional border relief with classical motifs.

13

14

15

13. Antonio Rossellino,
Tomb of Cardinal of Portugal, 1461-66.
Florence, San Miniato al Monte.

14. Luca della Robbia,
Tomb of Cardinal Federighi, 1457-58.
Florence, Santa Trinita.

**15-16. Desiderio da
Settignano, *Tomb of Carlo
Marsuppini* and detail
with putto, 1455-58.
Florence, Santa Croce.**

MEN, SAINTS AND HEROES

Renaissance man had faith in the possibility of shaping his own life and to measure his destiny against his abilities. He thought himself in command of the natural world, and sought to affirm his own power over his surroundings. Aware of his own potential, he extended his interest to the rest of nature and felt admiration for it as part of his search to understand his physical humanity. But praise for the active life and for personal success stemmed from the idea of the unity and harmony inextricably linking an individual's body and soul. This intellectual and philosophical outlook was reflected in the transformation of both the form

17. Andrea del Castagno,
Dante, **1449-51.**
Florence, Uffizi.

18. Domenico Ghirlandaio
and assistants, *Decius,*
Scipio e Cicero, **1482-84.**
Florence, Palazzo
Vecchio, Sala dei Gigli.

and content of works. And so together with the appearance of a new style of unified altarpiece, a new iconography emerged, that of the sacra conversazione, in which the figures appeared as increasingly convincing portrayals of recognizable people. At the same time, in Florence, the iconography of "famous men", of late-medieval origin, put them into their social context , with references to recent history, while in the courts of northern Europe the celebrative aspect was manifest in scenes of contemporary and court life. In Florence at the time of Lorenzo the Magnificent the members of the Medici family and their adherents even became the leading figures in paintings with religious themes.

19

20

19. Domenico Ghirlandaio and assistants, *Brutus, Muzio Scevola e Camillus*, 1482-84. Florence, Palazzo Vecchio, Sala dei Gigli.

20. Perugino, *Cato*, 1497. Perugia, Palazzo dei Priori, Collegio del Cambio.

THE SACRA CONVERSAZIONE

The formal innovations of the Renaissance, which gave rise to the invention of the unified altarpiece, one no longer divided into separate panels, was accompanied by changes in iconography. Fra Angelico provided the earliest examples of these new representations in which the Virgin and Child appear together with saints according to the formula known as the "sacra conversazione". These were intended to depict imaginary conversations among the saints on doctrinal issues conducted under the auspices of the Madonna and Child. The scene often takes place against a renaissance, architectural background, and this contributes to the humanity of the sacred figures. It is an interpretation unimaginable outside the Florentine Renaissance climate of renewed faith in man. The patrons themselves were depicted in the paintings to the same scale as the Virgin and saints but kneeling as a sign of devotion.

21

21. Fra Angelico, *Bosco ai Frati Altarpiece*, about 1450. Florence, San Marco Museum.

22. Facing page: Filippo Lippi, *Virgin enthroned with Christ Child and saints*, 1442-50. Florence, Uffizi.

MIANVS·   ŜOSMS·ŜA·

CYCLES OF "FAMOUS MEN"

The cycle of *Famous men*, depicted by Andrea del Castagno on the walls of the Villa Carducci at Legnaia and now in the Uffizi, is the earliest secular decorative cycle of the Florentine Renaissance.

The theme was not new as it had its roots in fourteenth-century humanist culture. New was the choice of figures, all of whom reflected some glorious aspect of the recent past in Florence: the condottieri *Pippo Spano*, *Farinata degli Uberti* and *Niccolò Acciaiuoli*, the three great Florentine poets *Dante*, *Petrarch* and *Boccaccio*. The female figures, on the other hand, conformed to traditional types. The cycle was clearly an expression of civic pride and of a secular interpretation of history. The same humanist spirit was to inform the decoration, inspired by Bramante, at the end of the century, of the Casa Panigarola, with *Men at arms* and the ancient philosophers *Democritus* and *Ieraclitus*.

23

24

25

23. Andrea del Castagno, *Niccolò Acciaiuoli*, 1449-51. Florence, Uffizi.

24. Andrea del Castagno, *Pippo Spano*, 1449-51. Florence, Uffizi.

25. Andrea del Castagno, *Boccaccio*, 1449-51. Florence, Uffizi.

THE TRIUMPHS OF MANTEGNA

Between 1486 and 1495 Andrea Mantegna painted a cycle of nine pictures of the Triumph of Caesar, for the Gonzaga family, now in Hampton Court. Never before had an antique theme been given such grandiose treatment. Each of the enormous canvases shows a portion of the triumphal procession which starts with the standard bearers and closes with Caesar's chariot.

All the scenes depict men in Roman costume, moving from right to left. Each episode is a compositional entity but is also part of the variegated and complex whole, which draws its inspiration from literary descriptions and depictions of classical triumphs as well as from contemporary celebratory processions. This cycle represents one of the highest achievements of Renaissance painting in the representation of movement and became a point of reference for future generations.

26

26. Ludovico Dondi,
Triumph of Caesar,
Trumpet players and
standard bearers, **copy on**
copper of Andrea
Mantegna. Siena,
Pinacoteca Nazionale.

THE BRIDAL CHAMBER IN MANTUA

The bridal chamber in the Ducal Palace in Mantua was decorated by Andrea Mantegna between 1465 and 1474 for Ludovico Gonzaga and his wife Barbara of Brandenburg. In keeping with its original function as a reception room rather than a bridal chamber, the figures painted on the walls are courtly and celebratory.

In the lunettes and bays on the ceiling the emblems of the Gonzaga appear together with monochrome treatments of mythological subjects.

Higher on the ceiling are framed portraits of the Roman emperors, which allude to the prowess of the Gonzaga.

At the centre of the ceiling a painted oculus opens to a view of a blue sky and marble parapet with women and putti looking over it. The walls are covered with scenes of court life: Ludovico Gonzaga, appears over the fireplace surrounded by members of his family. He is shown at the moment he receives the news that his son Francesco has been created a cardinal.

The figures are depicted faithfully and the scene is given solemnity by the gestures, as well as by the even and diffused lighting. The west wall, divided into three, has a dedicatory cartouche at its center, supported by a group of putti; on the sides are episodes of court life, set against landscapes filled with antique monuments, alluding to the continuity between past and present.

27

28

154

27. Andrea Mantegna, *Return from the Hunt*, detail, 1465-74. Mantua, Ducal Palace, Bridal chamber.

28. View of the Bridal chamber. Mantua, Ducal Palace.

29

30

31

29. Andrea Mantegna,
*Family and court of
Ludovico III Gonzaga,*
1465-74. Mantua, Ducal
Palace, Bridal chamber.

30. Andrea Mantegna,
*Putti with dedicatory
inscription,* 1465-74.
Mantua, Ducal Palace,
Bridal chamber.

31. Andrea Mantegna,
*Return from Rome of
Cardinal Francesco
Gonzaga,* 1465-74.
Mantua, Ducal Palace,
Bridal chamber.

OCULUS OF THE BRIDAL CHAMBER

Andrea Mantegna, 1465-74
Mantua, Ducal Palace, Bridal chamber

SUBJECT

In the Ducal Palace in Mantua Mantegna painted a room with frescoes to the glory of the Gonzaga family. The *camera picta* better known as the "Camera degli sposi", or bridal chamber, is the painter's most complex and mature work to have come down to us.

In the ceiling Mantegna created a feat of perspective allusion in an oculus opening onto the sky. The oculus is surrounded by a marble parapet around which Mantegna has positioned winged putti, women and a peacock depicted with brilliant foreshortening.

There is also the head of a black woman, further evidence of the existence of slaves in the court at Mantua.

A pale blue sky appears above with scudding, soft, white clouds.

The base of the oculus is surrounded by a beautiful festoon in which a variety of fruit and leaves are interwoven with ribbons.

There are many references to classical art in decorative elements, as the double row of intertwined bands at the edge of the ceiling, palmettes and the floral motifs.

COMPOSITION

Mantegna produced a highly virtuoso effect with his use of foreshortened perspective including human figures and architectural elements. The idea of an illusionistic opening is essentially a Renaissance one. It is based on the relationship between open and closed space, between the artifice and nature. The results were so accomplished and successful that they were repeated throughout the sixteenth century and well into the baroque period.

The foreshortening of the putto standing on the parapet is so extreme as to suggest a deformation of his limbs.

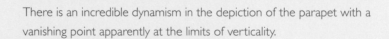

There is an incredible dynamism in the depiction of the parapet with a vanishing point apparently at the limits of verticality.

Among the objects depicted "di sotto in su", or from underneath, the wooden tub holding an orange tree and the apple clutched by a putto are particularly beautiful.

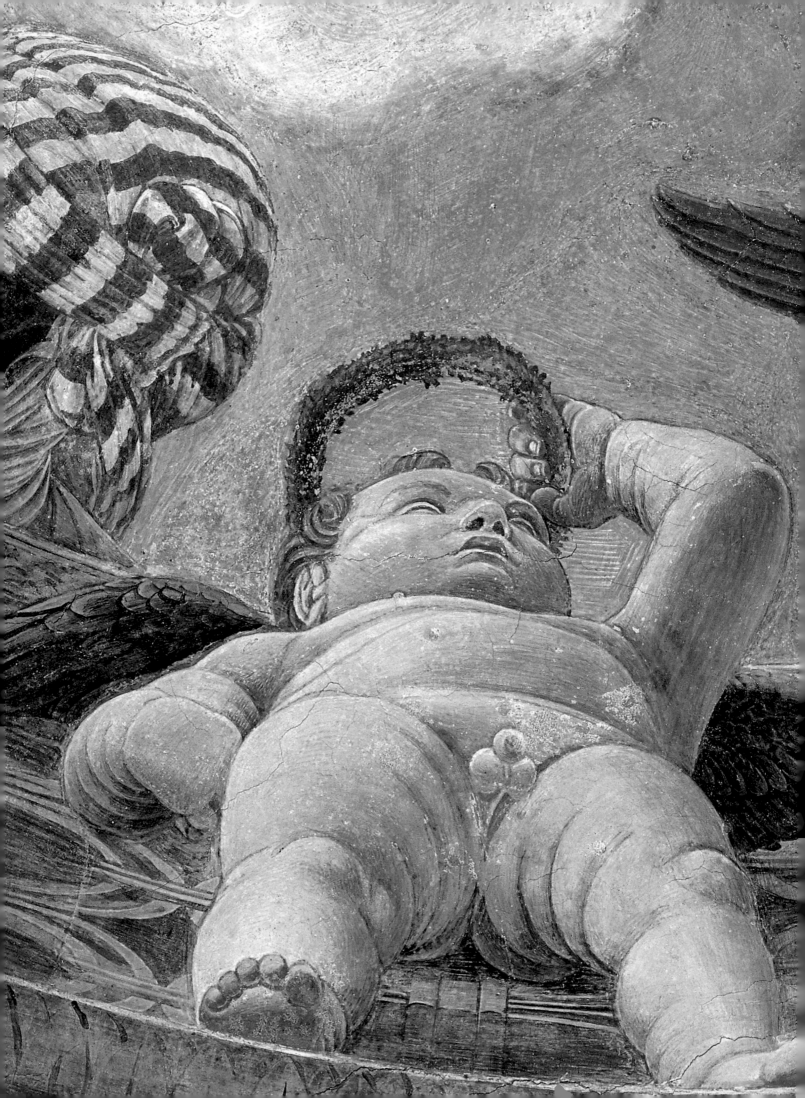

THE MEDICI FAMILY DEPICTED IN THE *ADORATION OF THE MAGI* BY BOTTICELLI

The altarpiece was executed in around 1475 for Guasparre Lami, an official in the Arte del Cambio, or Exchange guild, for his chapel in the church of Santa Maria Novella in Florence. The work was clearly painted in homage to Lorenzo the Magnificent and the Medici family as several of them appear as prominent figures in the sacred scene. The painting has a celebratory significance, but it is also linked to a custom, dear to the Medici, of parading through the streets of Florence every year at Epiphany dressed up as the three kings. To the left we can recognize Lorenzo with the poet Agnolo Poliziano leaning towards him, with the philosopher Pico della Mirandola next to him. The king kneeling in front of the Christ Child is Cosimo the Elder while the figure with his back to us wearing a red cloak is Piero the Gouty, the father of Lorenzo. Guiliano is shown to the right dressed in black. The figure in the yellow cloak to the right looking out of the painting is Botticelli himself.

32

32. Sandro Botticelli,
Adoration of the Magi,
about 1475.
Florence, Uffizi.

33-35. Sandro Botticelli,
Adoration of the Magi,
**details with Cosimo the
Elder, Giuliano de' Medici
and a self-portrait of
Botticelli, about 1475.
Florence, Uffizi.**

ANTONELLO DA MESSINA

Antonello da Messina is considered the greatest exponent of northern painting in Italy and is largely credited with the spread of the Flemish style south of the Alps. He probably received his training in both Naples and Palermo, where he assimilated the prevailing trends in Flemish, Catalan and Provencal painting. To these foundations he applied his understanding of Piero della Francesca, which gave his compositions a solid plasticism and a sense of volumetric space that tended towards geometrical simplification. But Antonello always retained the chromatic quality of Flemish painting, and therefore created a unique blend of color and monumental form, of poetic evocation together with a unified vision of reality. The most perfect example of Antonello's unique language is the Virgin Annunciate in Palermo. The Virgin is shown at the moment her reading is interrupted by the arrival of the angel. The depiction has all the qualities of portraiture with a vibrant realism and chromatic vitality in the contrast of the bright blue veil against the dark ground. At the same time we are aware of the volumetric study of her face with reference to abstract geometrical modules. In 1475 Antonello traveled to Venice where he stayed until the following year, a relatively short period but highly influential on his future production and also on the evolution of Venetian painting.

36

37

36. Antonello da Messina,
*Polyptych of St Gregory,
Virgin and Child*, 1473-75.
Messina, Museo
Nazionale.

37. Antonello da Messina,
Virgin Annunciate, 1476.
Palermo, Galleria
Nazionale della Sicilia.

38. Antonello da Messina,
*Polyptych of St Gregory,
St Benedict*, 1473.
Messina, Museo
Nazionale.

39. Antonello da Messina,
*Polyptych of St Gregory,
St Gregory*, 1473.
Messina, Museo
Nazionale.

MASTERPIECES

PIETÀ
Antonello da Messina, about 1476
Madrid, Prado

SUBJECT

The painting of the Dead Christ is offered to the contemplation of the onlooker by the angel supporting the body of Christ, made heavy by death. The iconography is a northern one which became widespread, and highly influential, in renaissance Italy through numerous engravings.

The body of Christ is treated with extraordinary naturalism, both in physical details such as his gashed side, as in the depiction of the emotional suffering on his face.

His face is strongly contrasted to the ideal beauty of the figure of the angel.

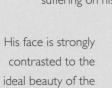

The scene takes place against a landscape, where, in the foreground dead tree trunks, skulls and bones symbolize death.

The green landscape immediately behind alludes to the Resurrection.

164

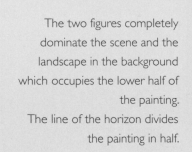

COMPOSITION

The composition is arranged on a diagonal which starts with the head of the angel and descends to Christ's knee in the lower right corner. Christ's body follows the same direction, and recedes in space, giving depth to the composition.

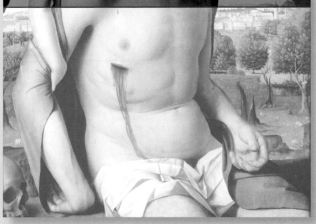

The two figures completely dominate the scene and the landscape in the background which occupies the lower half of the painting. The line of the horizon divides the painting in half.

PIETRO PERUGINO: A CULTURED AND PRODUCTIVE ARTIST

The personality and activity of Pietro Vannucci, known as Perugino, represents one of the most significant contributions to Umbrian art in the Renaissance. Perugino managed to synthesize the sophisticated and narrative style of Umbrian painting with the advances of Piero della Francesca and with the Florentine naturalism of Verrocchio, creating a new formula which enjoyed tremendous success in the whole of Italy.

Born in Città della Pieve, he established a workshop in Perugia, but also worked in other centers in Umbria and the Marches, in

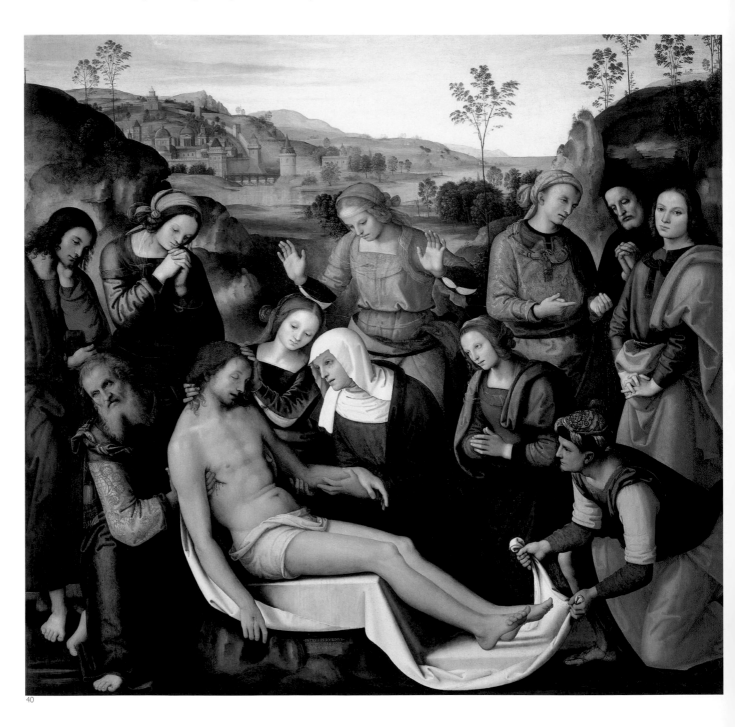

40

40. Perugino,
Lamentation, **1495.**
Florence, Palatine
Gallery.

Florence and in Rome; he also sent his work to Lucca, Bologna, Venice, Cremona, Ferrara, Milan, and Mantua. He gained the admiration of his contemporaries because he was able to interpret complex humanist iconographic programmes and political themes into a language that was both classical and modern at the same time. The elegant style of his religious paintings was particularly suited to attracting the faithful and inspiring devotion. In his early works, such as the *Adoration of the Magi* (1473) in the Galleria Nazionale dell'Umbria in Perugia he is clearly indebted to Verrocchio and to the luminosity of the work of Piero della Francesca.

But by the time he began work of the Sistine Chapel he had developed a mature style and was capable of orchestrating large compositions.

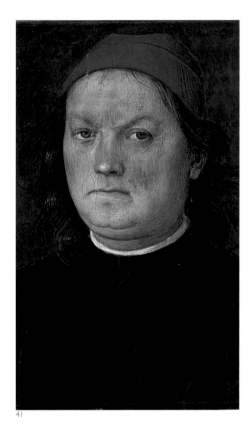

41

42

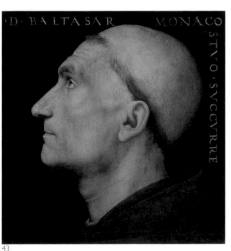

43

41. Perugino, *Self-Portrait*, 1496-1500. Perugia, Palazzo dei Priori, Collegio del Cambio.

42. Perugino, *Adoration of the Magi*, 1473. Perugia, Galleria Nazionale dell'Umbria.

43. Perugino, *Portrait of Baldassare, a Vallombrosan monk*, 1500. Florence, Uffizi.

The 1490s were his most fertile years, when he produced works such as the *Lamentation* in the Palatine Gallery in the Pitti Palace in Florence. In this work Perugino gives the composition his distinctive spatial calm, with the figures arranged in a landscape, depicted in all its natural detail.

Sometimes, however, especially in his later works, Perugino tended to reproduced successful formulae and his compositions became hackneyed. In his decoration of the Collegio del Cambio in Perugia, for example, where he frescoed the *Planets* on the ceiling, and *Famous Men* with the *Cardinal Virtues*, *Prophets* and *Sybils* together

with sacred subjects on the walls, he recycled old compositional devices, aligning the figures in the foreground and arranging them in layers. The decoration of the ceiling is more interesting, above all in the ornamental frames and grotesque work, derived from the recently unearthed *Domus Aurea* belonging to the Emperor Nero. Perugino continued working until 1512 in the major churches of Umbria and Tuscany, on the study for Isabella d'Este in Mantua and on the ceilings for the Stanza dell'Incendio in the Vatican. After this his activity was limited to the Perugia area and became increasingly bland and repetitive.

44

44. Perugino, *God the Father with Sybils and Prophets*, 1496-1500. Perugia, Palazzo dei Priori, Collegio del Cambio.

THE CYCLE OF THE MONTHS IN PALAZZO SCHIFANOIA

The frescoes in Palazzo Schifanoia were painted between 1467 and 1470 for Borso d'Este, lord of Ferrara. The best Ferrarese artists were engaged on the complex iconographical programme, devised by the court librarian Pellegrino Prisciani, who was also an astronomer. The walls of the room are divided by painted architectural elements into twelve panels, each with three layers. At the lowest level there are scenes related to the activities associated with each month: the subjects derived from medieval models are referred to Ferrara of the day and are a clearly designed to celebrate the Duke's benevolent government. The signs of the zodiac are painted in the middle band together with three astral personifications. The upper band encloses a triumph of pagan deities whose influence also determines the course of the months. *March* and *April* are by the hand of Francesco

45

45. Francesco del Cossa,
*March, Triumph of
Minerva and astrological
symbols*, 1467-70. Ferrara,
Palazzo Schifanoia.

46

47

48

46. Cosmè Tura, *Pietà*,
about 1460. Venice,
Museo Correr.

47. Ercole de' Roberti,
*September, Triumph of
Vulcan and astrological
symbols*, about 1467-70.
Ferrara, Palazzo
Schifanoia.

48. Francesco del Cossa,
*March, Borso d'Este sets
out for the hunt*, 1467-70.
Ferrara, Palazzo
Schifanoia.

del Cossa, the Ferrarese artist most influenced by Piero della Francesca. In his group of *Weavers* and in the scene of the *Pruning of the vineyard* in March, as in the *Conversing lovers* in April, Cossa gives us limpid narrative episodes with a serene insight into the real world. Borso d'Este and his court appear approachable and informal, especially when compared to the distant tone in the depiction of the Gonzaga by Mantegna in the Bridal Chamber in Mantua. The month of *September* was painted by Ercole de' Roberti, with his unmistakably agitated style and the sharp contours of his figures. In the group of Cyclops beating the metal at Vulcan's the Cyclops' legs are bent into energetic and dynamic poses, their bodies are twisted and their clothes ruffled. To the right of the fresco a sheet, apparently of marble, imprisons the lovers Mars and Venus in their bed. This is one of Ercole de' Roberti's earliest works and reflects the tormented manner of Cosmè Tura, the first real genius of the Ferrara school.

49

49. Ercole de' Roberti,
September, Triumph of
Vulcan, **detail of Vulcan's**
forge, about 1467-70.
Ferrara, Palazzo
Schifanoia.

ART AND SCIENCE

The Renaissance strove to unify artistic, scientific and theoretical knowledge. The same attitude which led artists of the fifteenth century to discover the mathematical laws of centralized linear perspective opened the way to the study of proportion and therefore of human anatomy.

In order to perfect representational techniques, the artist was compelled to enquire into the nature of man and to explore the world around him and to juggle the roles of anatomist, psychologist, zoologist, botanist and engineer.

Leonardo da Vinci is the most accomplished example of the Renaissance artist.

It would be wrong however to consider him as a genius isolated from the cultural climate of his day.

Starting with Brunelleschi, a large number of artists were also able

174

50. Leonardo, *Self-portrait n. 15741*, 1512. Turin, Biblioteca Reale.

51. Leonardo, *Bernardo Baroncelli hanged*, 1479. Bayonne, Musée Bonnat.

mathematicians, masters of the abstract sciences, then considered the highest branches of human knowledge.

Piero della Francesca, wrote a treatise on the abacus and another on perspective, and the Sienese painter Francesco di Giorgio Martini, like Leonardo, embodied the ideal of the universal man:

an architect, military engineer, sculptor and painter. He combined technical and technological, mathematical and practical knowledge and his *Treatise on military and civilian architecture*, with its drawings and inventions, sets an important precedent for the genius of Leonardo da Vinci.

52

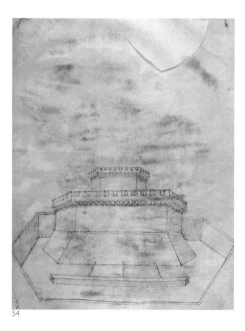

54

53

52. Piero della Francesca, *De prospectiva pingendi*, Corinthian capital. Parma, Biblioteca Palatina.

53. Francesco di Giorgio Martini, *Drawing of a war machine*. Siena, Collezione Chigi Saracini.

54. Francesco di Giorgio Martini, *Drawing of a fortress*. Siena, Collezione Chigi Saracini.

LEONARDO DA VINCI'S MANUSCRIPTS

In his will Leonardo left all his manuscripts to Francesco Melzi, the faithful disciple who followed him to France, but on the death of Melzi all the Leonardo papers were dispersed.

Today a large part of the manuscripts have been recovered and are to be found in museums and libraries throughout the world. A special feature of Leonardo's manuscripts is that they are painstakingly illustrated with the text constantly amplified by the image. A variety of subjects and problems covers each page, but

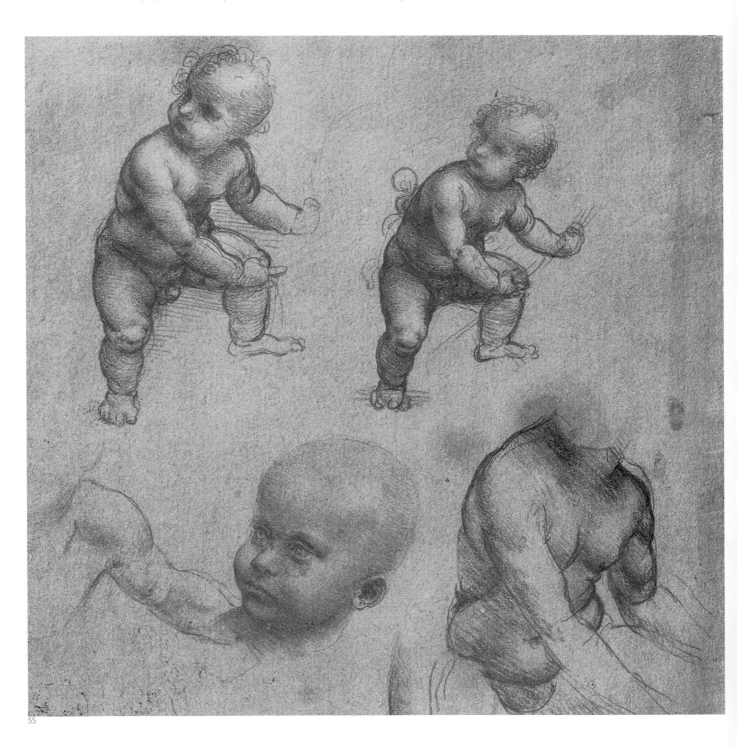

55

55. Leonardo,
Study of children.
Venice, Accademia.

there is a consistent approach and a tangible desire to understand the root of everything he tackled.

For Leonardo, who described himself as the "disciple of experience", knowledge was founded on the direct and creative observation of natural phenomena.

Following his observation of geometrical structures and his definition of universal laws governing them, he was able to move from general principles to the detailed observation of phenomena. His vast range of interests covered anatomy, optics, astronomy, mechanics, geometry, hydraulic engineering and technology, and he emblematically encompassed the symbiosis of art and science in Renaissance thought.

56

57

56. Leonardo, *Study of a flying machine, cod. B - Fol80R*. Paris, Bibliothèque de l'Institut de France.

57. Leonardo, *Assembling cannon in a foundry*. Florence, Uffizi, Gabinetto dei Disegni e delle Stampe.

5. The Venetian scene

B y the first half of the fifteenth century Venice had served as a bridge between the East and West for centuries and remained strongly tied to the late-gothic and Byzantine traditions. It was after the middle of the century, following the expansion of the Venetian territories on the mainland, that the city became aware of the innovatory language of the Renaissance, interpreting in an original way with modes that persisted and were developed well into the next century. The advances made in Padua were given a cautious reception in the workshops of Bellini and of the Vivarini, faithful adherents to late-gothic taste. The leading figure on the Venetian artistic scene was Giovanni Bellini who, after training in the workshop of his father Jacopo, was drawn to the humanism of Mantegna and to the advances made by Piero della Francesca, Antonello da Messina and the Flemish painters. In the wake of these influences he developed an atmospheric fusion of form, light, and color as a prelude to the "modern manner" of the early sixteenth century.

2

3

1. Facing page: Cima da Conegliano, *Virgin and Child with saints,* **about 1492. Venice, Accademia.**

2. Guadagnini, *Perspective chart of Venice.* **Venice, Museo Correr.**

3. Giovanni Bellini, *Sacra conversazione Giovanelli,* **detail of background landscape, 1500-04. Venice, Accademia.**

4

5

GIOVANNI BELLINI AND VENETIAN CLASSICISM

The revival of Venetian painting can be attributed to Giovanni Bellini, also known as "Giambellino". He was the son of Jacopo and trained as an assistant in his father's workshop but soon felt the need to update his manner by familiarizing himself with current trends. He studied the work of Andrea del Castagno in Venice, and of Andrea Mantegna, who married his sister Nicolosia. He then turned to Piero della Francesca, in a tireless search for improved ways of representing reality which remained with him throughout his long and active life. Even in his maturity he was inspired and encouraged by the advances made by Antonello da Messina, who arrived in Venice in 1475 and in the early sixteenth century he held his own against Titian and Giorgione. His paintings are built entirely on color and its relationship to light.

Through these elements Giovanni Bellini managed to attain the balance and harmony, most highly prized by Renaissance classicism, obtained by the masters of central Italy through drawing. Intuitively he created perspective in color, conferring a sense of distance through the gradual variation of tones. Bellini therefore laid the foundations for the development of tonal painting in Venice.

4. Giovanni Bellini,
Madonna and Child,
1480-90. Bergamo,
Accademia Carrara.

5. Giovanni Bellini, Frari
Altarpiece, detail, 1488.
Venice, Santa Maria
Gloriosa dei Frari.

6

7

8

6. Giovanni Bellini, *Pietà*. Rimini, Pinacoteca.

7. Giovanni Bellini, *Christ carrying the Cross*, about 1510. Rovigo, Pinacoteca dell'Accademia dei Concordi.

8. Giovanni Bellini, *Pietà*, about 1500. Florence, Uffizi.

PRESENTATION IN THE TEMPLE
Giovanni Bellini, about 1465
Venice, Galleria Querini Stampalia

SUBJECT
Bellini's painting of the presentation in the temple of the newly born Christ Child offered him a wonderful opportunity to execute a group portrait of his family.

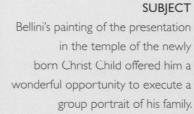

In the foreground resting against the balustrade are the most important figures in the scene: the Virgin and Child together with the priest.

Behind them, in the background are the members of the painter's family: from the left; his mother and sister, Nicolosia , the wife of Andrea Mantegna;

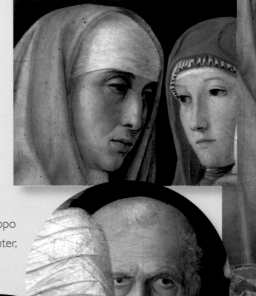

at the centre, his father, Jacopo Bellini, also a painter,

to the far right his celebrated brother-in-law and his own self portrait, with strong classical connotations, derived from Roman busts of the Republican period.

The bands swaddling the Christ Child are curious, being more reminiscent of the winding sheets used to wrap the dead.

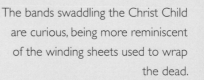

The painting alternates essential and fully modeled forms, together with elements described with analytical precision- witness the priest's rich, red, coat decorated with a raised pomegranate motif on a gold ground and the marble finish on the balustrade.

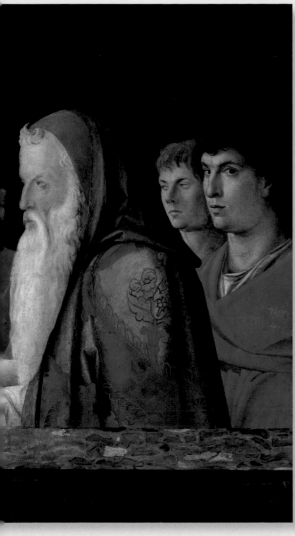

COMPOSITION

The scene is set against a dark ground which focuses our attention on the figures without the distraction of a landscape background.

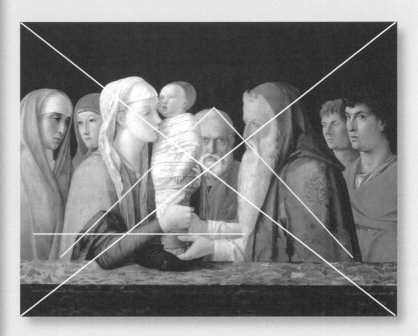

Despite the Christ Child's central importance he is not the focal point of the composition. This is rather in the middle ground and coincides with the figure of the painter's father, creating an unexpected jolt in the compositional arrangement. The position of the old Jacopo Bellini suggests the depth of the composition in which he is the vertex of a triangle and the Virgin and priest are at the base.

The other element to create a three-dimensional effect is the balustrade which is inclined towards the spectator, establishing a link between the external and internal space. Finally it is worth noticing the symmetrical arrangement of the figures in the scene in Bellini's search for an ideal compositional balance.

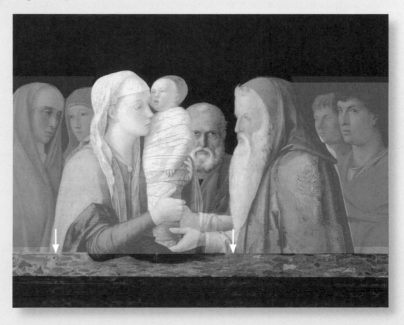

THE YOUNG BELLINI: HIS RELATIONSHIP
WITH MANTEGNA, NATURE AND THE ANTIQUE

Giovanni Bellini as a young man was profoundly influenced by the teaching of Andrea Mantegna whom he considered his first real master. Works like the *Presentation in the Temple* in the Galleria

Querini Stampalia were painted as an acknowledgement to his brother-in-law as his constant source of inspiration. Despite this act of homage Giovanni's art was quite different.

The tight, nervous and dramatic interpretation favored by Mantegna is made much more fluid and serene.

The narration is infused with an overpowering humanity with eloquent gestures and a melancholy yet controlled pathos, without any of the tense drama of Mantegna. In contrast to his master Bellini strove to establish an emotional dialogue between his figures and the landscape.

Bellini's interest in the antique also derives from Mantegna. Classical architectural elements are often to be found in his compositions, but they play a structural role within the composition and are not intended to recreate the antique world as they do in Mantegna. The *Pietà* in the Brera marks the end of Bellini's youthful activity as a painter, deepening the sense of *pathos* which was to become so typical of Venetian art in the late Renaissance.

9

10

9. Giovanni Bellini, *Saint.*
Florence, Uffizi, Gabinetto
dei Disegni e delle
Stampe.

10. Giovanni Bellini, *Pietà*,
about 1460. Venice,
Museo Correr.

COLOR, LIGHT, AND OPENING ONTO LANDSCAPE

Giovanni Bellini delighted in the description of nature, observing it with an attentive and a sensitive eye. In his early *Trasfiguration* in Venice, the emotion felt by the figures is echoed in the treatment of the landscape, creating a confluence between man and nature and raising Giovanni Bellini's art to new, and highly poetic, expressive heights. He includes passages of unprecedented lyricism and intimacy, finely orchestrated with softness of color and a warm golden light. In the *Trasfiguration* in Naples, everything is built on color and infused with light: warm tones in the foreground to draw us in, cooling gradually to create a sense of distance. This is the early example of what became known as tonal perspective.

In the distance there are glimpses of rural life and more distant villages and castles. Giovanni Bellini's painting signaled the beginning of an authentic enthusiasm for landscape which from then on characterizes Venetian painting.

11

12

11. Giovanni Bellini, *Transfiguration*, about 1487. Naples, Capodimonte.

12. Giovanni Bellini, *Transfiguration*, about 1455. Venice, Museo Correr.

PIETÀ
Giovanni Bellini, about 1460
Milan, Brera

SUBJECT

The three figures in the foreground are executed with an attention to volume and a sculptural plasticity typical of the art of Mantegna. This is particularly evident in the folds of the Virgin's clothing,

in the blue mantle worn by St John the Evangelist and in Bellini's treatment of the naked body.

Particularly remarkable are St John's curls: they appear to be almost sculpted but are rendered soft and vital by the warm coloring.

The iconography is of Flemish origin, as is the general pathos and the depiction of the Virgin.

The dramatic concentration of the scene is transfigured however by the soft coloring, by the diffused light in the sky and by the pictorial subtlety.

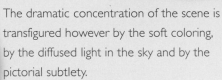

HAEC FERE QVVM GEMITVS TVRGEN
BELLINI POTERAT FLERE IOANNIS

The inscription in the centre front is taken from the *Elegies* by Propertius, and would appear to praise the eloquence of modern painting in expressing sorrow over the art and painting of antiquity.

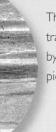

The deep sadness of the scene in the foreground is in contrast to the gentle landscape receding in the background. There we see a river wending through the meadows, with a road rising over a hill that is covered in vegetation and a view to a distant town.

COMPOSITION

The apparently simple and essential nature of the composition conceals a particularly complex scheme. The compositional balance is broken by the figure on the right being set back from the foreground which at the same time gains a plastic solidity.

The arrangement of the scene echoes the shape of the panel, giving emphasis to the structural composition of the figures.

The dramatic concentration of the foreground is in contrast to the bird's eye view of the background landscape and the movement of the streaky clouds.

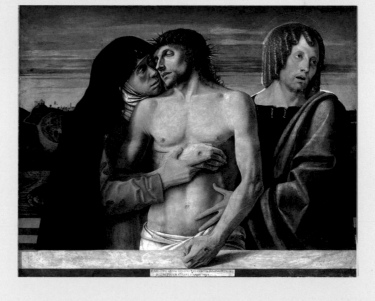

The half figure is used to bring the devotee as close as possible to the suffering of Christ and to the sorrow of those closest to him. We see the figures at very close range and they appear almost to be inclined towards us by the angle of the balustrade.

13

BELLINI'S ENCOUNTER WITH ANTONELLO DA MESSINA

Giovanni Bellini is distinctive for his life-long search for new modes of expression. When Antonello da Messina arrived in Venice in 1475, Giovanni, already in his maturity, did not shield himself from his innovatory style but rather absorbed Antonello's advances into his own style. It is worth comparing Antonello's *San Cassiano Altarpiece* with one by Bellini of the same period, the *Pesaro Altarpiece*, which shows the influence of the southern painter. Bellini uses color and not line and effects of light and shade to suggest form and volume as was the Florentine manner. And so the explorations of both artists proceeded at the same time and their line of enquiry was similar. Their achievements were filtered through the determining influence of the work of Piero della Francesca, especially with regard to the placing of the sacra conversazine within an architectural setting as in the *Sacra*

13. Antonello da Messina,
San Cassiano Altarpiece,
1476. Vienna,
Kunsthistorisches
Museum.

conversazione in the Brera. This arrangement is adopted by Antonello in the *San Cassiano Altarpiece*, of which only the central panel survives, and ten years later in the *San Giobbe Altarpiece* by Giovanni Bellini, reflecting his meditative absorption of Antonello's work. The Virgin, with the Christ Child on her knee, is seated on a high throne surrounded by saints and within a solemn architectural setting, reminiscent of Alberti. His interest in color is still crucial and has matured; a warm supernatural light floods the apse of the church and is used to build the figures of the saints and angels. The shadows are in deep color, devoid of light, and at the brightest passages are pure luminosity. Giovanni adopts Antonello's compositional scheme, with the saints grouped around the Virgin and Child who are enthroned in an architectural frame which in Bellini's case is the apse of the church of San Giobbe.

14

15

16

14. Antonello da Messina, *Pietà*, 1475. Venice, Museo Correr.

15. Giovanni Bellini, *San Giobbe Altarpiece*, 1487. Venice, Accademia.

16-17. Giovanni Bellini, *Pesaro Altarpiece*, and in the following pages, detail of the landscape, 1471-74. Pesaro, Museo Civico.

6. Lorenzo the Magnificent

The second half of the fifteenth century in Florence is dominated by the figure of Lorenzo de' Medici, known as the Magnificent, who was both an astute politician and great patron of the arts. In his artistic circle in the 1470s and 80s there was a concerted attempt to revive the forms and ideas of classical antiquity strictly associated with neoplatonic philosophy. Lorenzo, who also played a leading role on the wider Italian political scene, used his considerable diplomatic skills to exploit the artistic talent at home in order to increase his sphere of influence. Art was used as political propaganda and Lorenzo was perhaps even more ready to export his artists than to employ them on occasional projects in Florence. In this way the Florentine manner spread and enriched the artistic panorama in other Italian cities, notably Rome and Milan. And it was in Florence, under Lorenzo that two of the world's greatest artists emerged: Leonardo da Vinci and Michelangelo Buonarroti who influenced the whole course of European art from the sixteenth century on.

2

3

1. Facing page: Luca Signorelli, *Flagellation*, about 1480. Milan, Brera.

2. Sandro Botticelli, *St Augustine*, detail, 1480. Florence, Ognissanti.

3. Piero di Cosimo, *Portrait of Simonetta Vespucci*, about 1480. Chantilly, Musée Condé.

ARTISTS AT THE TIME OF LORENZO THE MAGNIFICENT

In addition to being a skilful politician and diplomat, Lorenzo the Magnificent was also a humanist, a collector of antiquities and a great patron of the arts. He gathered a brilliant circle of men of letters, artists and philosophers to his court and therefore succeeded to a large extent in directing the cultural development of the city as well as maintaining his predominant influence in politics and economics. Lorenzo treated the artists in his circle like members of his own family, and had considerable bearing on their choices and activities. And so works executed in Florence at this time, although by artists of different training and styles, have a particular stamp, influenced as they were by Lorenzo's taste and interests. The most famous example is the work of Botticelli which gave supreme expression to the ideals of the Platonic Academy in Careggi while glorifying the achievements of the Medici family. Piero di Cosimo and Filippino Lippi, were both fascinated by classical mythology and by the interpretation of intellectual allegories which they adopted in codified celebrations of their patron. Domenico Ghirlandaio offered the dynasty more explicit praise in his cycle of frescoes in the Sassetti Chapel in Santa Trinita. Here, under direct instruction, members of the Medici family were depicted together with the other key figures in the sacred scenes. Artists from outside Florence, such as Luca Signorelli in his *Triumph of Pan* and Pietro Perugino in his *Apollo e Daphne*, also painted complex allegories and mythological subjects.

4

4. Michelozzo di Bartolomeo, Villa Medici at Careggi, before 1459. Florence.

5

6

7

8

5. Cameo of Lorenzo the Magnificent. Florence, Museo degli Argenti.

6. Domenico Ghirlandaio, *Confirmation of the Franciscan order*, detail with Lorenzo the Magnificent, Antonio Pucci, Francesco Sassetti and his son, 1482-86. Florence, Santa Trinita, Sassetti Chapel.

7. Perugino, *Madonna and Child with saints*, 1493. Florence, Uffizi.

8. Piero di Cosimo, *Magdalene*, 1510. Rome, Galleria Nazionale d'Arte Antica.

SANDRO BOTTICELLI AND IDEAL BEAUTY

Sandro Botticelli was the artist most closely associated with neoplatonic philosophy after coming into direct contact with the men of letters at the Medici court. The Neoplatonists thought that man held a central and privileged position on a scale of being descending directly from God. He was therefore capable of reaching out to the Supreme Being if only he could free his spirit from matter in order to obtain universal harmony. Beauty, intended as a reflection of the Divine, and love, were seen as the means of advancing towards this goal. Botticelli's painting was designed to represent ideal beauty, by freeing form of any unnecessary naturalism. The two masterpieces in the Uffizi, *The Allegory of Spring* and the *Birth of Venus* are to be interpreted in the light of this philosophy.

It is significant that in both paintings the dominant mythological figure is Venus, the goddess of Love, who symbolizes both universal harmony and the culmination of man's most elevated qualities and aspirations. Another painting in the Ufizzi, *Pallas and the centaur*, also contains a hidden moral allegory of Platonic inspiration to be interpreted as the triumph of reason over man's more brutal instincts. Often however Botticelli's figures are characterized by a melancholy and detached air as though aware of some impending crisis.

9

11

10

9. Sandro Botticelli, *Portrait of a young man with a medal of Cosimo the Elder*, 1474. Florence, Uffizi.

10. Sandro Botticelli, *Pallas and the centaur*, 1482. Florence, Uffizi.

11. Sandro Botticelli, *Portrait of Giuliano de' Medici*, about 1480. Bergamo, Accademia Carrara.

196

12. Sandro Botticelli,
Virgin of the Magnificat,
1485. Florence, Uffizi.

THE ALLEGORY OF SPRING

Sandro Botticelli, 1478
Florence, Uffizi

SUBJECT

The *Allegory of Spring*, a mythological subject, is above all a hymn of praise to the continual rebirth of nature in love, even though it contains a wealth of other hidden meanings and allusions, derived from the neoplatonic philosophy and from the *Stanze per la giostra* by Agnolo Poliziano.

Immediately striking is Botticelli's close observation of nature. The painting reproduces the flowers and plants common in the area around Florence and in particular in the garden of the Medici Villa at Castello. This was the home of Lorenzo di Pierfrancesco Medici, Lorenzo the Magnificent's cousin, who commissioned the work..

The painting should be read from right to left. Zephyr, the breeze, pursues Flora; from their union Spring is born who moves forward scattering flowers.

Mercury, the final figure, shakes his caduceus, a symbol of peace and prosperity, to disperse the clouds.

Venus, the goddess of Love and Fertility, is at the center of the composition with the blind Cupid hovering above her head, shooting arrows from his bow.

To the left the Three Graces link hands in an harmonious dance of love.

COMPOSITION

Despite its obvious allusions to the classical world, the painting is in many ways out of keeping with the Renaissance. There is no real perspective depth of field nor solidity. The figures lack plasticity and there is no internal psychological rapport or understanding uniting them.

They are not arranged on different levels according to the rules of perspective but are placed in the near foreground, close to the spectator, against a background which limits the spatial depth rather like a theatrical backdrop.

The absence of spatial depth is apparent in the figure of Venus which, raised higher than the others, far from suggesting depth, reaffirms her central and dominant position.

The figures are arranged as in a frieze, as though dancing to a soft and elegant musical rhythm, which enhances their ethereal quality. This sense of movement, an essential component of Botticelli's world, is conveyed above all by the outline of the figures, which assumes far more importance than their volume.

BIRTH OF VENUS
Sandro Botticelli, about 1485
Florence, Uffizi

SUBJECT
The painting shows the birth of Venus Anadiomedes, meaning generated from the sea-foam.

Supported on an open shell, the goddess is carried by the winds towards the shore,

where a young woman, (either Flora or one of the mythological female deities) waits to envelope her in a crimson robe.

The work is remarkable for its harmonious and sophisticated design and the elegant linear modulation, creating impressive, abstract decorative effects. This enrichment is apparent in the treatment of the waves, the intermingling of the bodies,

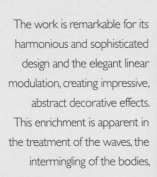

and in the view of the coast depicted in a succession of curving bays and promontories.

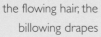

the flowing hair, the billowing drapes

The cold light colors, together with the pure and idealized form find perfect expression in the icy body of the naked goddess.

COMPOSITION

Botticelli arranges the figures on a single plane, prime importance being given to linear continuity. The sea and sky are arranged vertically to avoid the lines meeting at the vanishing point and intersecting the surface of the drawing which would otherwise be broken.

Venus is at the center of the composition at the point where the curved lines created by the figures of the wind and by the deity to the right converge.

The nude is classically conceived with a respect for symmetry: the straight and bent arms being counterbalanced in the arrangement of the legs. Her whole body is surrounded by a fine but quite evident uninterrupted line.

The small head is tilted to one side, without creating any folds in her long thin neck from which flow the raised and falling line of her shoulders. Her mass of fair hair, drawn strand by strand, softly billows around the contours of her body.

THE REPUBLIC OF SAVONAROLA AND BOTTICELLI'S LATE WORKS

After the death of Lorenzo the Magnificent in 1492 the fragile political equilibrium established among the Italian states was destroyed.

The invasion of Italy by Charles VIII of France opened an extended period of wars and invasions by foreign armies.

In Florence a popular uprising forced Piero de' Medici, the son of Lorenzo, into exile and set up a republic under the leadership of the Dominican friar Girolamo Savonarola. He had arrived in

Florence in 1489 and was originally well received by Lorenzo the Magnificent and the humanists in his circle who appreciated the friar's reforming spirit and moral integrity.

But soon the friar's teaching, with his censorious tone and religious asceticism, turned against the Medici and the humanists.

The culminating episode in this crisis was the bonfire of the vanities in Florence during the Carnival of 1497 when books, elegant clothing and pagan paintings were publicly burned.

Only a little more than a year later Savonarola himself was burnt at the stake, having been excommunicated by the Borgia pope Alessandro VI and abandoned by the people.

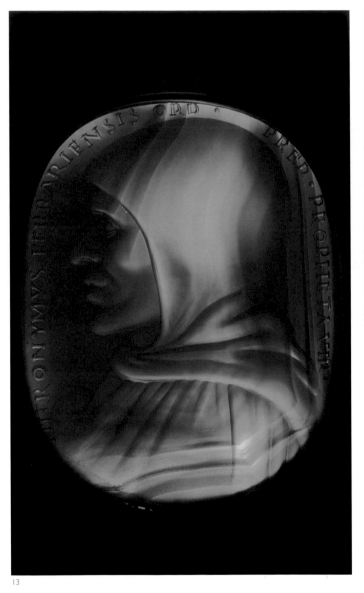

13. *Cameo portrait of Savonarola.* Florence, Museo degli Argenti.

14. Sandro Botticelli, *Mystical nativity*, 1501. London, National Gallery.

15

This social and religious crisis had profound repercussions in art: in Florence painting reverted to a more traditional manner, evident in the work of Lorenzo di Credi, who had trained in Verrocchio's workshop, and of Leonardo and Perugino.

Savanarola's mysticism overshadowed the late work of Sandro Botticelli. He rejected mythological subjects and his more graceful and elegant Madonnas in favor of darker, more dramatic religious subjects, making greater demands on the spectator.

The *Lamentation* in the Alte Pinakothek in Munich, and the National gallery of London *Mystical Nativity* are infused with a sense of religious disquiet expressed through a figurative language which negates the principles of Renaissance art.

Spatial depth and the correct proportional relationship are less crucial than apportioning size according to the devotional importance of the figures and plasticity is diminished by the rigid contours.

16

15. Sandro Botticelli,
Lamentation, 1495.
Munich, Alte Pinakothek.

16. Lorenzo di Credi,
Annunciation, 1480-85.
Florence, Uffizi.

17

19

18

THE INVENTIVENESS OF FILIPPINO LIPPI

In the troubled context of late fifteenth-century Florence Filippino Lippi's richly imaginative and anti-classical mature style reflects a desire to escape from the conflict between the ideal values of the great Florentine tradition and the dramatic reality of everyday life. In this he anticipated the palpable anxiety expressed by the early Mannerists. The son of Filippo Lippi and the pupil of Botticelli, Filippino developed his own individual style in fantastical, decorative compositions, reminiscent of the antique world but interpreted with a peculiar anti-classicism which occasionally verges on the grotesque. His period in Rome, where he worked on the frescoes in the Carafa Chapel in Santa Maria sopra Minerva, accentuated his taste for decorative detail which he further enriched by drawing on the city's vast archeological repertory. His paintings in the Strozzi Chapel in the church di Santa Maria Novella, executed on his return to Florence, are full of decorative elements with bizarre classical architecture and costumes, combined to create a fantastical theatrical impact. The impact of Flemish art on his style should not however be underestimated and is apparent in his love of naturalistic detail and in the analytical precision of the world he depicts.

17. Filippino Lippi, *Annunciation with St Thomas Aquinas presenting the Virgin to Oliviero Carafa*, 1488. Rome, Santa Maria sopra Minerva, Carafa Chapel.

18. Filippino Lippi, *Apparition of the Madonna to St Bernard*, 1486. Florence, Badia Fiorentina.

19. Filippino Lippi, *Self-portrait*. Florence, Uffizi.

20

21

22

20. Filippino Lippi, *Dispute with Simon Magus and Crucifixion of St Peter*, 1484-85. Florence, Santa Maria del Carmine, Brancacci Chapel.

21-23. Filippino Lippi, *Story of St Philip, the Saint chases the monster from the temple,* and in the following pages, detail, 1487-1502.

Florence, Santa Maria Novella, Strozzi Chapel.

ART IN ROME AT THE TIME OF SIXTUS IV AND ALEXANDER VI

After a long period of decline and cultural and artistic stagnation Rome in the fifteenth century experienced a renewal with commissions for artistic projects and monuments worthy of the ancient splendor of the city. This artistic revival, begun in the first half of the century, reached its climax under the della Rovere pope Sixtus IV (1471-84) and Alexander VI (1492-1503) of the Borgia family. Sixtus's plans to renew the city, he was referred to as *restaurator urbis*, offered employment to the best artists of the day, who were engaged on the restoration of ancient monuments, but also on the construction of new ones. He founded the Capitoline Museum and inaugurated the Vatican Library,

an event commemorated in the celebrated fresco by Melozzo da Forlì. During his pontificate the Sistine Chapel, named after him, was built on the design of Baccio Pontelli. Sixtus IV then commissioned the most highly acclaimed artists from Tuscany and Umbria, including Sandro Botticelli, Luca Signorelli and Pietro Perugino for its decoration. Remarkable too is the pope's tomb in the Grotte Vaticane, designed by Antonio Pollaiolo. Despite the political and religious crisis during the reign of Alexander VI, Sixtus's program of urban renewal was continued and Pinturicchio was commissioned to decorate the pope's private apartments in the Vatican. The convergence on Rome of so many artists of different backgrounds and formation contributed to the stimulating exchange of ideas, and to the fusion of the fifteenth-century schools.

24

25

24. Baccio Pontelli, Sistine Chapel, exterior, 1475-81. Rome.

25. Melozzo da Forlì, *Sixtus IV and Platina*, detail, 1477. Rome, Pinacoteca Vaticana.

THE FIFTEENTH-CENTURY DECORATION OF THE SISTINE CHAPEL

In 1481 Sixtus IV called to Rome the best painters in Tuscany and Umbria in order to decorate his new chapel. Sandro Botticelli, Domenico Ghirlandaio and Cosimo Rosselli with his pupil Piero di Cosimo, from Florence, Luca Signorelli from Cortona, and the Umbrians, Pietro Perugino and Bernardino Betti, known as Pinturicchio. The iconographic program, rich with symbolic episodes, illustrates the life of Moses and of Christ, drawing parallels between events in the Old and New Testaments. In the *Consigning of the keys* Perugino demonstrated his flair for spatial composition. Behind the static figures in the foreground the scene opens onto a wide piazza with a central

temple which pulls the rigorous perspective of the composition into focus. The ideology behind the painting makes it one of the most significant in the entire cycle as it illustrates the investiture of papal authority directly from Christ with St Peter as the first pope. For this reason Perugino chose to execute the fresco entirely in his own hand leaving his assistant Pinturicchio to work on the other scenes such as the *Journey of Moses into Egypt* and the *Baptism of Christ*. The dynamism of the composition in Sandro Botticelli's The *punishment of Core, Dathan and Abiron* reflects quite a different mood. Unity of space and time is sacrificed to the frantic and dramatic narration of events. There is a renewed sense of calm and monumentality in the *Death of Moses* by Signorelli. Its paced and solemn rhythm appears to demand the emotional involvement of the spectator.

26

26. Luca Signorelli,
***Death of Moses,* 1482.**
Rome, Sistine Chapel.

THE EARLY YEARS OF LEONARDO AND MICHELANGELO IN FLORENCE

The development of art in the sixteenth century was shaped by two figures of contrasting genius: Leonardo da Vinci and Michelangelo Buonarroti. In addition to their difference in age, they were divided by their intellectual and artistic outlook. Leonardo first served as an assistant in Andrea Verrocchio's workshop and his training moved him towards the naturalistic current in Florentine art. Leonardo based his understanding of the world on empirical experience and on the direct observation of natural phenomena. His artistic activity was also therefore a scientific exercise and painting the chosen instrument to investigate nature by representing its diversity: the effects of light, the movements and positions of the body and its

27

29

28

27-29. Leonardo,
Adoration of the Magi
and details, 1481-82.
Florence, Uffizi.

relationship to space. Michelangelo, the pupil of Ghirlandaio, was more a poet than a scientist, and came under the influence of the circle of Lorenzo the Magnificent, where he was profoundly moved by humanist and neoplatonic culture, and which became pivotal to his thought and work. His constant search for ideal beauty distanced him from the scientific exploration of the natural world conducted by Leonardo. These differences were reflected in their formal language: Michelangelo pushed drawing to the extreme, his painting resembling relief work, while Leonardo chose more pictorial means such as chiaroscuro and the creation of atmospheric effects. The ideals and ambitions of both artists are already apparent in their early works: in the *Baptism of Christ* and in the unfinished *Adoration of the Magi* by Leonardo; and in the *Madonna of the stairway* and the *Battle of the Centaurs* by Michelangelo.

30

31

32

30. Michelangelo, *Crucifix*, 1492. Florence, Santo Spirito. A comparison with the unfinished London *Pietà* reveals surprising similarities in the physiognomy of Christ.

31. Leonardo, *Study of plants*, copy of the original in the Royal Library at Windsor Castle. Florence, Uffizi, Gabinetto dei Disegni e delle Stampe.

32. Michelangelo, *Pietà*, detail, about 1500-01. London, National Gallery.

NATURALISM IN THE ART OF VERROCCHIO

The versatile painter, sculptor, and goldsmith Andrea Verrocchio was, like Pollaiolo, drawn to the naturalistic trend in Florentine art and this interest formed the basis of the training of his pupil, Leonardo.

Verrocchio's pronounced inclination towards naturalism was often interpreted with rich decorative detail, which was partly derived from his activity as a goldsmith.

His *David* in the Bargello stands in space and has multiple viewpoints. Young and aristocratic, the young boy's enigmatic smile has a psychological subtlety which resurfaces in the work of Leonardo. The *Tomb of Piero and Giovanni de' Medici*, in the

Florentine church of San Lorenzo, is unique; having a bronze net screen making the tomb visible from two separate areas and opening it to contrasting sources of light.

The variety of material used in the funerary monument reacts differently to the play of light, accentuating passages of luminosity and the pictorial impact of the entire work. Finally in his *Equestrian monument to Colleoni* the vigorous expressive power and the tension of the movement are designed to exalt the heroic pride of the subject. He died in Venice while working on the statue, which adopted the celebratory genre revived by Donatello in his *Equestrain statue of Gattamelata*, although Verrroccchio chose to highlight the statue's dramatic impact by the use of strong chiaroscuri.

33

34

214

33. Verrocchio, *Madonna and Child*, 1475-80. Florence, Bargello.

34. Verrocchio, *Young woman with a bunch of flowers*, about 1478. Florence, Bargello.

35

37

36

35. Verrocchio,
*Christ with the doubting
St Thomas*, 1476-83.
Florence, Museo di
Orsanmichele.

36. Verrocchio, *David*,
about 1475. Florence,
Bargello.

37. Verrocchio,
*Tomb of Piero and
Giovanni de' Medici*,
1469-72. Florence,
San Lorenzo.

THE BAPTISM OF CHRIST BY VERROCCHIO

Verrocchio's activity as a painter is problematical because of the frequent intervention of his workshop assistants. He does not appear to have been jealous of guarding his own name and recognized the talent and energy of younger artists in his studio such as Leonardo and Lorenzo di Credi. In this context the Uffizi *Baptism of Christ* is interesting.

The panel, originally in the Florentine church of San Salvi can be dated to about 1475 and is generally attributed to Verrocchio and to the young Leonardo. While the figures of the unfinished John the Baptist and of Christ bear all the traces of the master's work, the graceful depiction of the angel of the extreme left and the misty landscape in the background are attributed to Leonardo. The soft atmospheric quality is typical of Leonardo, obtained through his sfumato or soft shading technique, uniting the figures in the wide landscape. So too is the soft rendering of the face and the treatment of the angel's golden hair.

There is a pen drawing by Leonardo of 1473 which is referred to this painting, depicting a stretch of the Arno valley, and it would tend to confirm his hand in the background landscape. The contrast with Verrocchio's more sculptural treatment of the figures in the foreground is sufficient to demonstrate the different modes of the two artists. Vasari's anecdote confirms this: he relates how when Verrocchio saw Leonard's angel "he never wanted to touch paints again, indignant that a boy should know more than he did"..

38

39

40

38 and 40. Verrocchio and Leonardo, *Baptism of Christ* and detail, about 1470-75. Florence, Uffizi.

39. Leonardo, *Landscape*, n. 8P, dated 5 August 1473. Florence, Uffizi, Gabinetto dei Disegni e delle Stampe.

THE NARRATIVE FLAIR OF DOMENICO GHIRLANDAIO

In the second half of the fifteenth century, the workshop of Domenico Bigordi, known as Ghirlandaio, was one of the most active and prolific in Florence. The artist's vast figurative culture drew at the same time on the naturalism of the Flemish painters, on the Florentine models of the early Renaissance and on the work of his contemporaries. In 1481 Ghirlandaio was called to Rome by Sixtus IV in order to decorate the Sistine Chapel, where he was entrusted with two scenes: the Resurrection (destroyed) and the *Calling of St Peter and St Andrew*. His involvement in a project of such importance made him extremely popular with the powerful families associated with the Medici. These personalities were celebrated by Ghirlandaio in portraits inserted alongside the leading figures in the sacred scenes frescoed on the walls of the main Florentine churches: *Scenes from the Life of St Francis* in the Sassetti Chapel in Santa Trinita, painted in 1485, and *Scenes form the life of the Virgin* and of *St John the Baptist* in the choir of Santa Maria Novella between 1486 and 1490.

41

42

43

44

41-42. Domenico Ghirlandaio, *St Francis receives the stigmata* and detail, 1485. Florence, Santa Trinita, Sassetti Chapel.

43-44. Domenico Ghirlandaio, *Calling of St Peter and St Andrew* and detail, 1481-82. Rome, Vatican Palaces, Sistine Chapel.

45

46

47

45. Domenico Ghirlandaio,
Funeral of St Francis,
1485. Florence, Santa
Trinita, Sassetti Chapel.

46-47. Domenico Ghirlandaio,
Massacre of the Innocents
and detail, 1486-90. Florence,
Santa Maria Novella.

MICHELANGELO IN GHIRLANDAIO'S WORKSHOP: DRAWINGS BY THE GREAT MASTERS

In 1487, when just twelve, Michelangelo began his apprenticeship in Domenico Ghirlandaio's very busy workshop. He only stayed there for two years as he decided to train as a sculptor under the guidance of Lorenzo the Magnificent. His training with Ghirlandaio proved extremely useful and helped him cope later with the enormous strain of working in the Sistine chapel. Ghirlandaio specialized in fresco and under his guidance Michelangelo learned the technique and probably took part in the decoration of the Tornabuoni Chapel in Santa Maria Novella. With him Michelangelo also learnt drawing, a skill closely associated with the Florentine workshops and considered of prime importance in the formation of the artist. Michelangelo's training would have also included copying the works of the great masters of the past. The Florentine churches were better than any art manual and Michelangelo copied the frescoes by Giotto in Santa Croce and those by Massaccio in the Brancacci Chapel in the Carmine. He also copied sculpture, especially the work of Donatello, from whom he drew inspiration for his marble *David* now in the Bargello. As he developed Michelangelo also looked to other artists of the fourteenth and fifteenth centuries including Giovanni Pisano, Paolo Uccello, Pollaiolo and above all Jacopo della Quercia.

48

49

48. Michelangelo, *Study of figures*, from Masaccio. Vienna, Graphische Sammlung Albertina.

49. Michelangelo, *Study of two cloaked figures*, from Giotto. Paris, Louvre, Cabinet du dessins.

BRAMANTE AND LEONARDO IN MILAN

During the 1480s both Leonardo da Vinci and Donato Bramante were working in Milan.

The protection offered to Leonardo by Ludovico il Moro finally enabled him to explore his many disparate interests. He plunged into the study of engineering, mechanics, military and civil architecture, and the natural sciences. He made sets and designed costumes for court performances, worked on monumental sculptural projects including the *Equestrian statue to Francesco Sforza* and painted the masterpieces of the *Virgin of the Rocks* and the *Last Supper*. In his Last Supper, painted for the refectory of Santa Maria delle Grazie, Leonardo revitalized traditional iconography by arranging the Apostles in groups of three so that

Christ appears isolated in the center of the scene. This greatly increased the dramatic tension, fed too by the range of emotions on the faces of the Apostles: bewilderment, incredulity, fear and sorrow. These all bear witness to Leonard's study of physiognomy as the window to the soul. The extremely poor condition of the painting can also be attributed to Leonardo's insatiable desire to experiment which in this case failed to produce a durable solution for fresco.

Bramante too began working in Milan as a painter, but soon turned to architecture where he experimented with projects for centrally-planned churches, an interest which he brought to fruition in his design of San Pietro in Montorio in Rome. The artistic culture of Milan, although lively and distinctive, clearly felt the impact of these two artists and subsequent stylistic development was indebted to their presence.

50

51

220

50. Bramante, *Christ at the column*, 1480-90. Milan, Brera.

51. Leonardo, *Study of St Bartholomew for the Last Supper*. Florence, Uffizi, Gabinetto dei Disegni delle Stampe.

LEONARDO AND SFUMATO: THE *VIRGIN OF THE ROCKS*

The *Virgin of the Rocks*, in the Louvre is one of Leonardo's most celebrated works dating from his period in Milan. It was commissioned in 1483 by the Confraternity of the Immaculate Conception for their chapel in the church of San Francesco Grande. The painting depicts the encounter between St John the Baptist and the Christ Child In the presence of the Madonna and an angel. The figures, that are all interconnected through a series of glances and gestures, are placed at the entrance of a grotto with a soft half light filtering through to illuminate and unite the background with the foreground figures. This particular effect is obtained through Leonard's use of the sfumato technique which he developed from his observation of the natural world. He observed that the outline of objects became less distinct the more distant they became: atmospheric effects make objects appear veiled or indistinct removing contours through the gradual change of tone. It also breaks down the distinction between background and foreground. There is a copy of this painting in the National Gallery of London, painted by Leonardo and his assistants during his second Milanese period, between 1503 and 1506, presumably to replace the original which had been sent to France.

52

53

52. Leonardo, *Virgin of the Rocks*, 1483. Paris, Louvre.

53. Leonardo, *Virgin of the Rocks*, 1503-06. London, National Gallery.

MASTERPIECES

LAST SUPPER
Leonardo, 1495-97
Milan, Refectory of Santa Maria delle Grazie

SUBJECT
This large painting started to deteriorate soon after it was completed, not only because of the damp conditions, but also as a result of Leonard's experimentation with fresco technique.

The moment depicted in the fresco is that immediately following Christ's announcement to his apostles: *"one of you will betray me"*.

The position of the table and of the placing of the apostles of the far side has precedents in Florentine painting but Leonard's interpretation of the scene is quite different.

He broke with the traditional iconography of the Last Supper which placed the apostles symmetrically on either side of Christ by placing the apostles into smaller separate groups each with its own set of gestures and expressions.

The prevailing mood is of bewilderment but there are also some agitated passages and sharp exchanges. Leonardo offers us an extraordinary psychological survey as each apostle reacts in a personal way to the news of Christ's impending betrayal. Leonardo shows us the inner man and we understand the state of mind of each of them. By so doing Leonardo made visible one of the fundamental ideas of the Renaissance: that each man is a unique individual, different from any other.

The contrast between the noble calm of Christ and the excitement of the others is essential to the theme but is also testimony to Leonard's profound artistic sensitivity

COMPOSITION

The apostles are divided into four groups of three which roughly resemble four pyramids joined at the base. The central pyramid is formed by the lone figure of Christ: his arms are stretched out in a sign of devotion and he is isolated from the others.

The room is depicted in linear perspective. As it is an interior aerial perspective is rejected in favor of a single vanishing point: the sense of depth being created by all the lines converging above the head of Christ. These lines are suggested in the sides of the table, the embroidery of the tablecloth, by the coffered ceiling and above all by the upper edges of the tapestries hanging from the walls.

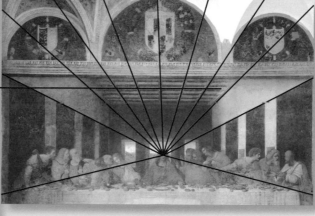

Beyond the open windows, in the rosy evening light, there is the familiar stretch of atmospheric landscape.

While the main source of light is from the left there is an alternative source of light from the background. This softens the outline of the head of Christ, alluding to his divine nature in place of the traditional halo.

MICHELANGELO: THE EARLY YEARS

After a brief apprenticeship in Domenico Ghirlandaio's workshop, Michelangelo became part of the Medici artistic milieu based on the San Marco garden. It was here that Lorenzo the Magnificent stored his collection of classical sculpture and where he gave young artists access to the garden in order to study them.

The legendary school of San Marco, under the direction of Donatello's disciple, Bertoldo di Giovanni, was of fundamental importance in Michelangelo's formative years. It was not long before he gave proof of his exceptional gifts and was welcomed into the Medici household where he made contact with the humanists and philosophers, Marsilio Ficino, Poliziano, and Pico della Mirandola.

There he absorbed the neoplatonist culture which was to color his thought and art for the rest of his life. Between 1490-92 he produced the *Madonna of the stairway* and the *Battle of the Centaurs*, which already demonstrate the strength of his genius, elaborated more fully in later works. In addition to the literary and philosophical culture of the Medici circle Michelangelo also absorbed the Florentine figurative tradition of the first half of the fifteenth century, notably the contributions made by his spiritual masters, Masaccio and Donatello, but also by Verrocchio, Bertoldo and Benedetto da Maiano.

The world of antiquity remained a vital source of inspiration and was reinterpreted by Michelangelo according to the humanist ideals of emulation but also in the hope of going beyond classical models.

54

THE MADONNA OF THE STAIRS AND THE *BATTLE OF THE CENTAURS*

In the Casa Buonarroti museum in Florence there are two works executed by Michelangelo when he was only a little more than fifteen that are startling not only for their precocity but also for their reflection of an individual and distinctive artistic personality. The low relief of the *Madonna of the stairway* draws its inspiration from Donatello, with the use of "stiacciato" or very low relief, and from classical funerary

sculpture, reflected in the clear profile of the Virgin. The detached and melancholy air of the Madonna would appear to allude prophetically to the death of Her Son, similarly the cloth being held by the two children in the background is often interpreted as symbolizing the Holy Shroud. The *Battle of the centaurs* is based on the study of Roman sarcophagi, but in this case the mythological scene suggested by Poliziano, is the pretext for demonstrating the artist's technical virtuosity. A mass of bodies is engaged in a conflict which is expressed with a vital energy and plasticity.

54. Bertoldo di Giovanni,
Battle, after 1478.
Florence, Bargello.

55. Facing page:
Michelangelo, *Madonna
of the staircase*, 1490-92.
Florence, Casa
Buonarroti.

56

THE STATUES ON THE *ARCA DI SAN DOMENICO* IN BOLOGNA

After the death of Lorenzo the Magnificent and the exile of the Medici from Florence, the young Michelangelo left for Bologna.

He was given a warm welcome by Gian Francesco Aldovrandi who commissioned him to finish the *Arca di San Domenico*.

The tomb, containing the remains of the founder of the Dominican order, was begun between 1265 and 1267 by Nicola Pisano, but after 1469 was dramatically altered by the southern Italian sculptor Niccolò da Bari known as "dell'Arca".

Left unfinished on his death, the tomb was completed by Michelangelo with three new statues representing *St Petronius, St*

Proculus and a very lovely *Candle-bearing Angel.*

Despite their small size, the figures have a monumentality and presence characteristic of Michelangelo's later works.

The angel is a particularly harmonious composition and the marble is highly finished, reflecting Michelangelo's s attempt to express the purely spiritual, typical of his young works.

The other two statues are more dynamic and vigorous , especially the St Proculus who with his expressive face and agile pose, with his body turned from the hips, prefigures, despite his limited size the heroic ideal and the "terriblilità" or awe inspiring quality of so much of Michelangelo's mature art.

56. Michelangelo, ***Battle of the centaurs***, 1491-92. Florence, Casa Buonarroti.

57. Michelangelo,
St Petronius, 1494.
Bologna, San Domenico.

58. Michelangelo,
St Proculus, 1494.
Bologna, San Domenico.

THE VATICAN PIETÀ

Executed in 1499, the *Pietà* in St Peter's reveals Michelangelo's admiration for Hellenistic sculpture, apparent also in the Bacchus of the same period in the Bargello in Florence. Characteristic of both works is the perfectly finished marble, worked to a translucent sheen with minute attention given to anatomical detail and also to conveying the emotional tone. This ability to express mood is most evident in the Bacchus where his drunkeness is suggested by his uncertain gait and his head weighed low by the weight of the grapes, while he peers vacantly into the distance. The iconography of *Pietà* is derived from northern art in homage to the work's patron, a French cardinal. Built on a harmoniously arranged pyramidical structure the body of the dead Christ lies in the Virgin's lap and she appears to support him with the same tenderness and as when he was a babe in arms. The emotional impact of the work lies in this very tenderness. The emotion however is always contained and never distracts us from the extraordinary beauty of both figures, in accordance with the neoplatonic ideal of the contemplation of beauty as a means of elevating the soul to God. Michelangelo's religious sensibility is reflected in the idealized forms and in the extraordinary finish of the marble and its highly translucent sheen.

59

60

61

59-62. Michelangelo,
***Pietà* and details, 1499.**
Rome, St Peter's.

BACCHUS
Michelangelo, 1496-97
Florence, Bargello

SUBJECT

Michelangelo created this *Bacchus* when he was only twenty-one for Cardinal Riario and it was immediately purchased by the Roman banker Jacopo Galli, a collector of curios, who placed it in the sculpture garden of his home in San Lorenzo in Damaso.

The pagan god is given an adolescent body, well rounded and with soft contours.

His expression is clouded by drink and his gait appears unsteady,

the cup of wine held high in his right hand.

Crouched behind him a young satyr nibbles at the grapes that Bacchus holds in his other hand, together with a tiger skin.

This statue accords perfectly with the taste for mythological subjects in the Medici circle in Florence at the end of the fifteenth century.

COMPOSITION

It appears clear that in the statue *Bacchus* the young
Michelangelo was eager to rival classical sculpture in expressing
naturalism and vitality in marble.

Michelangelo however surpasses his models, with his curved
and unsteady figure, far removed from the static equilibrium
of Hellenistic sculpture. In this pose Michelangelo conveys
Bacchus's drunken stupor but also alludes to the ambiguity of
the symbolism associated with the god of wine and fertility.

The natural pose of the body is highlighted by the tactile
quality obtained through Michelangelo's magisterial
treatment of the marble.

7. Florence and the birth of the "modern manner"

Leonardo, Michelangelo and Raphael, were all engaged on projects in Florence at the beginning of the sixteenth century for the head, or gonfaloniere, of the Florentine Republic, Pier Soderini. He reversed the policy of exporting Florentine talent for political reasons, promoted by Lorenzo de' Medici, and encouraged artists to remain in the city. The climate of fertile competition between these artists, who often interpreted the same subjects and themes, laid the foundations for a whole figurative language, that of the High Renaissance. Vasari described the "third" or "modern manner" as the artistic perfection reached by these masters, the culmination of the rebirth of painting started by Giotto, and which found its highest expression in Michelangelo. In Florence an eclectic style evolved in an attempt to reconcile the plasticity of Michelangelo's forms with Leonardo's sfumato and idealized classical figures were arranged in harmonious compositions devised by Raphael.

2

3

1. Facing page:
Michelangelo, *Tomb of*
Lorenzo de' Medici, duke
of Urbino, **detail with**
Dawn, 1524-34. Florence,
San Lorenzo, Medici
Chapel.

2. Andrea del Sarto,
St John the Baptist, **1517.**
Florence, Chiostro dello
Scalzo.

3. Raphael, *St George and*
the dragon, **1505. Paris,**
Louvre.

LEONARDO IN FLORENCE

Leonardo left Milan after the fall of Ludovico il Moro to stay in Mantua under the protection of Isabella d'Este, and then in Venice, before his return to Florence, the city he had left some eighteen years before and where his presence is again documented from August 1500. Although he remained there until 1506 he finished very few paintings. It was a period of intense artistic activity nevertheless and Leonardo introduced major stylistic and figurative innovations.

In 1501 in the cloister of the church of Santissima Annunziata Leonardo displayed a cartoon depicting the *Virgin and Child with St Anne*, which was immediately recognized as a masterpiece by artists and the wider public. The *group* combined an extraordinarily naturalistic representation of human experience and landscape in a harmonious composition. He developed this manner still further in the *Mona Lisa* and created a new model for portraiture. But in his last Florentine commission, the *Battle of Anghiari* in the Palazzo Vecchio, Leonardo's depiction of the anguished expressions already reflects his failing confidence in the harmony and balance which characterized the early Renaissance.

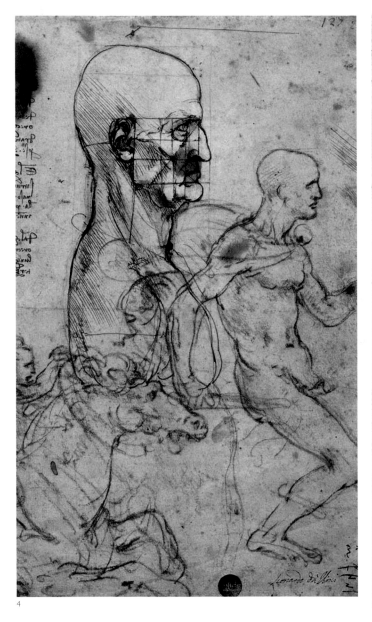

4

5

4. Leonardo, *Studies of human physiognomy and of horses*. Venice, Accademia.

5. Leonardo, *Study of horses for the battle of Anghiari*, 1503-04, copy of the original in the Windsor Royal Library.

SACRED SUBJECTS: THE DEPICTION OF FEELING

The theme of the Virgin and Child with St Anne emerged during his last years in Milan and was very dear to Leonardo. It was developed in two different cartoons and a painting, dated to the same period on stylistic considerations and according to information found in contemporary accounts.

The first cartoon, now in the National Gallery of London, probably dates from the end of the Milanese stay, from 1498 to 1500, and is distinctive for including the young St John the Baptist in the group. The figures are depicted in a compact composition and are interrelated though a series of affectionate gestures and gazes. Giorgio Vasari describes having seen a second cartoon in Florence, now lost, and drawn shortly after Leonardo arrived in the city. Exhibited in Santissima Annunziata, it received widespread admiration.

The theme was given unprecedented vitality and intimate tenderness with the figures set against an atmospheric background rather than constrained by a geometrical or architectural one.

The same interests resurface in a painting of the *Virgin and Child* in

6

8

7

6. Leonardo,
Head of St Anne. **Venice,**
Accademia.

7. Leonardo, ***Virgin and***
Child with St Anne,
1498-1500. London,
National Gallery.

8. Leonardo, ***Study for the***
Virgin and Child, St John
the Baptist and St Anne.
Venice, Accademia.

RENAISSANCE ART

241

which the Christ Child is playing with a lamb, identified by some art historians with the painting described by Pietro da Novellara in Florence in 1501, although others place it on stylistic grounds to around 1510. It seems probable that Leonardo began the painting in1501 in Florence but only finished it later after his move to France. The young St John the Baptist of the earlier cartoon has been replaced by a lamb and there is a stronger intermingling of the figures with the Virgin shown seated on St Anne's knee. The Christ Child who leans forward to play with the lamb is pulled back into the center of the group by his Mother. Everything is charged with symbolic meaning. For just as the Virgin sprang from the womb of St Anne, and Christ was born of Mary, his appearance signified rebirth through Christianity.

The lamb is also the *Agnus Dei* and alludes to the sacrifice on the Cross. The rocky landscape symbolizes the ever changing course of nature.

9

11

10

9-11. Leonardo,
Virgin and Child with St
***Anne** and details, 1510.*
Paris, Louvre.

LIFE FLOWING INTO PORTRAITURE: THE MONA LISA

The painting of the *Mona Lisa*, possibly the most famous art work of all time, portrays, according to Vasari, a woman of the same name who was married to the merchant, Francesco del Giocondo (in Italian the painting is known as the *Gioconda*).

The Mona Lisa appears in a raised position with regard to the background which offers a bird's eye view of a landscape. The apparent simplicity of the figure conceals an extraordinarily complex composition: the bust, head, and arms are not presented frontally and are not symmetrical but turn in opposing directions. This endows the figure with a natural quality and an animation quite unprecedented in Renaissance portraiture. Leonardo conveys an emotional depth and psychological complexity in her mysterious expression which appears transitory, extremely difficult to define, and therefore much closer to real life.

The *sfumato* technique with delicate passages of light and color further enhances the indeterminate quality of the forms. In the background landscape, sometimes identified with the Valdarno near Arezzo and Ponte Buriano, the rocky peaks, eroded by the continual passage of water, allude to the cyclical life of water and its continual mutation of the earth's surface. The main theme of the painting is therefore the flux present in all aspects of life, from human emotions to the eternal mutations in nature.

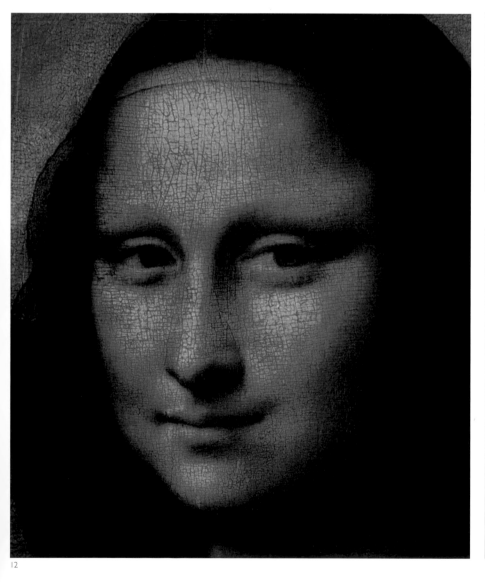

12

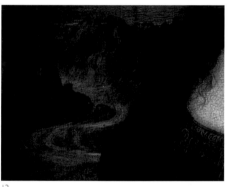

13

14

12-14. Leonardo,
***Mona Lisa* and details,**
1503-05. Paris, Louvre.

THE EXPLORATION OF NATURE

Leonardo's interests encompassed anatomy, physiology, mathematics, geometry, optics; mechanical, military and hydraulic engineering; botany, geology, hydrodynamics and flying. The diversity of his range and the probing nature of his research are reflected in the large number of manuscripts that still survive despite the dispersal which had already begun in the second half of the sixteenth century. Single and bound sheets and codices are now distributed in museums, libraries and private collections throughout the world.

Together with the notebooks which Leonardo carried about with him to jot down ideas and observations as they came to him, in which his writing covers all the available space around his sketches, – there are more ordered collections devoted to individual subjects (anatomy, optics, perspective, military machines, mechanical devices, the flight of birds, the movement of water).

These sheets, nearly all dating to the years after 1480, reflect the development in the Milanese years of Leonardo's speculations on scientific and technical problems. He saw no division between these interests and his "artistic" ones. Painting, drawing and perspective were to Leonardo tools for increasing our understanding of the natural world. Experimentation was vital: experience had to be systematically explored if causes and universal laws were to be discovered. And then the detail could be studied more fully.

Leonardo raised painting to the level of a science as, he argued, the painter reproduced the forms and appearances of reality, giving them rational representation. Painting was not to be considered a "*mechanical*" but rather a liberal or intellectual art ("*if you despise painting, which alone reproduces all works, you will certainly despise the philosophical and subtle enquiry intent on understanding the nature of all forms: air and land, plants, animals, herbs and flowers, which are enveloped in light and shade; and painting is truly a science and the daughter of nature*").

15

16

244

15. Leonardo, *Storm*, about 1506, copy of the original in the Windsor Royal Library.

16. Leonardo, *Cataclysm*, about 1515, copy of the original in the Windsor Royal Library.

THE TREATISE ON PAINTING BY LEONARDO

According to his friend, the mathematician Luca Pacioli, Leonardo had already completed the Treatise on painting in around 1498, when he was about to leave Milan.

Like so many of Leonardo's manuscripts the original *Treatise* has not survived, but a series of abbreviated versions have now been assembled into a unified text. Leonardo considered painting the highest of the arts . It was a *"truly a science and the daughter of nature [...] it springs from nature itself"*. He placed it above poetry *"for it depicts with more truth and certainty than do words and letters"* and *"has no need of interpreters in any other language, as do words, but satisfies human kind by reproducing all things found in nature"*.

Sculpture, on the other hand *"is not a science, but the most mechanical art because it entails sweat and fatigue"*, Leonardo noted that *"the sculptor endures great bodily fatigue but the painter labours with his mind"*.

In painting *"the painter's prime concern is to produce figures in relief on a flat surface"* ...*"created from shadow and light, or rather chiaroscuro"*. He therefore developed the sfumato technique, using the subtle gradation of shade to give form and shape to the image.

Leonardo's aim was to convey both the outer and the inner life of his subjects ,*"for if the physical depiction of the figures does nothing to suggest their thoughts and feelings, they are twice dead, firstly because the painting is in itself dead, and because figures depicted without vitality remain dead"*.

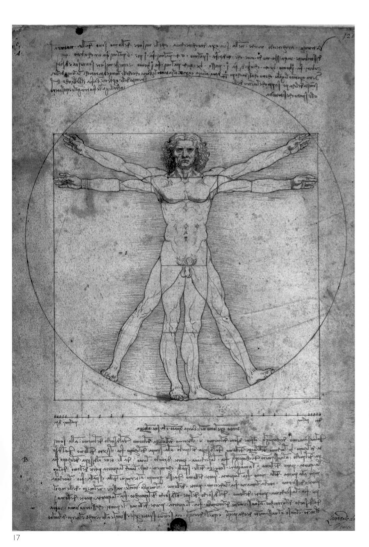

17

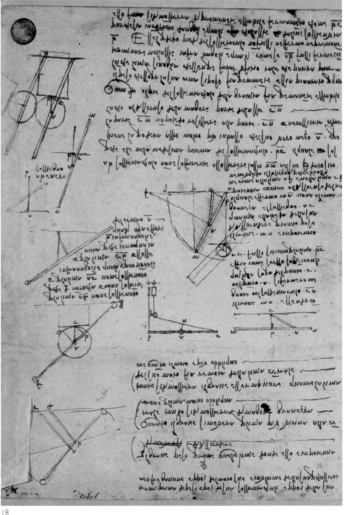

18

17. Leonardo, *Scheme of the proportions of the human body*, 1492. Venice, Accademia.

18. Leonardo, *Study of mechanical problems*. Venice, Accademia.

THE PRESENCE OF MICHELANGELO

Michelangelo returned to Florence in 1501, where the city offered him prestigious commissions because of his fame as the creator of the Roman *Pietà*. He was in the city until 1506 when Pope Julius II insisted on his return to Rome. On his arrival in Florence his republican convictions also helped secure his first commission for the statue of *David*, which was raised as a symbol of liberty and fortitude, the virtues embraced by the young Florentine republic. While working on the *David*, Michelangelo was struck by the group of the *Virgin and Child with St Anne* and he interpreted

Leonardo's compositional innovation in his two marble tondi, the *Pitti Tondo* and the *Taddei Tondo*. Between 1504 and 1506 Michelangelo painted the celebrated *Doni Tondo*, its sculptural strength and elaborate composition were centered on the spiral movement of the figures in the foreground which, together with the acidic coloring, mark the birth of the new pictorial manner, later referred to as Mannerism.

Michelangelo's most demanding project during these years was for the cartoon of the *Battle of Cascina* to be painted in the Council Chamber of the Palazzo Vecchio opposite and in competition with the *Battle of Anghiari* by Leonardo.

19

20

19. Michelangelo, *Study of Mercury and Apollo*, n. 688 R. Paris, Louvre, Cabinet des desseins.

20. Michelangelo, *Man's face*. Florence, Uffizi, Gabinetto dei Disegni e delle Stampe.

DAVID: REPUBLICAN IDEALS

According to Vasari, while Michelangelo was in Rome "*his friends wrote to him from Florence suggesting that he might obtain the spoiled block of marble in the cathedral workshop*" and "*Michelangelo came to Florence in an attempt to secure it*". The large block of marble had been left roughly hewn by Agostino di Duccio in 1463 but Michelangelo overcame the difficulties of working on a block abandoned by a previous artist to produce a powerfully expressive figure, recognized at the time as the embodiment of the artistic and cultural values of the Florentine Renaissance. The biblical hero and slayer of the giant Goliath is depicted as, "*a young David with slingshot in hand; and just as he had defended his people and ruled over them with justice so those who governed that city had to defend it fiercely and govern it with justice*". Sculpted between 1501 and 1504, the statue was placed in Piazza della Signoria. It was then moved in 1873 to the Accademia delle Belle Arti (now the Accademia gallery).

The *David*, emblematic of the civic virtues of "fortitude" and of "zeal", is an apparently static yet dynamic figure, his head characterized by intense intellectual concentration and with larger than life-size hands.

21

22

21-22. Michelangelo,
***David*, detail of the head,**
1501-04. Florence,
Accademia.

MICHELANGELO AND LEONARDO

The composition of both Michelangelo's Florentine low-relief marble tondi of the *Virgin and Child with the infant St John the Baptist*, owe much to the compositional innovations in Leonardo's *St Anne* which was put on public display in Florence at that time. The relationship between Michelangelo and Leonardo, as the sources record, was never easy and often confrontational and yet Michelangelo was clearly indebted to the older master's pictorial inventions. While the *Pitti Tondo* is built on the classically inspired, pyramidal composition, adopted by Leonardo in the first cartoon of the *Virgin and Child with St Anne*, executed in Milan (now in the National Gallery, London), the *Taddei Tondo* experiments with the dynamic arrangement of juxtaposed volumes and with the fluid movement evident in the Leonard's version of the same theme, now in the Louvre. Lastly, in the Doni Tondo, the only panel painting attributed with certainty to Michelangelo, he boldly surpasses Leonardo's model by interpreting the central group of the Virgin and Child with St Joseph in a spiral movement articulated within the compact block of the Holy Family.

23

25

24

248

23. Michelangelo, *Madonna and Child with St John the Baptist* known as the *Pitti Tondo* detail with the face of the Madonna, 1504. Florence, Bargello.

24-25. Michelangelo, *Madonna and Child with St John the Baptist* known as the *Pitti Tondo* and detail with the face of the Christ Child, 1504. Florence, Bargello.

THE ST MATTHEW

On 23 April 1503 Michelangelo was commissioned to sculpt a series of twelve apostles for the piers in Florence cathedral. He began work on *St Matthew*, which was interrupted in 1506 when he returned to Rome at the insistence of Julius II, but resumed a year later following his disagreement with the pope over the progress of the papal tomb.

Although external reasons prevented the completion of the statue it allows us to trace all the stages of work from its original conception. From that point on, Michelangelo purposefully left all his sculpture incomplete: the roughly hewn block revealed the ideal image imprisoned within it, an image the artist could only free from the surrounding matter.

And so the *St Matthew* is caught at the dynamic moment of struggling to break free from the inert and raw block. The determined concentration of the face and taut body muscles are designed to convey the immense suffering of man's earthly existence.

26

27

26. Michelangelo,
St Matthew, detail with
the face of the saint, 1503-
06. Florence, Accademia.

27. Michelangelo,
St Matthew, 1503-06.
Florence, Accademia.

HOLY FAMILY, THE DONI TONDO
Michelangelo, 1504-06
Florence, Uffizi

SUBJECT

The subject of the Holy Family was chosen to commemorate the wedding between Agnolo Doni and Maddalena Strozzi, whose portraits were painted at the same time by Raphael.

Raphael, *Portrait of Agnolo Doni*, 1506. Florence, Uffizi.

Raphael, *Portrait of Maddalena Strozzi*, 1506. Florence, Uffizi.

There has been much discussion about the hidden meaning of this painting which shows the Christ Child raised high against a background peopled with five young nude figures.

The Virgin is seated on the ground, according to the medieval iconography of the Madonna of Humility, but with greater dynamic tension as she is depicted at the moment of receiving the Christ Child from the hands of St Joseph.

The young St John the Baptist with his camel skin looks up from behind the wall on the right. The space separating him from the Holy Family perhaps indicates the division between the world of the Old Testament, which he represents, and the Redemption, personified by the Virgin and Christ Child.

COMPOSITION

The spiral movement of the Holy Family composition is in keeping with the circular shape of the painting.

The three figures form a single mass that can be schematically reduced to a triangle with its apex at the head of St Joseph. The verticality of the composition is balanced by the horizontal line delimiting the space occupied by the Holy Family.

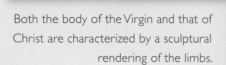

Both the body of the Virgin and that of Christ are characterized by a sculptural rendering of the limbs.

The naked figures in the background might represent humanity before the receiving of the tablets of law from God. If the subsidiary theme is read as the three ages of man then the painting depicts the pagan, and biblical ages, preceding the Redemption.

The colors are bright and even garish, as in the juxtaposition of the orange and pink of the robes of Joseph and Mary.

PALAZZO VECCHIO: THE "SCHOOL OF THE WORLD"

The cartoons for the frescoes of the *Battle of Anghiari* by Leonardo and of the *Battle of Cascina* by Michelangelo, designed to celebrate the victories of the Florentine Republic in the Palazzo Vecchio, are now both lost and are only known to us through copies. They were the guiding lights for generations of artists in the development of a whole new pictorial language which is why Benvenuto Cellini described them as "*the school of the world*". In the ferocity of the encounter depicted by Leonardo he refers metaphorically to the collapse of the values of balance and harmony and the dissolution of the certainties of Renaissance civilization. Michelangelo on the other hand pushed the classical theme of the battle to its limits in his brilliant studies of the naked human figure in action.

28

29

30

254

28. Salone dei Cinquecento. Florence, Palazzo Vecchio.

29. Giovanni Francesco Rustici, *Fighting knights from the battle of Anghiari by Leonardo*, 1504-15. Florence, Bargello.

30. Arnolfo di Cambio, Palazzo Vecchio, 1299-1314. Florence.

THE *BATTLE OF ANGHIARI* BY LEONARDO

In 1503 the Florentine Republic commissioned Leonardo to execute a fresco in the Council Chamber of the new republican government formed after the exile of the Medici from Florence.

The Palazzo Vecchio fresco was intended to record the famous victory by the Florentine and papal forces over the Milanese on June 29, 1440. Leonardo worked on the project until his return to Milan in 1506, having completed the cartoon and started on the fresco. Both are now only known to us though copies, including a drawing by Rubens, in the Louvre.

This unfortunately only reproduces the central section of the drawing showing a group of warriors fighting to capture the captain's standard.

31

RENAISSANCE ART

31. School of Leonardo,
Horses in battle. **Florence,**
Uffizi, Gabinetto dei
Disegni e delle Stampe.

Leonardo highlights the dynamic and emotional tension in the depiction of the frenzied cruelty and violence of the opposing forces.

Some of the surviving preparatory sketches of groups of knights with powerfully expressive details of their faces portray man at his most bestial.

32

32. Leonardo, *Horses in battle*, 1503-04. Venice, Accademia.

THE *BATTLE OF CASCINA* BY MICHELANGELO

Vasari describes how Soderini, the head of the new Florentine Republic, because of "*the great virtue he recognized in Michelangelo*" immediately commissioned a fresco for the Council Chamber, as a pendant to the one by Leonardo. The subject was to be the victory of the Florentines over the Pisans at Cascina in 1364. Michelangelo never painted the fresco and the original cartoon, finished in 1506, has not survived although there are a number of copies of the central section, including one by Aristotile da Sangallo. It depicts the episode when the Florentine soldiers, while bathing in the Arno, are suddenly called to arms and are shown hastily pulling on their garments. The work represents a modern interpretation of a classical theme, the representation of the naked human figure in movement, which in Michelangelo's translation places emphasis on the extraordinary dynamism and plastic tension of the bodies.

33

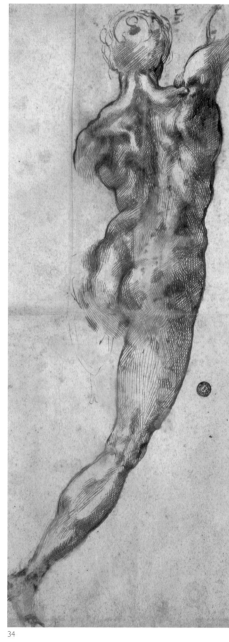

34

33. Michelangelo, *Study for the battle of Cascina*, detail. Florence, Uffizi, Gabinetto dei Disegni e delle Stampe.

34. Michelangelo, *Study of a nude for the battle of Cascina*, Florence, Uffizi, Gabinetto dei Disegni e delle Stampe.

RAPHAEL IN FLORENCE

Having received his early training in Umbria and the Marches and after a probable journey to Rome in 1503, the young Raphael stayed in Florence between 1504 and 1508.

Although attentive to the lessons of Leonardo and Michelangelo he developed a distinct personal language in his portraits and in his treatment of the Virgin and Child theme.

Despite the influence of his father the painter Giovanni Santi, and of more notable Umbrian artists such as Perugino, Pinturicchio and Luca Signorelli, it was only in Florence that Raphael, in just a few years, evolved a distinctive, intellectual, pictorial style.

35

35. Raphael, *Madonna Conestabile*, 1504. St Petersburg, Hermitage.

36

37

38

THE *VIRGIN AND CHILD*: VARIATIONS ON A THEME

Raphael's emerged as a distinctive artist because of his various depictions of the Virgin and Child, the addition of other figures, and the experimentation with various formal and compositional solutions. The influence of Leonardo is immediately apparent in the *Virgin of the goldfinch* and in the *Virgin of the meadow*, which are elaborations of the pyramidal composition of the *St Anne* cartoon. In the *Virgin and Child*

with the young St John the Baptist known as *La Bella Jardinière* Raphael, inspired by Michelangelo, was seeking to give his figures greater monumentality. These objectives were reached in the Tempi Madonna of 1508, an admirable confluence of various impulses into a personal and mature style.

In the *Madonna del Baldacchino*, the only altarpiece painted in Florence his adoption of a grandiose architectural setting created a model for Florentine altarpieces in the second decade of the century.

36. Raphael, *Madonna del baldacchino*, 1507-08. Florence, Palatine Gallery.

37-38. Raphael, *Madonna and Child with St John the Baptist* known as *La Belle Jardiniere* and detail, 1507. Paris, Louvre.

MADONNA OF THE GOLDFINCH
Raphael, 1505-06
Florence, Uffizi

SUBJECT

Raphael painted this masterpiece on panel soon after his arrival in Florence. It was commissioned to celebrate the wedding between the cloth merchant Lorenzo Nasi, and Sandra, of the prosperous Florentine Canigiani family. The Mother and Child was a traditional theme for such occasions and Raphael gives it a particularly joyous interpretation.

The Virgin is shown seated on a rock and has turned away from her book to gaze tenderly on the children at play.

The young St John the Baptist, patron saint of Florence, is also included and holds a goldfinch in his hand. This symbol of the Redemption is being held out towards the Christ Child who strokes it lovingly.

Vasari describes how the painting was broken int[o] seventeen pieces in about 1547, following the co[l]lapse of the ceiling in casa Nasi. The fragments w[ere] carefully pieced together and the painting restore[d] by Michele di Ridolfo del Ghirlandaio.

COMPOSITION

Raphael organizes the figures in a pyramidal structure according to a scheme that both respects the block and accentuates the monumentality of the group.

Soft curves predominate, exemplified in the oval of the Madonna's face and in the soft rendering of the children's' bodies, further enhanced by the use of sfumato.

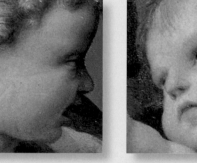

There is a serene landscape in the background, with a distant renaissance city and a bridge over the river to the left behind the Virgin. All is merged in a spatial harmony of color and form and the whole work is infused with a sense of beguiling serenity.

THE PSYCHOLOGICAL PORTRAIT

Raphael, while eager to obtain public commissions in Florence was almost exclusively engaged on projects for the nobility and merchant classes; painting portraits and private devotional works. Among these was the *Portrait of Agnolo Doni*, a rich merchant and patron of the arts, who also commissioned the companion portrait of his wife, Maddalena Strozzi. The three-quarter arrangement of the figures,

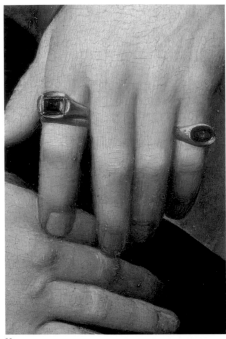

39

41

40

262

39-40. Raphael, *Portrait of Agnolo Doni* and detail, 1506. Florence, Uffizi.

41. Raphael, *Portrait of a veiled woman* known as *La Velata*, 1516. Florence, Galleria Palatina.

set against a wide landscape, is derived form Leonardo's *Mona Lisa*. Raphael, however, fails to achieve the expressive complexity of Leonardo's portrait in which the human figure becomes a universal symbol of the flow of life and emotion. He chose rather to concentrate on the physical characteristics of the couple, showing them in all their material splendor and eager to have their social standing recognized. This new treatment became the prototype for portraits throughout the sixteenth century.

42

43

44

42-43. Raphael, *Portrait of Maddalena Strozzi* and detail, 1506. Florence, Uffizi.

44. Raphael, *Double portrait*, detail, 1518. Paris, Louvre.

MICHELANGELO'S LAST YEARS IN FLORENCE

THE FACADE OF SAN LORENZO

With the death of Julius II and the election of the Medici pope Leo X in 1513, Michelangelo returned to Florence where he was given important sculptural and architectural commissions. In 1516 the pope charged him to design a facade for the Medici church of San Lorenzo. Michelangelo's solution was totally innovative but unfortunately the project was never realized. Following this disappointment, Cardinal Giuliano dei Medici (the future Pope Clement VII) commissioned Michelangelo to build a new chapel in San Lorenzo to house the tombs of the Medici, also designed by the artist. His third and final architectural scheme, again commissioned by the Medici, was for the Laurentian Library, destined for the precious collection of the family's manuscripts and books.

A number of drawings and a wooden model are all that survive of Michelangelo's innovative project for the facade of San Lorenzo. His design, far from adapting to the existing shape of the nave and side aisles, is conceived as an independent and richly modulated, architectural structure.

A complex arrangement of pilasters, columns and architraves unites the various sections and creates a perfect balance between the vertical and horizontal elements.

The difficulties encountered in the early stages and the deaths of Leo X's brother and nephew, Giuliano, duke of Nemours and Lorenzo, duke of Urbino, put an end to the project, much to Michelangelo's disappointment.

45

45. Michelangelo,
Model of the facade
***of San Lorenzo**, 1518-20.*
Florence, Casa Buonarroti.

THE NEW SACRISTY IN SAN LORENZO

In 1519 Michelangelo began building a mausoleum in Brunelleschi's church of San Lorenzo for Giulio de' Medici. The symmetrically arranged building, now referred to as the New Sacristy, and the four tombs within it were conceived as a unified creation.

Michelangelo drew inspiration from Brunelleschi's architecture with regard to the ground plan and the division of the walls into three bays and in the choice of materials - the grey *pietra serena* set against whitewashed walls.

But Michelangelo unites these elements in a much tighter rhythm with the walls articulated with projections and recessions in which he plays freely with the classical orders. The tombs of the Medici dukes Giuliano of Nemours and Lorenzo of Urbino face each other: the figures of the dead, in military costume, are placed within raised niches set into the walls above the tombs. The building serves to celebrate the triumph of the Medici over Time.

Pairs of allegorical figures lie on the covers of the sarcophagi, personifications of *Night* and *Day* on the tomb of Giuliano, *Dawn* and *Dusk* on that of Lorenzo. The extraordinary plastic vigor of these melancholy figures is at one with the architecture.

The statue of the *Virgin feeding the Christ Child* by contrast symbolizes eternity. The work was continually interrupted and came to a definitive halt in 1534 when Michelangelo made his final departure for Rome. The project remained incomplete as the tombs of the "magnificent" Lorenzo and Giuliano were never incorporated.

46

46. Michelangelo, *New Sacristy*, 1520-24. Florence, San Lorenzo, Medici Chapels.

47. Michelangelo,
Virgin feeding the Christ Child, 1521-34.
Florence, San Lorenzo,
Medici Chapels.

48-49. Michelangelo, *Tomb of Giuliano, duke of Nemours* and detail, 1524-34.
Florence, San Lorenzo,
Medici Chapels.

50

52

51

50-51. Michelangelo,
Tomb of Lorenzo, duke of
Urbino **and details,**
1524-34. Florence,
San Lorenzo, Medici
Chapels.

52. In the following pages:
Michelangelo, ***Tomb of***
Giuliano, duke of Nemours,
detail, 1524-34. Florence,
San Lorenzo, Medici Chapels.

THE LAURENTIAN LIBRARY

Work on the building of the Laurentian Library, begun in early 1524, is documented in a number of drawings presented to Giulio de' Medici, later Clement VII.

The building, designed to house the Medici collections of books and manuscripts, had to fit in with the pre-existing buildings in the cloister complex of San Lorenzo.

Michelangelo adopted the model of the fifteenth-century reading room in the convent of San Marco by Michelozzo but abandoned the divisions of the room into bays and chose to give light to the structure by opening windows on both sides.

He also created a modulated rhythm in the application of pietra serena elements along the walls.

In the vestibule the classical orders are used without any regard for their traditional function: the triple stairway flows from the reading room into the space lined with indented columns, blind windows and irrational projections.

53

53. Michelangelo, reading room, 1524-34. Florence, Laurentian Library.

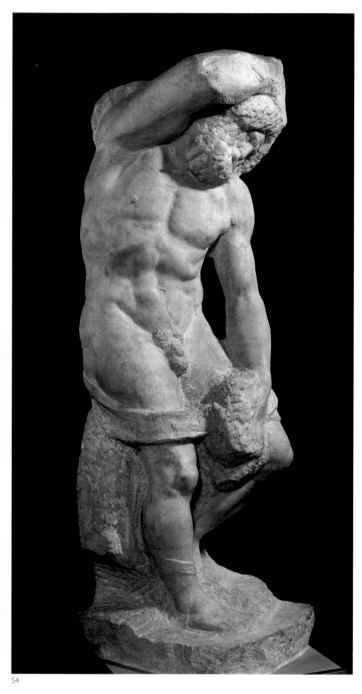

54

55

MICHELANGELO'S AESTHETICS: "UNFINISHED" WORKS

In Michelangelo's poetry he reveals his aesthetic ideas which are bound up with neo-Platonist philosophy. In a celebrated sonnet he elaborates the concept of the "unfinished", exemplified in the four

Prisoners sculpted for the tomb of Julius II:

"Not even the best artist has any conception
of what a single marble block contains
within, and that is only attained
by hand that obeys the intellect".

Michelangelo, "*excavating*" the form from his block believed that

54. Michelangelo,
***Prisoner* known as**
***The awakening slave*,**
1530-34. Florence,
Accademia.

55. Michelangelo,
Prisoner* known as *The
***bearded slave*, 1530-34.**
Florence, Accademia.

infinite forms existed to be liberated in order to reveal the image, of divine origin, innate within the stone. The figure emerges from the block almost like a body surfacing in the water, as Vasari noted: *"you take a figure in wax or some other solid material and you lay* *it horizontally in a vessel of water, which water being by its nature* *flat and level at the surface, lifting the said figure gradually, first we* *see the most salient features then little by little the hidden parts are* *revealed"*.

56

57

56. Michelangelo,
***Prisoner* known as *Atlas*,**
1530-34. Florence,
Accademia.

57. Michelangelo,
***Prisoner* known as**
***The young man*, 1530-34.**
Florence, Accademia.

SELF-PORTRAITS OF PAINTERS

The growth in popularity of portraiture in the sixteenth century was accompanied by an increasing number of self-portraits. This phenomenon is also linked to the increased social standing of the artist and his awareness of the intellectual and spiritual importance of the visual arts and therefore of his role in society. Painting, sculpture and architecture were all elevated above their medieval status as mechanical arts to become liberal ones, on the same intellectual level as poetry and literature. Leonardo, Michelangelo, Raphael, Bramante, Titian, Vasari and others brought intellectual and spiritual value to their calling by exalting the conceptual idea and removing the work of art from the repetitive routine of the workshop.

The 'divine' Michelangelo was exemplary in this process and was, even in his lifetime, something of a cult figure. The prestige of Italian artists is reflected in anecdotal accounts of more or less legendary episodes, such as the one describing Leonard's death in France in the arms of Francis I or the emperor Charles V stooping to pick up the paint brush dropped by Titian, with the words: "*Titian is worthy to be waited on by Caesar. There are many princes, but only one Titian*".

Indicative of this new status was the inclusion of portraits of artists in the series of famous men assembled in about 1545 in the villa belonging to Paolo Giovio on lake Como, known as the "Gioviano Museum". The series was later copied by Cristofano dell'Altissimo for Cosimo I de' Medici to be hung in the Uffizi corridor and including a substantial number of painters, sculptors and architects.

It was not until the seventeenth century that Cardinal Leopoldo de' Medici made a collection of self-portraits of artists. Before then a valuable sixteenth-century selection of engraved portraits of artists had accompanied the Lives by Giorgio Vasari, the first literary work to celebrate art through the lives of artists.

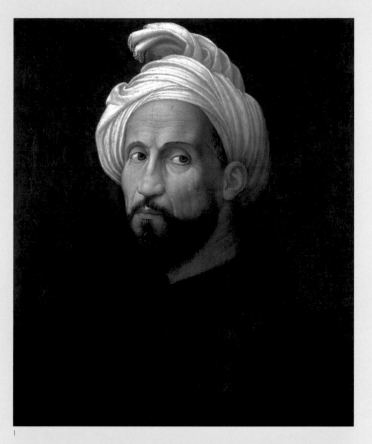

I

II

I. Giuliano Bugiardini,
Portrait of Michelangelo
Buonarroti with a turban.
Florence, Casa Buonarroti.

II. Uffizi Gallery, view of
the first corridor.
Florence. in the upper left
are the "Gioviana" series
of portraits.

III. DÜRER, SELF-PORTRAIT WITH A THISTLE
Paris, Louvre

This self-portrait by Durer, easily recognizable from his distinctive features and shoulder-length fair hair, was probably painted to mark his engagement to Agnes Frey, whom he married in 1494. A theory reinforced by his holding a thistle flower between his fingers, a symbol of marital fidelity. Another allusion to the vow about to be made is perhaps the phrase written above his head which roughly translates; "My life enfolds according to God's will".

IV. RAPHAEL, SELF-PORTRAIT
Florence, Uffizi

Raphael painted this celebrated self-portrait in 1506 when he was almost twenty and while he was still dividing his time between Urbino and Florence. Some believe it to be a copy of his self-portrait in the fresco of the *School of Athens* in the Stanza della Segnatura in the Vatican. Recently the traditional attribution to Raphael's own hand has been seriously questioned but the extremely poor condition of the painting makes it impossible to decide either way.

V. ANDREA DEL SARTO, SELF-PORTRAIT
Florence, Uffizi

This self-portrait, painted in fresco on a tile, according to Vasari was done while Andrea del Sarto was in Vallombrosa between 1528-29, using material left over from another job and records his appearance when he was about forty. It belonged to Andrea del Sarto's widow, Lucrezia del Fede, until 1569 when it was bought by the Medici. It is a superb example of the painter's skill as a portraitist reflected also in his *Portrait of a sculptor*, probably a portrait of Jacopo Sansavino, in the National Gallery di London, and his *Girl with a copy of Petrarch* in the Uffizi.

III

IV

V

VI. TITIAN, SELF-PORTRAIT
Madrid, Prado

Titian was almost seventy-five when he painted this portrait in 1565. He appears very much as he was in the engraving done by Cornelis Cort two years later, taken from the *Adoration of the Holy Trinity* painted for the Emperor Charles V. He is shown in profile and dressed in black, holding a paint brush in his right hand to indicate his profession. His style is of restrained elegance, his only ornament being a simple gold chain. The palette is limited to dark brown shades, conveying an almost abstract quality despite the pronounced naturalism of the portrait.

VIII. TINTORETTO, SELF PORTRAIT
Florence, Uffizi

In the self-portrait, painted in oil on panel, Tintoretto with his long white beard, is already an old man. He holds a small book in his right hand in reference to the intellectual nature of his calling. His deeply lined forehead, his sunken cheeks, and the shadowy cavities of his eyes intensify the melancholy mood of the portrait. The painting is dated to about 1585 and is thought to be a copy of the self-portrait in the Louvre.

VII. GIORGIO VASARI, SELF PORTRAIT
Florence, Uffizi

Vasari here appears a little older than in the *Feast of Esther and Ahaseurus* in the Museum of Medieval and Modern Art in Arezzo, which is dated to 1563. The medal around his neck bears the arms of Pope Pius V, who was pope from 1566 and Vasari's patron. But the portrait may well be earlier as it appears to be the one reproduced in the engraving in the second edition of his *Lives*. The panel was part of Leopoldo dei Medici's collection, but there is disagreement surrounding the attribution to Vasari himself.

VII

VI

VIII

8. The artistic supremacy of Rome

During the pontificates of Julius II della Rovere (1503-13) and of Leo X de' Medici (1513-21) Rome became the most important cultural center in Italy. The artistic activity promoted by these two popes, and their employment of the best artists of the day, resulted in the highest expression of the central themes of humanism. The interchange between artists coming from various parts of Italy, who worked together on projects in Rome, led gradually to the disappearance of distinctive local traits and the formation of a unified artistic language. Julius, who planned an ambitious political program to increase the power of the papacy, hoped to restore Rome to its past imperial grandeur, and embarked on a series of monumental projects including the decoration of the Sistine Chapel by Michelangelo and the Vatican Stanze by Raphael. Under Leo X the papal court became increasingly interested in archeological and scholarly research, creating something of a Golden Age with Raphael as its presiding genius.

2

3

1. Facing page: Raphael, *Triumph of Galatea*, 1511. Rome, Farnesina.

2. Baldassarre Peruzzi, *Apollo and the Muses*, detail. Florence, Palatine Gallery.

3. Michelangelo, *Tomb of Julius II*, detail of the face of Moses, 1515. Rome, San Pietro in Vincoli.

THE ARCHITECTURE OF BRAMANTE

After the fall of the Sforza, Bramante left Milan and in 1500 arrived in Rome where he made a direct and detailed study of antiquity, exploring classical remains and monuments in order to understand their proportions and construction. His familiarity with the techniques of classical architecture combined with his sensibility for the visual and spatial effects of antique monuments enabled Bramante to devise a universal architectural language perfectly suited to the plan for reviving the temporal power of the papacy initiated by Julius II. His first commissions in Rome – his work on Santa Maria della Pace and on San Pietro in Montorio – although both quite small projects, had a resounding impact on the development of sixteenth-century architecture. His meeting with Julius II, in 1503, opened the way to more prestigious projects, starting with the Belvedere courtyard in the Vatican and culminating in his design for St Peter's, renewing the symbol of universal Christianity and bringing his reflections on centrally-planned buildings to fulfillment.

4

5

4. Federico Barocci, *Tempietto in San Pietro in Montorio*. Florence, Uffizi, Gabinetto dei Disegni e delle Stampe.

5. Bramante, spiral staircase connecting the Belvedere Courtyard with the gardens below, 1505. Rome, Vatican Palaces.

RULES AND PROPORTIONS

In his Roman buildings Bramante strove to create a perfectly coherent affinity between the plan and volume and the relationship of the individual parts to the whole. This idea is first evident in the courtyard and cloister of Santa Maria della Pace, where the architect chose the square as his geometrical module and used it to plan all the architectural elements whether on the ground or in elevation. References to Lombard cloisters and his referral to classical models express his desire to confer monumentality on the building despite its limited scale.

In 1502 the king of Spain commissioned him to build a small church in the cloister of San Pietro in Montorio on the traditional site of St Peter's martyrdom. A Doric colonnade surrounds the *cella*, or inner building, covered by a hemispherical dome which is surmounted on a drum opening onto a balcony.

The original project called for the construction of a circular cloister around the building, to emphasize the ideal form of the circle, a metaphor for divine perfection. Bramante was inspired by Roman architecture, especially the centrally-planned Pantheon and the temple of Minerva Medica in Rome, already cited as ideal models for churches by Leon Battista Alberti.

6

7

6. Bramante, cloister, 1500-04. Rome, Santa Maria della Pace.

7. Bramante, Tempietto in the cloister of San Pietro in Montorio, 1502. Rome.

THE BELVEDERE AND THE ARCHITECTURE OF ANTIQUITY

In 1505 in response to Julius II's request for Bramante to devise a scheme for linking the old Vatican palace with the buildings created by Innocent VIII he designed the Belvedere courtyard. He enclosed it on two sides with long wings, housing corridors, while exploiting the natural slope of the land to create three terraces joined by a series of ramps and steps. Inspired by classical ruins such as the temple at Palestrina and the parks of the Roman Imperial villas as well as by literary sources, he furnished the courtyard with plants, fountains and most notably with the classical statues excavated in Rome at the time (the *Belvedere Torso* and the *Apollo Belvedere*, both named after their new location, together with the *Laocöon*), and so created an open-air museum. The three levels are drawn into a visual unity by the longitudinal axis, which leads dramatically into the grand exedra on the upper terrace.

Despite numerous alterations to Bramante's original design over the years, some of the most inventive features still remain, much imitated by sixteenth-century architects: witness the spiral staircase to the side of the villa with its use of the superimposed Tuscan, Ionic and Corinthian orders, inspired by the Coliseum.

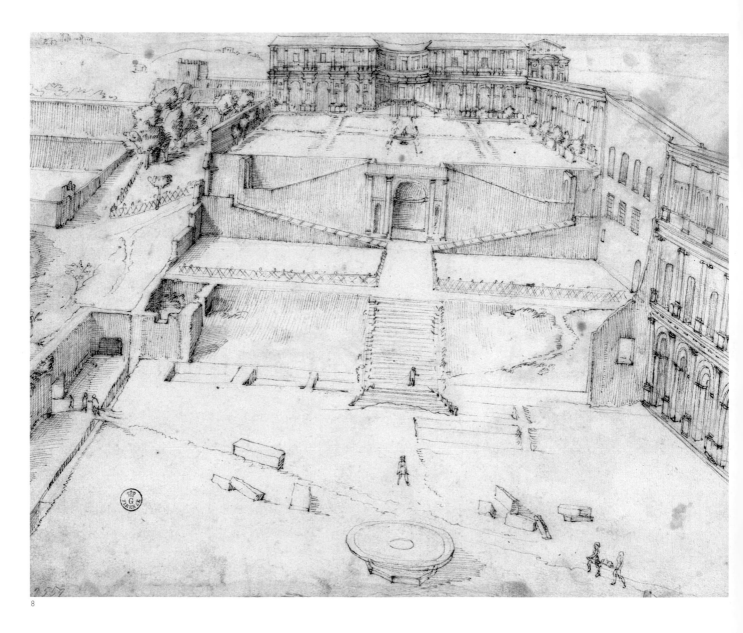

8

8. Giovanantonio Dosio, *Belvedere Courtyard.* Florence, Uffizi, Gabinetto dei Disegni e delle Stampe. The drawing documents the state of work in the middle of the sixteenth century.

**9. Bramante, Courtyard of
the Pigna, exedra, 1505.
Rome.**

THE PROJECT FOR ST PETER'S

In about 1505 Julius II made the bold decision to demolish the old San Peter's, which was threatening to collapse of its own accord, in order to build a new church, intended to become the new symbol of the universal and triumphant church. Bramante's design, documented in a number of sheets and in a medal on the first pier in the basilica, was for a grandiose Greek-cross building inscribed in a square and covered by a series of domes. The immense space of the interior was to enclose four corner chapels interconnected around the large central space. Bramante chose the central plan, the favorite of Renaissance architecture, to express the concept of divine perfection by translating it into a monument representing the universality of the Church of Rome and Christian Humanism. He had already employed it to great effect in the tempietto of San Pietro in Montorio, where it not only referred explicitly to antiquity but represented the highest achievement of the Renaissance search for spatial harmony.

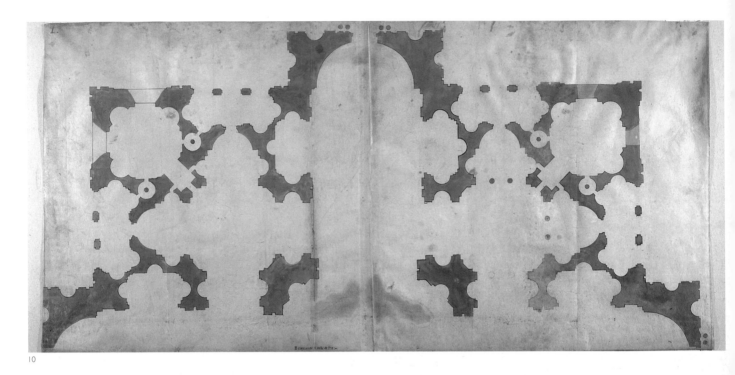

10

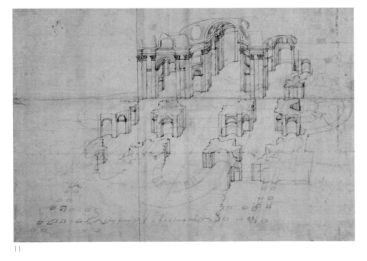

11

12

10. Bramante, *Plan for the new St Peter's*, n. 1A, 1505. Florence, Uffizi, Gabinetto dei Disegni e delle Stampe.

11. Bramante, *Plan for the new St Peter's*, n. 2A, 1506. Florence, Uffizi, Gabinetto dei Disegni e delle Stampe.

12. Maarten Van Heemskerck, *New St Peter's and the Constaninian Basilica*, n. 0210. Florence, Uffizi, Gabinetto dei Disegni e delle Stampe.

13. Facing page: St Peter's, coffered vault. Rome.

In their enthusiasm for antiquity many artists in the sixteenth century turned their attention to classical buildings on a central plan. The monuments of ancient Rome, such as the Pantheon, but also Eastern and Byzantine buildings like Hagia Sofia in Constantinople were taken as models for decades.

Once the choice was made the model was loaded with symbolic meaning: the circle, for example, the basis of every centrally-planned building, was crowned by the construction of a cupola which came to represent heaven. In the early fifteenth century Brunelleschi's plan for the church of Santa Maria degli Angeli in Florence, had incorporated an octagonal space (modified when the building was completed after his death), while Michelozzo intervened in the gothic church of Santissima Annunziata to create a tribune which amounted to a literal quotation from the temple of Minerva Medica. It was Leon Battista Alberti who had laid down the theory, citing the central plan as the model for the church-temple, but who also applied it with austere solemnity in his building of the church of San Sebastiano in Mantua, designed with three short naves built around a central crossing covered by a cross vault. Experimentations and variations on the theme continued over the years with increasing fervor from the late fifteenth to the early sixteenth century. Alongside the theories of Filarete and Francesco di Giorgio Martini, Giuliano da Sangallo made a fundamental contribution to the development of the centrally-planned theme. Disciple and interpreter of the Brunelleschi tradition, he was actively engaged in the culture of his day and devised innovatory solutions based on the close study of antique form.

In the restrained and elegant church of Santa Maria delle Carceri in Prato, his masterpiece on the Greek-cross plan, above the intersection of the arms he built an a square attic supporting the drum, dome and lantern. Leonardo experimented imaginatively on the theme although none of his many plans were realized. Taking as his point of departure the dome of Milan cathedral he explored the plan of the church of Santa Maria ad Perticas in Padua and the dome of Florence cathedral in order to develop numerous designs for complex centrally-planned buildings, articulated with endless variety. While Leonardo continued to experiment with plans, during his Milanese sojourn Bramante had already realized centrally-planned constructions in the dome of Santa Maria at San Satiro and in the tribune of Santa Maria delle Grazie. When he arrived in Rome, his building of the tempietto in San Pietro

I. San Vitale, mid-6th century. Ravenna.

II. Santa Maria della Consolazione, from 1504. Todi.

in Montorio extended the idea of a Roman circular temple, recalled in the very word tempietto, and gave it perfect expression. So successful was it that architectural theorists of the sixteenth century, Serlio and Palladio presented Bramante's little temple as an exemplary modern building alongside drawings of the architecture of antiquity. Bramante's reflection on the theme culminated in his plan for St Peter's, also conceived as a "temple" to Christianity.

Attention focused for so long on plans for the new St Peter's produced further reflections and imaginative interpretations of the theme. The artists who succeeded one another in directing operations sometimes opted for more traditional schemes based on the longitudinal plan (Raphael and Antonio da Sangallo) while others pursued the centrally-planned idea, clearly derived from Bramante (Peruzzi and Michelangelo), a concept that persisted throughout the century. Among its most striking developments were the church of San Biagio in Montepulciano, built in 1518 by Antonio da Sangallo the Elder, on a Greek-cross plan, and Santa Maria della Consolazione in Todi. The monumental harmony of the Todi church has lead many to detect the hand of Bramante himself.

Begun in 1508, the building proceeded slowly for nearly a century, on the designs of Baldassarre Peruzzi, Vignola and Michele Sanmicheli, until it was completed on a central plan surmounted by a high dome raised on a drum, with four hemispherical domes at the sides covering the apses.

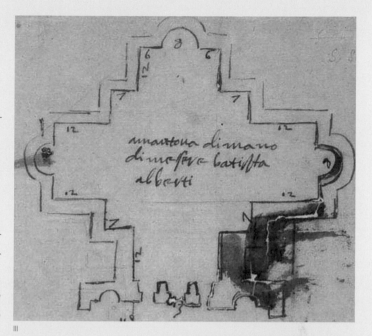

III

IV

III. Leon Battista Alberti, San Sebastiano in Mantua. Florence, Uffizi, Gabinetto dei Disegni e delle Stampe.

IV. Catena map, 19th century copy, detail of Santissima Annunziata in 1480. Florence, Museo di Florence com'era.

MICHELANGELO IN THE SERVICE OF JULIUS II

In 1505 Michelangelo left Florence for Rome, where Julius II, who had already engaged Bramante on designs for the new St Peter's, entrusted him with creating his tomb, a highly ambitious project, really more like a mausoleum, to be built in the new basilica. Michelangelo's design, after a long and agonizing gestation, was never completed but the sculpted figures he provided are the finest expression of the philosophical and aesthetic thought driving all his work. In addition to his sculptural activity, these years in Rome witnessed Michelangelo's highest achievement as a painter following his early success in Florence with the *Doni Tondo*. He was commissioned to fresco a vast area charged with historical and symbolic power where his work could be compared with some of the greatest contributions to Christian art. After heated discussions with Julius II arising from misunderstandings about the papal tomb Michelangelo was entrusted with decorating the ceiling of the Sistine Chapel in the Vatican. Here in four solitary and extremely demanding years he created magnificent painted architecture peopled with biblical figures. If this splendid cycle recalls the energetic forms and acidic colors of the *Doni Tondo*, it also clearly reflects Michelangelo's progress towards a more striking monumentality. These frescoes were studied by the young Raphael, who was working on the decoration of the Vatican Stanze at the same time, and by generations of artists after him.

14

15

14. Michelangelo, *Delphic Sibyl*, 1509. Rome, Vatican Palaces, Sistine Chapel.

15. Michelangelo, *Tomb of Julius II*, detail of *Leah* or the *Active life*, 1542. Rome, San Pietro in Vincoli.

THE TOMB OF JULIUS II

Julius II intended his funerary monument to stand in Bramante's new Basilica above the tomb of St Peter in order to stress the symbolic union between the present head and the founder of Catholic Church and the universal role of Christianity. Michelangelo's first scheme, dating to 1505, was for a grand pyramidal structure on three levels and isolated in space like a temple. It was to enclose a sepulchral *cella* and to be adorned with more than forty statues of figures from the Old and New Testaments together with allegories of the Arts and Virtues triumphing over the Vices (the so-called *Prisoners*), the whole dominated by the figure of Julius II lying on a bier. He had already prepared a number of figures to be placed on the base against the pilasters when, in 1506, Julius decided to abandon the project in order to concentrate on the construction of the new St Peter's.

Michelangelo left Rome extremely disappointed by the turn of events and only embarked on a second project at the request of the della Rovere family when the pope died in 1513. Over the next three years he created two figures of slaves known as the *Dying slave* and the *Rebel slave*, together with the *Moses*. But the second project too was destined to remain unfinished and it was not until 1545 that the final version of the monument was entrusted to assistants and transformed into a wall tomb for the church of San Pietro in Vincoli. *Moses* is seated in the central niche, the only figure to have survived from the original conception of the project.

16

17

16. Michelangelo and assistants, *Tomb of Julius II*. **Rome, San Pietro in Vincoli.**

17. Michelangelo, *Tomb of Julius II*, **detail, Moses, 1515. Rome, San Pietro in Vincoli.**

DYING SLAVE AND REBEL SLAVE
Michelangelo, 1513-14
Paris, Louvre

COMPOSITION

The Dying slave, considered one of Michelangelo's greatest masterpieces, represents the painful overpowering of the spirit in the oblivion of sleep or death. The beautiful young man is falling into an exhausted slumber with his head tilted slightly backwards and his body stretched out in an almost lifeless state. His delicate body has an ephebic quality.

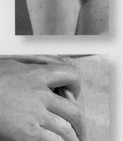

His right hand gently caresses the surface of his chest, lifting his garment as if to free his body for his final breath.

The surface of the marble is covered in the marks and grooves left by Michelangelo's chisel, hammer and drill, for although he finished the front of the figure the back of the figure was left in its rough state.

SUBJECT

When the tomb of Julius II was finally set up in the church of San Pletro in Vincoli, problems related to expenditure and limited space led to the rejection of the two slaves.

These pieces, allegories of the soul imprisoned by the earthly concerns of the body, are colossal figures inspired by classical models depicted in their attempt to free themselves of incumbent matter. Michelangelo himself presented them to the Florentine Roberto Strozzi, who took them with him into France where they were then presented to the king.

Michelangelo and assistants, *Tomb of Julius II*. Rome, San Pietro in Vincoli.

His face has perfect features, crowned by a fine head of curls.

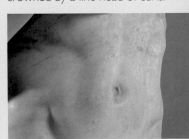

The long and sinuous forms are delineated with an apparently infinite tension. In this naked creature movement and statis are counterposed in a play of lines to give warm to the human body as it emerges from the inert block of marble.

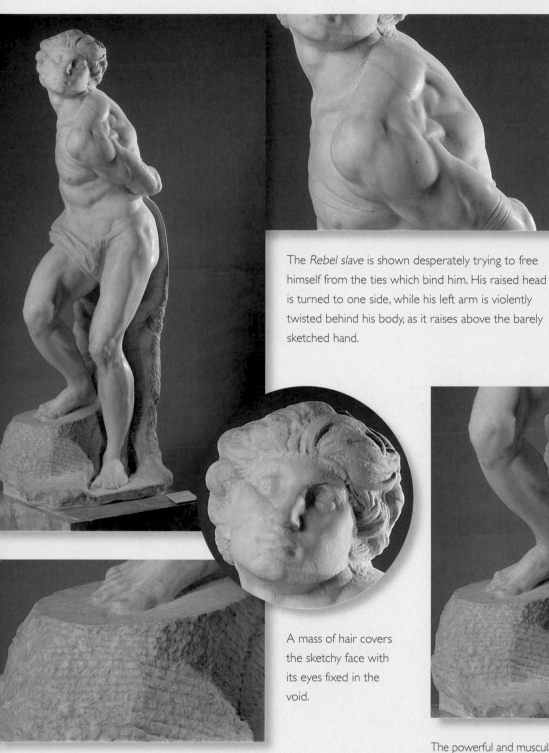

The *Rebel slave* is shown desperately trying to free himself from the ties which bind him. His raised head is turned to one side, while his left arm is violently twisted behind his body, as it raises above the barely sketched hand.

The spiral movement suggested by this arm is continued by the other and repeated in the twisted drapes.

A mass of hair covers the sketchy face with its eyes fixed in the void.

nly the legs and torso appear completely finished, while the other nbs are still reminiscent of the block, indicating his vain struggle against s captivity.

The powerful and muscular legs serve to accentuate the evident suffering of this athletic figure: his right left is bent and his foot is raised while the left one appears firmly anchored to the ground.

THE CEILING OF THE SISTINE CHAPEL

Following Julius II's insistent requests Michelangelo decided to return to Rome in March 1508, where he accepted the commission to decorate the ceiling of the Sistine Chapel even though he realized that he had very limited experience as a painter. From 1508 to 1512 he worked on this enormous project in order to create the most magnificent fresco cycle in the Western world. He divided the vast surface (42.64×118.8 ft) into three sections: the first, at the center of the ceiling, was covered with nine episodes from the book of Genesis, (*Separation of the light from darkness, Creation of the stars, Separation of the earth from the waters, Creation of Adam, Creation of Eve, Original sin and the Expulsion of Adam and Eve from Paradise, Sacrifice of Noah, Flood, Drunkenness of Noah*), painted within fictive marble frames and separated by pairs of naked figures (*ignudi*) flanking decorative medals. The architectural framework continues in the lower order with thrones containing seven *Prophets* and five *Sybils*, while the lunettes rising from the walls and the corners contain the *Ancestors of Christ*. The painted architecture is conceived as an independent structure, with the magnificent marble framework providing the perfect backdrop to Michelangelo's energetic male and female figures. These figures are represented in isolation like enormous painted sculptures, the twists and turns of their bodies dramatically enhancing their relationship to the architecture. The theme of the cycle is man's spiritual ascent to God, depicted first through Revelation (lunettes, vault segments, spandrels), then in the earliest awareness of the Divine (*Prophets, Sybils, Ignudi*), until man's encounter with God (*Scenes from Genesis*). The frescoes also allow us to follow Michelangelo's artistic development from his earliest paintings of the last biblical scenes. In August 1511 work was interrupted, the ceiling uncovered and Michelangelo was finally able to view the frescoes from the ground. When he resumed painting, he adopted a noticeably more pronounced language: the figures became much larger, while at the same time the compositions were simplified. In comparison with the first scenes, which appear somewhat cramped and more like classical reliefs, the later episodes are bare and dynamic while the larger figures are characterized by simpler, clearer, but nevertheless eloquent gestures.

18

18. Sistine Chapel, ceiling, 1508-12. Rome, Vatican Palaces.

19

20

21

19. Michelangelo,
Creation of Adam,
1508-12. Rome, Vatican
Palaces, Sistine Chapel.

20. *Torso Belvedere,*
Ist century B.C. Rome,
Vatican Museums.

21. Michelangelo,
*Creation of the moon
and the stars,* detail of a
nude holding a festoon,
1508-12. Rome, Vatican
Palaces, Sistine Chapel.

22

23

24

22. Michelangelo, *Joel*, detail with a nude, 1509. Rome, Vatican Palaces, Sistine Chapel.

23. Michelangelo, *Judith and Holofernes*, detail, 1508-12. Rome, Vatican Palaces, Sistine Chapel.

24. Michelangelo, *The Flood*, detail, 1508-12. Rome, Vatican Palaces, Sistine Chapel.

RAPHAEL FOR JULIUS II

At the end 1508 Raphael moved to Rome, where he had been summoned together with a large group of artists from all over Italy, to assist in the decoration of the rooms refurbished for Julius II, known as the Vatican *Stanze*. It was not long before he was given complete responsibility for the *Stanza della Segnatura* and later, as the head of a large workshop for the *Stanza di Eliodoro*, decorated with scenes relating to the history of the papacy and of the Church. This commission was extraordinarily ambitious and painstaking for the young artist.

The walls were irregular, and were interrupted at odd intervals by windows and doors. There were also compositional difficulties aris-

ing from the large number of figures to be included. Raphael's tackling of these problems clearly reflects the impact of Michelangelo's work on the Sistine Chapel – witness the pronounced and twisted poses of some of the figures, especially in the *Expulsion of Heliodorus from the Temple* – and of Bramante, evident in the spacious architectural setting.

During these years in Rome Raphael also produced some of his finest portraits: in his *Julius II* and *Baldassar Castiglione*, for example, he perfected his talent for the psychological insight already apparent in his earlier works. When he left Florence for Rome the *Madonna del baldacchino* was incomplete but Raphael continued his research into altarpieces, elevating sacred scenes to new levels of idealization and technical accomplishment.

25

26

25. Raphael, *Portrait of Baldassar Castiglione*, 1514-15. Paris, Louvre.

26. Raphael, *St Cecilia*, 1514. Bologna, Pinacoteca Nazionale.

RENAISSANCE ART

LA *STANZA DELLA SEGNATURA* AND THE CELEBRATION OF HUMANIST CULTURE

In the *Stanza della Segnatura*, the pope's study, Raphael celebrated humanist culture and the fulfillment of humanist ideals in the Renaissance Rome of the papacy by painting, between 1508 and 1511, in the *Disputation of the Sacrament*, the *School of Athens*, *Parnassus* and the *Virtues* (*Fortitude*, *Prudence*, *Temperance*). Facing one another, the *Disputation of the Sacrament* and the *School of Athens* represent respectively Christian revelation and the wisdom of antiquity, the affinity between them reflected in the symmetrical arrangement of the compositions and their corresponding elements. At the center of the *School of Athens* stand Plato and Aristotle, the greatest philosophers of antiquity, who represent the two main systems of classical thought. Arranged around them are a crowd of famous thinkers and philosophers. In the *Disputation of the Sacrament*, the host displayed on the central altar is the focus of three superimposed semicircular layers: the Church Militant with its lay and religious representatives (below), the Church Triumphant with saints and patriarchs in the center, and the Trinity with the Virgin and St John (above). In *Parnassus*, poetry is celebrated as the highest faculty of the spirit in which Apollo and the Muses among the ancient and modern poets allude to an accord between the classical and Christian humanist world. Raphael synthesizes the complex iconography in a harmonious and highly symbolic composition. The themes are elaborated in a sophisticated and controlled vein but rendered with a lively naturalism.

27

27. Raphael, *Disputation on the Sacrament*, 1508-11. Rome, Vatican Palaces, Stanza della Segnatura.

28

29

30

28. Raphael, *Parnassus*, 1508-11. Rome, Vatican Palaces, Stanza della Segnatura.

29. Stanza della Segnatura, 1508-11. Rome, Vatican Palaces.

30. Raphael, ceiling, 1508-11. Rome, Vatican Palaces, Stanza della Segnatura.

SCHOOL OF ATHENS
Raphael, 1508-11
Rome, Vatican Palaces, Stanza della Segnatura

SUBJECT
The spacious architecture is crowded with figures: famous philosophers and thinkers of antiquity together with modern artists and men of letters.

To the left is Pythagoras, seated in the foreground hunched over a book; behind him is Averroes , wearing a white turban. Epicurus is seen standing further to the left crowned with vine-leaves.

In the group at the top of the stairs stands Socrates in discussion with his disciples. His face is taken from classical portrait busts which provide a convincing record of his features.

The person in the foreground, seated and facing forwards with his arm resting on a block, is Heraclites, often taken to be a portrait of Michelangelo: an act of homage by Raphael to the artist who had by then uncovered part of his work on the Sistine Chapel.

At the center of the painting, Plato points his finger up towards the realm of ideas while Aristotle stretches his hand over the terrestrial sphere to indicate the world of experience. Plato bears a striking similarity to Leonardo da Vinci.

COMPOSITION

The scene takes place within a building which appears to be planned on a Greek cross with a dome rising above the square crossing. The axis of the composition, indicated by the perspective lines, coincides with one of the arms of the cross, its receding arches creating spatial depth.

The building has the solemnity of Roman buildings in the sixteenth century, built in conscious emulation of antique basilicas and is perfectly suited to housing the great philosophers. The motif of the wide coffered arched vaulting is probably derived from the basilica of Maxentius.

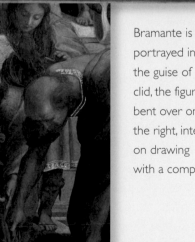

Bramante is portrayed in the guise of Euclid, the figure bent over on the right, intent on drawing with a compass.

Finally, the young man to the extreme right, looking out of the painting and wearing a black hat, is a self-portrait of Raphael.

The two fundamental schools of ancient and renaissance thought are represented in Plato and Aristotle. They appear to move slowly forward, their figures set against a luminous patch of sky, and framed by the final arch, at the point where the groups of figures reverently converge.

THE *STANZA DI ELIODORO* AND THE CELEBRATION OF CATHOLIC DOCTRINE

Between 1511 and 1514 Raphael painted the *Stanza di Eliodoro*, the papal audience chamber, to record historical moments when Divine intervention had responded to the Church in need, thereby exalting Catholic doctrine and the activities of Julius II. The wall paintings depict the *Expulsion of Heliodorus from the Temple*, the *Liberation of St Peter*, *Leo the Great stopping the progress of Attila the Hun* and the *Miracle of the Mass at Bolsena*.

In the *Expulsion of Heliodorus*, and this fresco lends the room its name, to the right we see Heliodorus who had been sent to Jerusalem in order to take the treasures from the Temple of Solomon but is punished by God with the apparition of a terrifying horseman.

The event is witnessed by Julius II, the patron of the project, who is portrayed on the left.

The fresco therefore celebrates the pope's political success, and recognizes the importance of Divine intervention, which on several occasions had helped the Church overcome interference

31

31. Raphael, *Leo the Great halts the progress of Attila,* 1511-14. Rome, Vatican Palaces, Stanza di Eliodoro.

from foreign powers. The style adopted in this room is noticeably different from that in the *Stanza della Segnatura*. The dramatic tension of the composition, the use of light and color, and the agitated dynamism of the group surrounding Heliodorus are reminiscent of Michelangelo's figures on the Sistine ceiling.

The *Miracle of the Mass at Bolsena* depicts an event which occurred in 1263, when a Bohemian priest who had doubts about the doctrine of transubstantiation, (the real presence of Christ in the bread and wine of the Eucharist), saw the host bleed and stain his corporal. This event too is witnessed by Julius II, who is shown kneeling before the altar. The painting was designed to respond powerfully to questions raised by Lutheran schismatics at a critical time for the Church. Raphael's harmonious composition is a perfect combination of form, drawing and color. His use of warmer and denser tones suggests the influence of Venetian painting, as does the extraordinarily natural, psychologically acute, and expressive depiction of the five figures kneeling in the lower right. In the scene showing the *Liberation of St Peter* from prison in Jerusalem Raphael's research into the effects of light achieved extraordinarily dramatic results.

32

32. Raphael, *Expulsion of Heliodorus from the Temple*, 1511-14. Rome, Vatican Palaces, Stanza di Eliodoro.

33. Raphael, *Miracle at Bolsena*, 1511-14. Rome, Vatican Palaces, Stanza di Eliodoro.

34-35. Raphael, *Liberation of St Peter* and detail with St Peter and the angel, 1511-14. Rome, Vatican Palaces, Stanza di Eliodoro.

PORTRAITS AND ALTARPIECES

Raphael was also actively engaged as a portraitist during his stay in Rome, a career he had begun in Florence, and an activity he combined with the production of altarpieces. His portraits capture both the physical and psychological traits of his subjects as in his wonderful portrait of Julius II.

The remarkable personality of the pope, endowed with both political insight and artistic sensibility, is revealed in his lowered gaze which manages to convey both the determination of his personality and the fatigue of a grand old man. The slightly elevated viewpoint and the diagonal thrust of the composition create the illusion of being in the actual presence of the pope. The same device is used in the portrait of Baldassar Castiglione, Raphael's homage to his friend and to the author of The Courtier, with whom he shared

the same courtly ideals of elegance and spiritual elevation. After his youthful experimentation with the emotional tension of the *Deposition*, executed in 1507 during his stay in Perugia, Raphael continued his research into altarpieces, his constant aim being to solicit the emotional involvement of the spectator through elevating compositional arrangements.

In his private commissions on the other hand he aimed for natural and tender interpretations of the emotions, best exemplified in the *Madonna della seggiola*. In his Sistine Madonna, painted between 1513 and 1514 for the high altar of the church of the Benedictines in Piacenza, he broke away from the architectural framework of the altarpiece to present a moment of direct, personal experience of the Divine. The Virgin, no longer enthroned or surrounded by a throng of angels and saints as the queen of heaven, appears as a miraculous vision in the clouds, and draws the faithful towards her

36

37

36. Raphael, *Sistine Madonna*, 1513-14. Dresden, Gemäldegalerie.

37. Raphael, *Portrait of Julius II della Rovere*, detail, 1511-12. Florence, Uffizi.

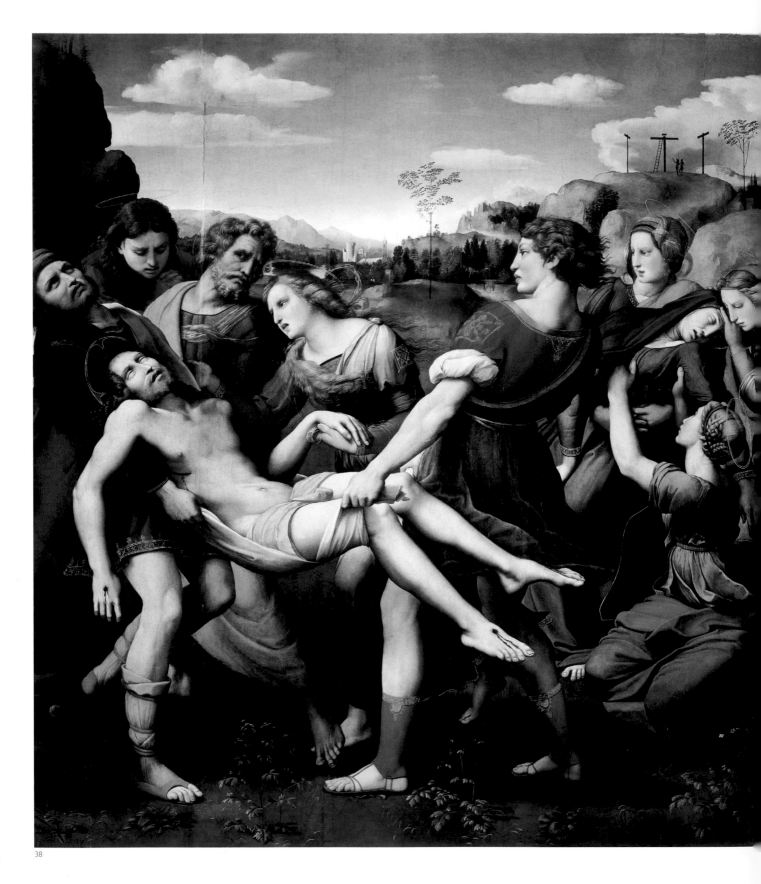

38

38. Raphael, *Deposition*,
1507. Rome, Galleria
Borghese.

through the devotional gestures of both St Barbara and St Sixtus. The *Transfiguration*, left unfinished when Raphael died, is his most ambitious altarpiece.

It is divided into two quite distinct zones: the higher heavenly sphere, luminous and symmetrical, and the lower earthly one, darker, and crowded with gesticulating figures. Raphael created a new highly dramatic type of sacred painting which had a tremendous impact and was much imitated throughout the sixteenth century.

39

40

39-40. Raphael, *Transfiguration* and detail, 1518-20. Rome, Pinacoteca Vaticana.

MADONNA DELLA SEGGIOLA

Raphael, 1514
Florence, Palatine Gallery

SUBJECT

The circular form reflects the domestic origin of this painting, undoubtedly destined for private devotion and which was probably painted to commemorate a wedding or birth.

The scene is both intimate and informal, and centers on the affectionate gesture of Mary depicted with her arms clasped around the Christ Child.

The work is entitled the Madonna della seggiola after the rich chair with its carved back, gold decoration and heavy fringe.

The Virgin wears an exotic silk shawl over her traditional blue gown, an unexpected addition to the sacred scene. Her hair is also worn in the contemporary style, wrapped in a striped scarf.

COMPOSITION

The composition reflects the circular shape of the panel.

Even the Christ Child's feet are aligned to echo the circular border of painting.

The curved pose of the Mother and Child is in contrast to the vertical arm of the chair.

On the right, and slightly behind, is the young St John the Baptist, dressed in a camel skin.

The compositional unity and the affectionate intimacy between Mother and Child are also achieved through the play of color, cold on the fringes and warm at the heart of the painting.

RAPHAEL AND LEO X: THE REBIRTH OF ANTIQUITY

Leo X de' Medici, who succeeded Julius II in 1513, was intent on maintaining peace and consolidating papal power, and appeared more interested in promoting culture and art at home than dealing with the religious divisions north of the alps.

Raphael was Leo X's favorite artist and he loaded him with commissions which Raphael was only able to carry out with the help of a large and highly skilled workshop.

He continued the decoration of the Vatican apartments, painting with assistants the *Stanza dell'Incendio di Borgo*, before turning his attention to the cartoons for the tapestries destined for the Sistine Chapel.

His public activities became increasingly demanding when in 1514 he became master of the works for St Peter's and, a year later, his archeological expertise, led to his nomination as superintendent of marbles and Latin inscriptions with control over excavations and responsibility for the conservation of the Roman monuments. Inevitably then the study of the antique assumed a role of central importance in Raphael's work with numerous references to classical motifs in his decorative projects.

41

42

41. Raphael, *Leo X between cardinals Luigi de' Rossi and Giulio de' Medici*, 1518. Florence, Uffizi.

42. Raphael, *Prospetto di teatro Drawing of a theater*, n. 560 A. Florence, Uffizi, Gabinetto dei Disegni e delle Stampe.

THE STANZA DELL'INCENDIO DI BORGO

Between 1514 and 1517 Raphael worked with his assistants on the decoration of the Stanza dell'Incendio di Borgo, intended as a formal dining room. The scenes depicted are episodes from the lives of popes Leo III and Leo IV and allude to similar events in the life of Leo X. The political authority and cultural prestige of the papacy were celebrated through examples from ancient history. The depiction of the *Fire in the Borgo*, the only scene for which Raphael was personally responsible illustrates a miraculous episode described in the *Liber Pontificalis*. In the Roman quarter of the Borgo, directly in front of St Peter's, there was a violent fire in 847 miraculously extinguished by the prayers of Leo IV, who is seen in the background in the process of blessing the troubled area. Raphael is most interested in the human aspects of the tragedy, dwelling on the people desperately trying to escape the flames, and to the left, inserts the tender passage of the escape of Aeneas from Troy bearing his aged father Anchises on his shoulders and accompanied by his wife Creusa and son Ascanius. The fresco therefore alludes to the achievements of Leo X in bringing peace to the Italian peninsula. Changes are detectable in Raphael's mature style: the composition is no longer strictly contained within the architectural framework and the dramatic pathos has become more emphatic in the gestures of the figures who appear to be in more isolated groups and placed in theatrical settings Raphael's part in the *Coronation of Charlemagne*, in the same room, was limited to the preparatory drawings while the execution, not of the highest quality, was entrusted to his assistants, Gian Francesco Penni and Raffaellino del Colle, who worked on the fresco after Raphael's departure. The episode showing Leo III crowning the Holy Roman Emperor on Christmas day 800, refers indirectly to the peace signed in Bologna in 1516 between Leo X and Francis I of France. This explains why Leo III and Charlemagne appear to be portraits of the Florentine pope and the French king.

43

43. Raphael, *Fire in the Borgo*, 1514. Rome, Vatican Palaces, Stanza dell'Incendio di Borgo.

RENAISSANCE ART

45

46

44. Facing page: Raphael and assistants, *Stanza dell'Incendio di Borgo,* **1514-17. Rome, Vatican Palaces.**

45. School of Raphael, *Coronation of Charlemagne,* **1516-17. Rome, Vatican Palaces, Stanza dell'Incendio di Borgo.**

46. School of Raphael, *Justification of Leo III,* **1514-17. Rome, Vatican Palaces, Stanza dell'Incendio di Borgo.**

47

Between 1515 and 1516 Raphael devoted his attention to cartoons for the creation of a series of tapestries depicting *Episodes in the Lives of St Peter and St Paul*, made in Brussels and supposed to decorate the lower part of the Sistine Chapel walls. Raphael, who was both inspired by the prestigious commission, and aware of the comparisons to be made with Michelangelo's painting of the ceiling, adopted spacious compositions characterized by eloquent gestures and by figures with a wide variety of expressions. These set the tone for a more rhetorical language that became widely disseminated in Europe.

48

47. Raphael, *St Paul preaching in Athens,* n. 540 E. Florence, Uffizi, Gabinetto dei Disegni e delle Stampe.

Preparatory drawing for the cartoon and tapestry.

48. Raphael, *Miraculous draft of fishes,* 1515-16. Rome, Vatican Picture Gallery.

RAPHAEL AND ANTIQUITY: THE LETTER TO LEO X

Raphael was stimulated by his contact with the court of Leo X to pursue his passionate interest in the world of antiquity.

At the papal court he met writers and collectors including Cardinal Bibbiena, Pietro Dovizi and Baldassar Castiglione, and was able to follow first hand the excavations of classical statues and Roman monuments.

The pope was in complete sympathy with Raphael's conception of the "classical", detailed in a letter sent to Leo X explaining the artist's ideas and practical approach to antiquity.

He proposed a detailed study, with accompanying drawings, of all that survived in order to determine the best way to embark on the reconstruction of classical Rome.

It is a surprisingly modern document, pleading the case for ending the plundering of the classical sites and the destruction of the surviving monuments.

Raphael even invented a kind of compass or rose of the winds in order to help plot the position of the various buildings.

There are three versions of the letter with different dates but it was presumably written following Raphael's appointment as the papal keeper of antiquities.

49

49. Raphael, *Interior of the Pantheon*, n. 164 A. Florence, Uffizi, Gabinetto dei Disegni e delle Stampe.

50

51

GROTESQUE DECORATION IN THE SCHOOL OF RAPHAEL

Raphael's determined and passionate research into classical architecture was later continued by his followers in Rome and the surrounding countryside. The excavation of classical buildings decorated with paintings and stuccoes was the direct inspiration for a whole series of decorative motifs in Raphael's new projects including the so-called *Stufetta* of Cardinal Bibbiena (his bathroom), the Vatican Logge, the Psyche Loggia in the Farnesina and Villa Madama. The large workshops directed by Raphael specialized in grotesque decoration, much imitated by his followers. The term *a*

grottesche, also adopted by Vasari, refers to the fact that most of the Roman monuments, such as Nero's *Domus Aurea*, where these highly decorative elements were found, were still underground and hard to explore, and so were like grottoes.

These grotesque elements were bizarre, fantastic and often monstrous forms drawn from a rich human, animal and vegetable repertory. Although these decorative motifs had been known since the fifteenth century and interpreted by previous artists (witness the Renaissance "candelabre"), in Raphael workshops the master's detailed archeological research led to the revival of the essential technique with rapid brushstrokes and the use of bright colors against white, black and red grounds.

50. Raphael, Loggetta, detail, 1517-19. Rome, Vatican Palaces.

51. *Stufetta* of Cardinal Bibbiena, 1516-20. Rome, Vatican Palaces.

RAPHAEL THE ARCHITECT IN THE SERVICE OF AGOSTINO CHIGI

Raphael's activity as an architect began in 1509 in the small church of Sant'Eligio degli Orefici, which pays homage to Bramante in the spacious centrally-planned interior surmounted by a dome. Following this the Sienese banker Agostino Chigi secured Raphael's services in the decoration of part of his villa, known as the Farnesina, and in the project for his family chapel in Santa Maria del Popolo.

The Chigi chapel, successfully integrated decorative and structural elements, at a stage when Raphael was intensely involved with a number of architectural projects and his innovative solutions were widely adopted by his pupils.

Later, following Bramante's death in 1514 when Raphael was put in charge of building operations at St Peter's, he adopted more monumental and grandiose forms, mirrored in his painting, and exemplified in the Villa Madama on Monte Mario and in Palazzo Branconio dell'Aquila, destroyed in the seventeenth century.

52

53

RENAISSANCE ART

52. Raphael, Sant'Eligio degli Orefici, dome, 1509. Rome.

53. Raphael, *Section of the church of Sant'Eligio degli Orefici and sketch of the lantern.* Florence, Uffizi, Gabinetto dei Disegni e delle Stampe.

54

55

56

54. Raphael, Loggia
of Psyche, detail with
Venus, *Ceres* and *Juno*,
1517-18. Rome,
Farnesina.

55. Raphael, Loggia of
Psyche, 1517-18. Rome,
Farnesina.

56. Palazzo Chigi, known
as the Farnesina, from
the garden. Begun 1509.
Rome.

THE DECORATION OF THE VILLA FARNESINA

In 1509 Agostino Chigi commissioned Baldassarre Peruzzi to build his new villa, the Farnesina, intended as a "place of delight" where he might enjoy the pleasures of the worldly, but also of the contemplative life, hold parties and gatherings of intellectuals, and house his collection of art and antiquities. The rooms were decorated between 1511 and 1518 by all the best artists in Rome starting with Raphael and his assistants, who chose mythological subjects and astrological scenes including the horoscope of his patron.

In the east loggia facing the garden, Raphael painted the *Triumph of Galatea*, taken directly from a classical painting based on the description provided by Philostratus. This work succeeded in reviving the classical myth by freely adapting antique motifs while imitating the original coloring – witness the Pompeian red of Galatea's mantle and the brilliance of the waves.

In the Loggia of Psyche, Raphael created the perfect decorative confluence of nature and architecture as the tale of Cupid and Psyche by Apulleus, executed between 1517 and 1518 entirely by Raphael's assistants, unfolds within an airy pergola laden with festoons of fruit and flowers.

Sebastiano del Piombo painted the lunettes with mythological subjects evidently indebted to Michelangelo's figures, while Sodoma decorated the first floor with the *Wedding of Alexander and Roxanne* and Baldassarre Peruzzi in the *Salone delle Prospettive*, created a breathtaking illusionistic open colonnade and loggia.

57

57. Baldassarre Peruzzi,
Salone delle Prospettive,
1515-16. Rome,
Farnesina.

58

58. Sodoma, *Wedding of Alexander and Roxanne*, detail, 1515-16. Rome, Farnesina.

THE CHIGI CHAPEL IN SANTA MARIA DEL POPOLO

In the family chapel built in 1515 for Agostino Chigi in Santa Maria del Popolo, Raphael adapted Bramante's design for the dome of St Peter's to a single room. While the architectural components are in white marble, the other surfaces are faced in marble in tones of red and brown while the dome is covered in bright mosaic with gold on a blue ground. The two Chigi tombs rise like pyramids on either side, while the niches between the pilasters were intended to house statues designed by Raphael (only one of these was carved, by Lorenzetti, while the others were carved in the seventeenth century by Bernini). The iconography brings together the sacred and profane, including the signs of the zodiac on the ceiling referring to the horoscope of Agostino Chigi.

59

**59. Cappella Chigi,
interior, 1515. Rome,
Santa Maria del Popolo.**

RENAISSANCE ART

60

61

62

THE MODEL VILLA: VILLA MADAMA

Between 1517 and 1518 Raphael designed the residence on Monte Mario, known as Villa Madama for Cardinal Giuliano de' Medici. Contemporary enthusiasm for classical mythology and the ideals of antiquity turned Raphael's attention to Pliny the Elder's description of the Villa Laurentiana, which he used as his model. His alleged ability to completely recreate the antique world was given concrete visibility in this building so perfectly in keeping with its surroundings. Certain areas such as the large bathrooms, the circular central courtyard and hippodrome were faithfully reproduced from Pliny's account of the villa. The same search for classical harmony is apparent in the arrangement of the external space divided into terraces and gardens. Although left unfinished Villa Madama was fundamental to the subsequent development of the villa in the sixteenth century.

60. Loggia di Raphael, 1518-25. Rome, Villa Madama.

61. Villa Madama, north facade, 1518-25. Rome.

62. Fish pond, 1518-25. Rome, Villa Madama.

ROME AT THE TIME OF BRAMANTE, RAPHAEL AND MICHELANGELO

During the pontificates of Julius II and Leo X the greatest artists of the day were drawn to Rome, attracted by prestigious papal commissions and the lavish patronage of the papal court. From all over Italy artists flocked to work in proximity with Bramante, Raphael and Michelangelo, and to find those ready to pay for their services. Most notable of the architects were Baldassarre Peruzzi and Antonio da Sangallo the younger, while among the painters the Venetian Sebastiano del Piombo was particularly adept at assimilating Michelangelo's innovations. Of the sculptors, Jacopo Sansovino interpreted the new classicism in the wake of Bramante and Raphael. Strangely enough Leonardo's stay in Rome appears to have had limited repercussions. He arrived in 1513 attracted by the patronage of the Medici Leo X but he lived apart from the other artists and worked on projects to improve the Pontine marshes and on the port at Civitavecchia. Although he also painted *St John the Baptist* he took it away with him when he left for France. Leonardo also decided to take the *Monna Lisa* and the *St Anne*, both now in the Louvre, when he retreated to the French court.

63

63. Baldassarre Peruzzi, Palazzo Massimo alle Colonne, facade, 1532-36. Rome.

BALDASSARRE PERUZZI AND ANTONIO DA SANGALLO THE YOUNGER

The Sienese architect and painter, Baldassarre Peruzzi, entered Bramante's studio in 1505. He immediately devoted his attention to the study of historical monuments and, through his drawings and detailed reliefs, acquired a thorough understanding of classical monuments, which he used with freedom and confidence in his own designs. The Villa Farnesina is a fine example of Peruzzi's extension of the classical theme. It was built for his friend, Agostino Chigi, between 1509 and 1511, with direct reference to the villas of Imperial Rome. Peruzzi nevertheless created an original building, articulated behind with two projecting wings, and connected by a loggia on the ground floor, which also served to bring the garden and the house into closer proximity. In his decoration of the *Salone delle Prospettive* he opted for highly theatrical effects with his illusionistic columns and loggias revealing his architectural accomplishment. For his part, Antonio da Sangallo the Younger who arrived in Rome in 1505, continued the family line of architects, being the third Sangallo to practice after Giuliano and Antonio the Elder. His training in the family workshop led him to concentrate on developing a distinctive type of urban palazzo, the most notable example being the Palazzo Baldachin.

64

64. Baldassarre Peruzzi,
Stage design with the
symbolic monuments of
Rome. **Florence, Uffizi,**
Gabinetto dei Disegni e
delle Stampe.

THE ARCHITECTS OF ST PETER'S

The construction of the new St Peter's, initiated by Julius II, was based on the plan devised by Bramante. When Julius died in 1513 the first four enormous piers had been raised together with the arches destined to support a dome some forty meters in diameter. From 1514, at Bramante's own request Raphael was engaged to superintend the work on the basilica, with the help of Fra' Giocondo, of Giuliano and later of Antonio da Sangallo. Raphael worked on a plan in keeping with Bramante's project, lengthening the nave from the original crossing. Following Raphael's death the building of St Peter's was entrusted to Antonio da Sangallo the Younger, who was assisted by Baldassarre Peruzzi. Their plans were criticized by Michelangelo, who considered them too dispersive, with an excessive use of superimposed columns on the exterior. The dispute was settled when Michelangelo took charge in 1547 and when he reaffirmed his confidence in Bramante's centrally-planned design. He then drew up plans for the giant dome which was only completed after his death.

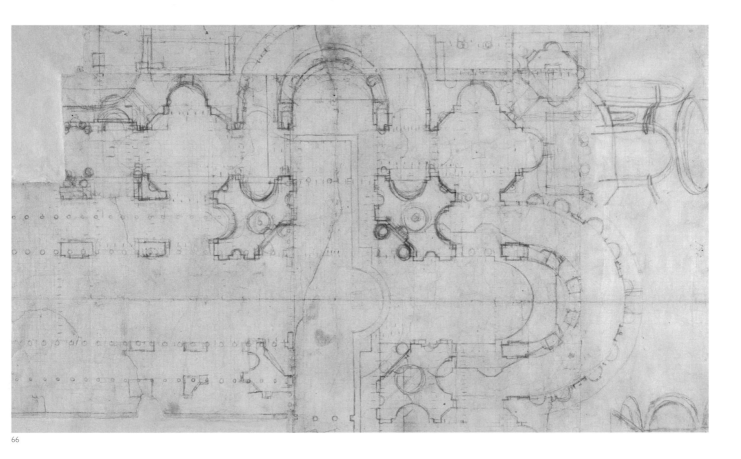

65

66

65. Michelangelo, St Peter's, interior of the dome, from 1547. Rome.

66. Bramante, *Plan for the new St Peter's*, 1520. Florence, Uffizi, Gabinetto dei Disegni e delle Stampe.

THE PAINTINGS OF SEBASTIANO DEL PIOMBO

The Venetian Sebastiano Luciani – known as del Piombo after he became chancellor of the papal *piombatura* or seal – moved to Rome in 1511. He was immediately engaged to work on the decoration of the Villa Farnesina, where he painted the Sala di Galatea with mythological subjects taken from Ovid's *Metamorphoses* in the lunettes, and revealed his adhesion to the monumental forms adopted by Michelangelo. His portraits from the same period also reflect the influence of Raphael but by the time he left Rome to return to Venice in 1526 he had become much more closely allied to the manner of Michelangelo. They were also close personal friends so that Michelangelo occasionally provided Sebastiano with drawings such as the one for the *Raising of Lazarus* which he was commissioned to paint for Cardinal Giulio de' Medici in competition with the *Transfiguration* by Raphael. In his *Pietà* a profound religious sensibility is expressed in the dark and lifeless tones which serve to underline the sorrow at Christ's death. There is also a sense of heroism in the monumental figures arranged in a triangular composition.

67

69

68

67. Sebastiano del Piombo, *Sketch for a portrait of Portrait Clement VII*, about 1526. Napoli, Capodimonte.

68-69. Sebastiano del Piombo, *Pietà* and detail, 1516-17. Viterbo, Museo Civico.

THE TRAINING OF JACOPO SANSOVINO IN ROME AND FLORENCE

Jacopo Tatti, known as Sansovino, in recognition of his master Andrea Sansovino, returned to work for a number of years in his native city of Florence, after a highly influential period in Rome between 1506 and 1511. His early sculptural work reflects his debt to Michelangelo - witness the *Bacchus with a faun* in the Bargello, a highly accomplished piece full of grace and harmony, and the *St James the Apostle* for the cathedral. At the same stage Sansovino became active as an architect and worked with Andrea del Sarto on the temporary facade for Florence cathedral, created especially for the ceremonial entry of pope Leo X into the city. During his second Roman period, between 1516 and 1527, Sansovino was actively involved in the architectural debate led by Bramante on the one side, and the more conservative Sangallo on the other. Sansovino planned the church of San Giovanni dei Fiorentini in a conciliatory style incorporating certain of Bramante's innovatory modes into the traditional Florentine language. From 1527 Sansovino was in Venice, and the Veneto, where he worked primarily as an architect but also produced some fine sculpture.

70

71

70. Jacopo Sansovino, *Bacchus and a faun*, 1511-12. Florence, Museo del Bargello.

71. Jacopo Sansovino, *St James the Apostle*. Florence, Duomo.

9. Venice and the birth of tonal painting

A manner of painting developed in Venice in the early sixteenth century quite distinct from the prevailing trends in Florence and Rome. The Venetian painters offered a rich alternative to the High Renaissance of Central Italy but one shaped on quite different principles. The city's enormous wealth, its unique site and the cultural ideals formed there produced a figurative language steeped in fascination for the material world and visual sensation. Giorgione helped bring about this transformation of Venetian painting by rejecting the conventions of fifteenth-century art in order to concentrate on imitating the natural world. He created a new way of interpreting space based on superimposed layers of color, using the intensely luminous tones to convey the natural vibrations of the open air, giving birth to the "tonal painting". His innovation was taken up by a whole generation of Venetian painters, from Titian on, and affected the late work of Giovanni Bellini.

2

3

1. Facing page: Titian, *Flora*, 1515. Florence, Uffizi.

2. Giorgione (attributed), *Leda and the swan*, detail of the landscape. Padua, Museo Civico.

3. Giorgione, *Knight with his page*, about 1509. Florence, Uffizi.

THE REVOLUTIONARY WORK OF GIORGIONE

Giorgione's invention of a new pictorial style in Venice can be compared with the innovatory role played by Leonardo in Florence. Like Leonardo, he realized the need to search beyond the fifteenth-century manner in order to concentrate on the problems related to the imitation of nature. This led to his creation of "tonal painting", painting without drawing, in which color for the first time became an independent means of expression. The individual colored mark, or brushstroke, without any outline, was built up to shape soft and atmospheric compositions. Space was no longer conveyed though orthogonals, but shaped through layers of color which, within a unified tonal composition, were differentiated according to their luminous intensity. Our knowledge of Giorgione's career is very limited. Of his recorded works only the very badly damaged fragments of the frescoes for the facade of the Fondaco dei Tedeschi, the German Exchange building, can be clearly identified. For the rest we rely in part on the description of a number of his works in private Venetian collections compiled by the Venetian noble Marcantonio Michiel, and on the information in Giorgio Vasari's *Lives*. Now only six or seven works are unanimously attributed to the master, one of the earliest works being the Castelfranco Altarpiece, painted between 1504 and 1505. His most celebrated paintings are of modest proportions, their meaning is opaque, executed for a select circle of aristocratic intellectuals: the *Three Philosophers*, the *Sleeping Venus* and the *Tempesta*. To these are added the *Portrait of an Old Woman* and two paintings discovered as a result of late nineteenth-century scholarship; the *Judith* in the Hermitage and the *Portrait of a young man* in Berlin.

4

5

328

4-5. Giorgione, *Trial of Moses* and detail, 1505. Florence, Uffizi.

GIORGIONE IN THE *LIVES* OF VASARI: THE PAINTER WHO DID AWAY WITH DRAWING

Vasari considered Giorgione among the founders of "the third manner which we choose to call modern" that is the High Renaissance manner. Historians often attribute Giorgione's innovations in painting to his understanding of the advances made by Leonardo, emphasizing the importance of Florentine culture on Venetian painting. It is true that like Leonardo, Giorgione focused on overcoming the difficulties in representing nature and in particular on an atmospheric unification, harmonizing figures with their settings. Giorgione's solution was markedly different to Leonardo's however. According to Vasari he "would never use anything in his works which he had not drawn from life. These he would represent as best as he knew how with colors, without drawing; maintaining that painting with colors alone, without any drawing on paper, was the true and best way to proceed".

6

7

6. Giorgione, *Judith*, about 1504. St Petersburg, Hermitage.

7. Giorgione, "With Time", *Portrait of an old woman*, about 1508. Venice, Accademia.

8

418.

9

8. Giorgione (attributed),
Fête champêtre.
Padua, Museo Civico.

9. Giorgione, *Madonna
and Child with saints*.
Madrid, Prado.

THE *SACRA CONVERSAZIONE* IN A LANDSCAPE

An early work of fundamental importance, the *Virgin and Child with St Liberale and St Francis* known as the *Castelfranco altarpiece*, of 1504-05, was probably painted for the funerary chapel of Matteo Costanzo (whose coat of arms appears on the base of the throne) in the church of San Liberale in Castelfranco Veneto, Giorgione's birthplace. The altarpiece appears to follow the traditional fifteenth-century Venetian model both in the subject of the "sacra conversazione", and in the symmetrical arrangement of the saints on either side of the Virgin.

The composition is reduced to the essential triangular scheme and the space is defined by a balanced arrangement of parallel surfaces. The unusual height of the throne is taken from the *San Cassiano Altarpiece* by Antonello da Messina, but Giorgione's invention is to transport the scene into a natural open-air setting instead of confining the group in an architectural framework. The group of figures serves as a pivot between the two halves of the painting, the lower half with the saints and the upper one opening onto an airy landscape. The free, soft, application of the paint, without any drawing, creates the vibrant natural atmosphere.

10

11

12

10-12. Giorgione, *Castelfranco Altarpiece* and detail of the landscape and of the coat of arms, about 1504-05. Castelfranco Veneto, Duomo.

THE CLASSICAL STYLE OF THE FONDACO DEI TEDESCHI

In 1507-08 Giorgione was engaged in decorating the facade of the Fondaco dei Tedeschi, or German Exchange, on the Grand Canal in Venice. This ambitious cycle would have told us much about his monumental style but unfortunately it has been almost totally destroyed after years of exposure to damp and adverse conditions. The space between the horizontal friezes and the windows was painted with classically inspired human figures of which only one detached fragment survives depicting a *Young female nude*. The rest we can only imagine from an eighteenth-century engraving. What is clear is Giorgione's intention to expand on the theme of the classical nude in highly articulated studies of the human body and especially through his exploitation of color to give vitality to the flesh tones. The young Titian assisted Giorgione in the decoration of the Exchange.

HIDDEN MEANING IN PAINTINGS FOR A SELECT FEW

Giorgione's inventiveness was not limited to the technique of painting "without drawing", based exclusively on gradations of color. He also influenced the important development of new figurative themes. Both the sources and the surviving works make it quite clear that Giorgione mainly painted small pictures for a select circle of intellectuals. The subject matter was secular and his patrons were cultivated individuals who delighted in complex allegories and veiled symbolism. Giorgione himself belongs to this group and was also a highly accomplished poet, lute player and singer. The themes treated in the *Three philosophers*, the *Tempesta*, and the *Sleeping Venus* were probably developed after learned discussions with those who commissioned them and after Giorgione's searching enquiry into the concepts of nature and life, female beauty, and the idyllic rapport between man and nature.

13

14

13. Giorgione, *Young female nude*, 1508. Venice, Ca' d'Oro, Galleria Giorgio Franchetti.

14. Fondaco dei Tedeschi. Venice.

15

16

17

15. Giorgione, *The Three Ages of Man*, 1505-10. Florence, Palatina Gallery.

16. Giorgione, *Three philosophers*, 1507-10. Vienna, Kunsthistorisches Museum.

17. Giorgione, *Sleeping Venus*, about 1510. Dresda, Staatliche Gemäeldegalerie.

THE TEMPESTA
Giorgione, 1506-08
Venice, Accademia

SUBJECT

This celebrated painting by Giorgione depicts a wild landscape with two figures:

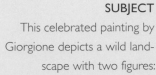

to the left a man standing holding a long staff at his side, his head turned towards the center of the painting;

to the right, seated on a white sheet which is drawn up over her shoulders, a naked woman breast feeds a child.

The interpretation of this scene, despite relentless critical attention, remains a mystery. Among the many theories it is worth recalling the Venetian patrician, Marcantonio Michiel, who saw the painting in 1530 and described it in his Information on works and drawings: "the landscape on canvas with the Storm with the gypsy [cingana] and soldier". The difficulty in identifying the painting's meaning stems largely from the limited importance Giorgione himself appears to give it. The man and woman are components on the scene, they are part of the natural order and are witnesses to the event which is about to take place.

Out attention is however drawn to the sudden flash of lightening in a sky heavy with threatening clouds.

The buildings in the background with their long chimneys and decorative detail have been recognized as typically of Venice.

COMPOSITION

The painting, despite its apparent natural facility, is built up on an extremely sophisticated composition. The figures on either side serve as theatrical wings leading into the main drama: the depiction of nature.

The painting is constructed along the diagonals, which converge below the mirrored surface of the water,

Beneath the surface of the painting, instead of the standing man we now see, there was originally another seated female nude which also suggests that Giorgione had not planned a specific subject and had no determined theme, but rather invented freely as the work progressed.

In a startling reversal of the old order the real protagonist becomes the landscape itself, nature with a life and power of its own.

while in the background two trees frame the flash of lightening, a narrative passage of great pathos.

THE LATE WORKS OF GIOVANNI BELLINI

Giorgione's work accelerated a process begun in Venice more than two decades earlier.

There was evidently a desire to integrate figures more harmoniously into the landscape which previously had only served as a backdrop to the human drama. This search had also been conducted by a great painter of the previous generation, Giovanni Bellini, who was, according to Vasari, Giorgione's early master.

From the beginning of the sixteenth century, in fact, there are signs of a profound shift in paintings by Bellini, who was always alert to the innovations of the younger generation, many of whom had trained in his studio and who greatly admired his work.

18

18. Giovanni Bellini, *Sacra conversazione Giovanelli*, detail, 1500-04. Venice, Accademia.

19

21

20

LIGHT AND COLOR IN THE VENETIAN TRADITION

In his mature period, and until his death in 1516, Giovanni Bellini continued the Venetian tradition of light and color while remaining alert to the innovative work of other artists, especially to Giorgione. Among Bellini's late works, the *San Zaccaria Altarpiece* of 1505, depicting a group of saints in meditation around the enthroned Virgin, with all the figures sheltered under an imposing architectural structure, adopts the model furnished by Antonello da Messina in his *San Cassiano Altarpiece*. But Bellini's adaptation of the model also transforms it through the soft, suffused light that permeates the architectural setting. This treatment of light also pays homage to the new style of painting introduced by Giorgione with its naturalistic atmospheric effects. In his altarpiece of *St Jerome between St Christopher and St Augustine*, painted in 1515 for the church of San Giovanni Crisostomo, Bellini moved even closer to the pictorial language of the younger generation. The fusion of architectural and natural elements recalls Giorgione's *Castelfranco altarpiece* but it also draws on the one painted by Sebastiano del Piombo in 1510 for the same church.

19. Giovanni Bellini,
St Jerome with
St Christopher and
***St Augustine,* 1515.**
Venice, San Giovanni
Crisostomo.

20-21. Giovanni Bellini,
San Zaccaria Altarpiece
and detail, 1505. Venice,
San Zaccaria.

MYTHOLOGICAL SUBJECTS

While biblical subjects remained popular, in the last years of Bellini's life private patrons increasingly demanded mythological paintings and others treating non-religious themes. Bellini adapted to the change in taste producing such works as the *Feast of the gods* for Alfonso d'Este's Camerino d'Alabastro in the castle of Ferrara. The painting – in which the landscape was later altered by Titian who completed the cycle for the Camerino – is characterized by intense chromatic tones and by a new compositional dynamism. In the *Woman looking in the mirror* Bellini explores the Flemish interest in reflected images by introducing two mirrors and uses a softly modulated light to shape the form of the woman's body which is set off by the chiaroscuro of the background.

22

22. Giovanni Bellini,
Woman looking in the
***mirror**, 1515. Vienna,*
Kunsthistorisches
Museum.

EARLY TITIAN: NATURALISM AND CLASSICAL RESTRAINT

Born in Pieve di Cadore in about 1490, the young Titian was the pupil in Venice first of Giovanni Bellini and then of Giorgione. He worked with Giorgione on the frescoes on the Fondaco dei Tedeschi and assimilated his innovatory pictorial language, based on the independent use of color. Titian continued to experiment with the possibility of creating form through color which resulted in very different effects from those achieved in the soft and veiled atmosphere of Giorgione's painting. Of fundamental importance in the early years was his work on the frescoes of the *Scenes from the Life of St Anthony*, painted in 1511, in the Scuola del Santo in Padua, where he revealed his tal-

ent for dramatic narration. In the meantime, moved by Giorgione's example, Titian painted such allegories as *Sacred and Profane Love*, a work of classical inspiration with a perfectly balanced composition *The Assumption*, painted for the church of the Frari in Venice, represents the end of his early output. In this highly successful altarpiece Titian's work reflects a familiarity with the manner of Raphael and Michelangelo while he retains his facility for the expressive handling of color. Together with the rich production of altarpieces in the third decade of the century Titian worked on projects for the Italian courts, including a series of mythological paintings for the court of Ferrara. His portraits earned him renown, he established contacts with the duke of Mantua, the Emperor Charles V, and the court of Urbino where in 1538 he painted the wonderful *Venus of Urbino*.

23

23. Titian, *Presentation in the Temple*, detail, 1534-38. Venice, Accademia.

EARLY WORK: THE FONDACO DEI TEDESCHI

Titian worked as an assistant to Giorgione on the frescoes for the Fondaco dei Tedeschi. While working on the German exchange building he assimilated Giorgione's style so completely that, as the sources record, he was then able to paint "such a beautifully conceived and colored Judith that everybody thought it was the work of Giorgione, and all his friends congratulated him for having produced his best

work by far". Although the frescoes are all but destroyed the Judith, reveals a dynamism and treatment of form quite distinct from the manner of Giorgione.

In his frescoes of *St Anthony* Titian highlights the key events of the narrative. In the *Miracle of the woman wounded by her jealous husband*, for example, he places the violent scene between husband and wife and the miracle itself in the background with large patches of color from a vibrant palette.

24

25

26

24-25. Titian, *Scenes from the life of St Anthony, Miracle of the woman wounded by her jealous husband* and detail, 1511. Padua, Scuola del Santo.

26. Titian, *Judith*, 1508-09. Venice, Ca' d'Oro, Galleria Giorgio Franchetti.

ALLEGORICAL PAINTINGS

It has always been difficult to distinguish Giorgione's late works from Titian's early ones, for Titian absorbed, in addition to Giorgione's style, his intellectual approach to allegorical subjects which he painted for a select group of private patrons. The *Fête Champêtre*, which alludes to the transcendental quality of music is still disputed between the two great artists. Another complex allegorical picture *Sacred and Profane Love*, develops the theme of Love according to Neo-Platonist thought.

27

27. Titian, *Fête champêtre*,
1511. Paris, Louvre.

MASTERPIECES

SACRED AND PROFANE LOVE
Titian, 1514
Rome, Galleria Borghese

SUBJECT

Despite the endless attempts to interpret this allegorical painting its meaning still escapes us. It is best known as *Sacred and Profane Love*, but also as *Adorned and unadorned Beauty* or the *Three Loves*. None of the figures have a specific identity.

The seated naked figure is most probably Venus, the goddess of Love, and the lantern held up in her hand, the sacred flame of love. Her nudity is symbolic of love's purity.

The other elegantly dressed woman with gloved hands is more difficult to identify. She has been interpreted as earthly love, or the generative power of nature, exemplified in the luxuriant greenery behind her. Alternatively, her white dress, her belt and her gaze fixed ahead, indifferent to the overtures of Venus, have led some to see her as the personification of Chastity.

Behind the antique sarcophagus, decorated in relief with mythological subjects, Cupid bends over to dip his small arm into the water.

The coat of arms of Niccolò Aurelio, the secretary to the Republic of Venice, who probably commissioned the work, is attached to the middle of the front of the sarcophagus.

COMPOSITION

The horizontal arrangement of the composition, built around the sarcophagus, is repeated in the shape of the canvas. The figures are placed on a plane parallel with that of the spectator.

The gentle inclination of the two female bodies forms an ideal triangle with its apex outside the picture frame. Despite being in the background, the broad sweep of open countryside is a dominant element. The high line of the horizon gives ample opportunity to explore the natural setting in which the figures are harmoniously arranged.

The plant growing in front of the sarcophagus offers a more detailed study of nature.

The painting would appear to celebrate the marriage of Laura Bagarotto to Niccolò Aurelio, in 1514, as her coat of arms appears at the bottom of the metal dish resting on the edge of the sarcophagus.

The countryside behind the main allegory is peopled with hunters, animals and a pair of lovers.

The tall dark trees, in the center of the background, screen and filter the golden light which creates a sophisticated play of light on the material of the robes and drapes.

THE RENEWAL OF RELIGIOUS SUBJECTS

Between 1516 and 1518 Titian executed his first public religious commission, an altarpiece of the *Assumption*, for the high altar of one of the most important churches in Venice, Santa Maria Gloriosa dei Frari. In this monumental work Titian is no longer bound to the lessons he had learnt from Giorgione but creates a completely new model

for treating this subject. Space is constructed on three superimposed levels that rotate vertically around the Virgin on her ascent into heaven. The supernatural event which is witnessed by onlookers is depicted with strongly contrasting luminous effects and passages of color ranging from the brilliant and deep reds of the robes to the glowing golden light of the sun. The painting's heroic and monumental language reflects Titian's familiarity with the work of Raphael and Michelangelo. The

28

28. Titian, *Averoldi Polyptych*, 1520-22. Brescia, Santi Nazzaro e Celso.

Averoldi Polyptych painted between 1520 and 1522 commissioned by bishop Altobello Averoldi for the church of Santi Nazaro e Celso in Brescia, reveals Titian's particular enthusiasm for Roman art. The figures of the resurrected Christ and of St Sebastian refer respectively to the *Laocoon* – a Hellenistic sculptural group discovered in Rome at the beginning of the century, of which Titian had a copy – and to a *Prisoner* by Michelangelo. He also renewed the interpretation of the "sacra conversazione" in his second altarpiece for Santa Maria Gloriosa dei Frari, the *Pesaro Altarpiece*. The sacra conversazione takes place in an open space defined by the diagonal arrangement of the columns, suggesting movement, and by the viewpoint from below, conferring majesty on both the figures and the architecture. Jacopo Pesaro, victorious over the Turks at Santa Maura and who commissioned the altarpiece, is shown with members of his family in the bottom right hand corner.

29

30

29. Titian, *Assumption*, 1516-18. Venice, Santa Maria Gloriosa dei Frari.

30. Titian, *Pesaro Altarpiece*, 1519-26. Venice, Santa Maria Gloriosa dei Frari.

THE MYTHOLOGICAL PAINTINGS

Titian completed the *Feast of the Gods*, left unfinished by Giovanni Bellini in 1516, for the study of duke Alfonso d'Este in his castle in Ferrara, for which he also painted three other works: the *Worship of* *Venus*, a *Bacanal* and *Bacchus and Ariadne*. These mythological subjects, immortalized in the Latin poems of Catullus and Philostratus, reflect the duke's archeological interests but Titian interprets them with animated sensuality. The *Triumph of Bacchus and Ariadne* is inspired by the models of classical antiquity and Michelangelo's sculpture. They are

31

31. Titian, *Bacanal*,
1518-19. Madrid, Prado.

surrounded by an absolutely original use of intense and brilliant color in a natural setting strongly reminiscent of the Veneto. In 1538 Titian painted, for his patron Guidobaldo della Rovere, duke of Camerino and later of Urbino, the *Venus di Urbino*, adapted from the Giorgione's earlier prototype, the *Sleeping Venus*.

This masterpiece painted at the height of Titian's creativity, reaffirms his ties to the Venetian tradition but the mythological overtones of Giorgione's version have vanished in Titian's choice of a contemporary palace setting and in his insistence on the physical sensuality of the female figure.

32

32. Titian, *Worship of Venus*, 1519. Madrid, Prado.

VENUS OF URBINO
Titian, 1538
Florence, Uffizi

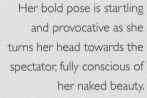

with the little dog curled up at her feet.

SUBJECT
The scene is set in a spacious and finely furnished bedroom. The splendid Venus holds our attention as she lies stretched out on her bed

Her bold pose is startling and provocative as she turns her head towards the spectator, fully conscious of her naked beauty.

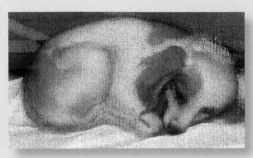

Two women at the back of the room are searching through a richly decorated chest for suitable clothes for the goddess.

Titian exploits the expressive potential of the color to the full, contrasting and juxtaposing in order to draw attention to the smallest details. The red bedcover embroidered with flowers is set off beautifully against the white sheets and pillows.

Similarly the heavy green curtain abov contrasts with the soft luminous flesh tones, Venus's lovely face and her cop blond curls falling over her shoulders.

COMPOSITION

The painting has an extremely complex composition with the two-dimensional foreground intersecting the three-dimensional treatment of the background. The elongated body of Venus stretched out on the bed determines the horizontal emphasis of the foreground. The spectator's gaze is concentrated on Venus who is further isolated from the scene behind by the heavy curtain behind her body. This device serves to create an atmospheric and highly effective emotional tension.

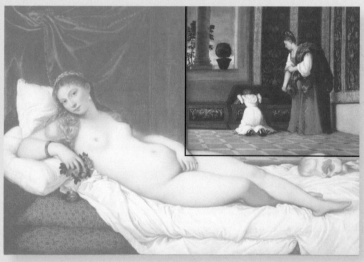

back right corner the painting opens
d is given depth by the traditional
d renaissance floor.

The figure of the woman in the corner further enhances the sense of depth and offers a dramatic contrast to the voluptuous Venus.

A typical Venetian window divided by a column opens onto the glow of the evening sky.

THE PORTRAITS

Titian began his brilliant career as a portraitist in about 1515, but it was only in the following decade that he received commissions to paint portraits of the leading figures in the Italian courts and abroad.

These portraits both interpret and document the personalities of the day, offering an insight into the physical and psychological dimension of political, religious and cultural figures.

Titian managed, at the same time, to produce ideal portraits of his subjects, the image which doges, popes, and emperors chose to present to the world. From the earliest portraits (*Ariosto*, *Vincenzo Mosti* and the *Man with a glove*) the strong physical presence of his subjects is in startling contrast to the traditional manner of Gior-

33

354

33. Titian, *Portrait of duke Federico II Gonzaga*, 1525. Madrid, Prado.

gione, as are the use of color and the new relationship of the figure to the surrounding space.

The *Portrait of Duke Frederick II of Gonzaga*, painted in Mantua in 1525, exemplifies the new model – the subject is depicted standing against a neutral background that dissolves into the dark – as seen in the *Portrait of Francesco Maria della Rovere* 1536-38.

In 1530 Titian first met the Charles V in Bologna where he had come to be crowned by the pope and in the following years he painted a number of portraits of Charles as emperor.

In the 1533 *Portrait* the emperor is depicted in full figure to display all his physical and psychological qualities as a leader, highlighted by his regal bearing and sumptuous clothing. This was the first of many portraits of the Imperial court which brought Titian twice to Augsburg where he painted the emperor and his family.

34

35

36

34. Titian, *Portrait of a man* also known as *Man with a glove*, 1523. Paris, Louvre.

35. Titian, *Portrait of the Emperor Charles V*, 1532-33. Madrid, Prado.

36. Titian, *Portrait of a man with gray eyes*, 1545. Florence, Palatine Gallery.

RENAISSANCE ART

THE CONTRIBUTIONS OF GIORGIONE AND TITIAN

Giorgione and Titian represent the two points of renewal in Venetian painting at the beginning of the sixteenth century. They were soon joined by other artists eager to spread the new Venetian manner through the territories on the mainland. In some instances the success of Giorgione and Titian can be attributed to the revival of mythological subjects, while some of their followers ignored their advances in "tonal painting" as was the case with Palma il Vecchio who produced mythological scenes and "sacre conversazioni" with opulent female figures in atmospheres vaguely reminiscent of Giorgione. Sebastiano del Piombo took a different and more original course. He was working in Venice at the time of the decoration on the Fondaco dei Tedeschi, and while adhering to the advances of the new "tonal painting", he favored a more monumental classical interpretation of his figures and architecture. This led him to leave Venice for Rome in 1511 to make a closer study of antique art.

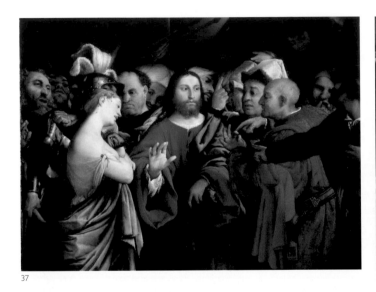
37

38

39

40

37. Lorenzo Lotto, *Christ with the woman taken in adultery*. Paris, Louvre.

38. Sebastiano del Piombo, *Death of Adonis*, 1511-15. Florence, Uffizi.

39. Palma il Vecchio, *Sacra conversazione*. Napoli, Capodimonte.

40. Palma il Vecchio, *Judith*, 1525-28. Florence, Uffizi.

SEBASTIANO DEL PIOMBO AND THE MONUMENTAL STYLE

Sebastiano del Piombo was pupil of Giovanni Bellini and Giorgione. From the beginning he embraced the new "tonal painting", although he chose to interpret it in a more monumental manner both with regard to the architectural dimension in his organization of space, and in his volumetric rendering of form. The figures of St Sinibald and St Louis of Toulouse on the organ cover painted in 1508 for the church of San Bartolomeo a Rialto, appear in niches borrowed from the facade of the Fondaco dei Tedeschi, while the figures of St Bartholomew and St Sebastian are enclosed within classically inspired architectural frames. In the *San Giovanni Crisostomo Altarpiece*, painted in about 1510 for the Venetian church of the same name, the painter depicts St John under a gigantic colonnade and surrounded by other monumental figures. A soft light pervades the painting and unifies the colors in a tonal harmony. In 1511 Sebastiano del Piombo moved to Rome where he was offered employment by the Sienese banker Agostino Chigi, and where he was attracted by the opportunity to explore the classical world at first hand.

41

42

41. Sebastiano del Piombo, *San Giovanni Crisostomo Altarpiece*, detail, about 1510. Venice, San Giovanni Crisostomo.

42. Sebastiano del Piombo, *St Sinibald*, 1507. Venice, Accademia.

CONTACT WITH THE NORTH: ALBRECHT DÜRER IN VENICE

Relations between German and Italian artists from the late fifteenth to the first half of the sixteenth century represent one of the most complex and intriguing chapters in the history of European culture. A fundamental figure in this exchange of ideas is the Nuremburg painter, engraver, and art theorist, Albrecht Dürer. He made his first trip to Venice through the Tyrol in 1494-95 where he was struck by the harmonious combination of color and form in the spatial

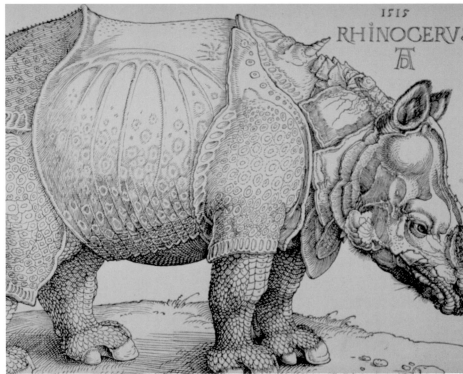

43

44

45

43-44. Albrecht Dürer, *Paumgärtner Altarpiece, Nativity with donors and St George and St Eustace* and detail of *St George*, 1498-1504. Munich, Alte Pinakothek.

45. Albrecht Dürer, *Rhinocerus*, 1515. London, British Museum.

arrangements of Giovanni Bellini and of Carpaccio, while at the same time his contact with Italian art was further enriched by his study of the engravings of Mantegna and of Pollaiolo. The *Adoration of the Magi* in the Uffizi, show an awareness of spatial problems combined with a typically northern preoccupation with realistic details. During his second visit from 1505 to 1507, Dürer developed a more secure grasp of the fundamental principles of the Italian Renaissance, in particular of the rules of perspective and proportion which he considered sadly lacking in German art and "without which nobody can become, or be, a real artist".

46. Albrecht Dürer, *Christ among the doctors*, 1506. Madrid, Thyssen-Bornemisza.

ADORATION OF THE MAGI
Albrecht Dürer, 1504
Florence, Uffizi

Although the Virgin is dressed very simply, in the contemporary style, Dürer has clearly enjoyed depicting the fine robes of the Magi in all their opulence and splendor.

SUBJECT
The adoration of the Magi takes place in the foreground, arrayed directly with extraordinary attention to detail.

Their cloaks have a material base but are richly decorated with leather, feathers, and with raised metal bosses inlaid with precious stones. Even the boxes containing their gifts are represented as fine goldsmiths' work, inspired by contemporary reliquaries.

The scrupulous and scientific attention Dürer devotes to the depiction of the real world, is particularly noticeable in his treatment of the plants growing among the ruined buildings.

The same care is exhibited in his representation of such creatures as the white butterfly with the delicate wings in the lower left.

The architectural setting is a fantastic combination of contemporary buildings on the distant hills with ruins of classical inspiration in the foreground.

COMPOSITION

The composition is built around the horizontal line created by the figures in the foreground arrayed directly in front of the spectator.

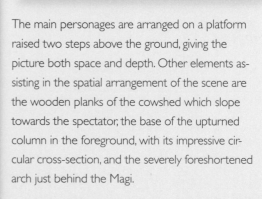

A sense of depth is created by the diminishing size of the figures as they recede into the distance. This is also true of the architecture and natural elements, of the clouds and vegetation.

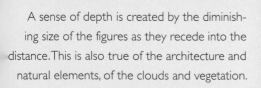

e painting is signed and dated by the artist on e gray block of stone in the foreground.

The main personages are arranged on a platform raised two steps above the ground, giving the picture both space and depth. Other elements assisting in the spatial arrangement of the scene are the wooden planks of the cowshed which slope towards the spectator, the base of the upturned column in the foreground, with its impressive circular cross-section, and the severely foreshortened arch just behind the Magi.

DÜRER AND ITALIAN ART

In 1506 Dürer completed the *Feast of the Rosary* for the church of the German community in Venice, San Bartolomeo a Rialto.
In this painting Dürer moves closer to the Venetian tradition in his sumptuous palette built around a clear, cold blue.

His novel approach to composition is both monumental and perfectly controlled. Inspired by his study of Italian art and the physical precision of depiction typical northern painting, his assembled figures appear to be portraits from life.
Also to be noted is Dürer's evident delight in the decorative rhythms of the contours. This work had a tremendous impact in

47

47. Albrecht Dürer,
Feast of the Rosary,
1506. Prague,
Narodni Museum.

Venice, on Lorenzo Lotto most noticeably. He was very taken by the lively gestures, by the festive gathering of figures in a rural land- scape, in which Dürer preserved certain iconographic references popular in engravings north of the Alps.

48

48. Albrecht Dürer,
The Four Apostles,
1526. Monaco,
Alte Pinakothek.

DÜRER AND THE SPREAD OF NORTHERN PRINTS

In the sixteenth century the growth of printing and the increased circulation of engravings made it possible for artists to increase their understanding of developments beyond their own sphere and therefore to enrich their own figurative language. They, in turn, could circulate their own models. In the German-speaking lands, following the Lutheran reformation, such major talents as Lucas Cranach devised elaborate anti-papal and anti-catholic allegorical compositions for engraving with the intention of reaching a wide audience. Albrecht Dürer too devoted much of his life to the production of prints adopting a variety of techniques. These works, disseminated throughout Europe, were also highly prized and sought after in Italy. Prints such as the *Knight, death and the devil* were sold by the sheet, while others – the *Large Passion*, la *Small Passion* and the *Life of Mary* – appeared in series. Italian artists including Lotto, Aspertini, Giorgione, Titian, Gaudenzio Ferrari, Andrea del Sarto and Pontormo, were struck by the dramatic tension in these subjects and by their profound religious sentiment. They were remarkable too for their extraordinary technical precision and clarity.

49

50

49. Albrecht Dürer, *A knight, death and the devil*, 1513. Karlsruhe, Staatliche Kunsthalle.

50. Albrecht Dürer, *Melancholy*, 1514. Karlsruhe, Staatliche Kunsthalle, Kupferstichkabinett.

51. Albrecht Dürer,
St Jerome,
1514. Karlsruhe,
Staatliche Kunsthalle.

10. The Renaissance in crisis: the emergence of Mannerism

I n his Vite de' più eccellenti architetti, scultori e pittori, Vasari uses the term "maniera" to indicate the style adopted by the masters of the early sixteenth century who had reached the summit of their artistic achievements and therefore felt compelled to provide models for the following generation. They came to be known as "manieristi" or Mannerists by seventeenth-century theorists of classicism who criticized their artificiality in repeating formulas derived from the great masters as essential to the development of an intellectual and academic art. Today the same term is used to indicate the restless generation of artists who, in the 1520s, in Siena and Florence, openly broke with the classical canons of Renaissance art. These artists reflected a crisis of confidence already apparent in the artists referred to by Vasari, but which was demonstrated in formal exasperation and eccentric experimentation.

1. Facing page: Francesco Salviati, *Charity*, 1554-58. Florence, Uffizi.

2. Scuola di Fontainebleau, *Gabrielle d'Estrée and one of her sisters*. Paris, Louvre.

3. Giuseppe Arcimboldi, *Autumn*, 1573. Paris, Louvre.

JACOPO PONTORMO; AN UNSTABLE GENIUS

Jacopo Carucci, Pontormo, was a contemporary of Rosso Fiorentino and they were both trained in the workshop of Andrea del Sarto. In 1516 they assisted in the decoration of the Chiostrino dei Voti of the church of Santissima Annunziata, where their style veered from the studied balance of their master's compositions. Pontormo's *Visitation* is much closer to the formal questioning derived from Michelangelo.

In 1518 the *Pucci Altarpiece* in San Michele Visdomini, an elusive and disturbing work, breaks with the serene harmony of the Florentine genre to present figures, with vacant gazes and ambiguous smiles, grouped untidily around the Virgin. In the cycle of *Scenes from the Life of Joseph*, commissioned by Pier Francesco Bogherini, the small panels by Pontormo are crowded with figures, and blatantly ignore the rigorous rules of renaissance perspective. In the scene of *Joseph in Egypt* the composition is cut in two by an improbable stairway which winds around a circular building, while the background landscape recalls the northern prints of Lucas Van Leyden and of Dürer.

In the Medici Villa at Poggio a Caiano, between 1520 and 1521, Pontormo painted a lunette of *Vertumnus and Pomona*, where the mythological theme, taken from Ovid's *Metamorphoses,* is interpreted with originality, and transformed into a serene depiction

370

4

5

4. Pontormo, *Visitation,*
detail, 1516-17.
Florence, Santissima
Annunziata.

5. Pontormo, *Pucci
Altarpiece,* 1518.
Florence, San Michele
Visdomini.

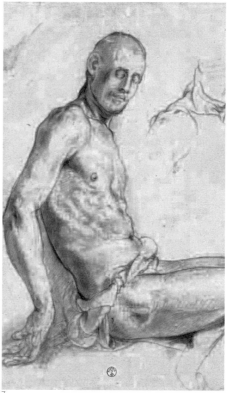

6

7

8

6. Pontormo, *Scenes from the Passion, the Resurrection*, 1523-25. Florence, Certosa del Galluzzo.

7. Pontormo, *Nude figure* or *Christ for the Deposition*, n. 6619 F. Florence, Uffizi, Gabinetto dei Disegni e delle Stampe.

8. Pontormo, *Vertumnus and Pomona*, 1520-21. Poggio a Caiano, Villa Medicea.

of rural life devoid of classical references and rendered in clear, transparent colors. Following the outbreak of plague in Florence in 1523, Pontormo moved to the Cistercian convent at Galluzzo, where he worked for about two years on the *Scenes from the Passion*, inspired by the iconography and tormented spirituality witnessed in the *Small Passion* by Dürer. The outstanding masterpiece

of his late years is the altarpiece of the *Deposition* in the Capponi Chapel in the church of Santa Felicita: the spatial disorientation is underlined by the spiral swell of weightless, grieving figures dressed in pink, yellow, blue, and red. Anguish, profound suffering, and a new form of extenuated beauty are expressed by Pontormo in a startlingly unexpected language.

9

10

9-10. Pontormo, *Annunciation*, 1526-28. Florence, Santa Felicita, Cappella Capponi. The figures of the Annunciation are on the counter-facade, on either side of the window, in a position to exploit the natural light.

11. Facing page: Pontormo, *Visitation*, 1528-29. Carmignano, San Michele.

ART IN EUROPE FROM THE RENAISSANCE TO MANNERISM

Art in countries beyond the Alps became gradually influenced by the Renaissance and Mannerism through the spread of Italian culture from the late fifteeenth, and especially after the end of the second decade of the sixteenth century.

In Germany the painter, engraver, and art theorist Albrecht Dürer was one of the first to embrace the Italian humanist ideals of the fifteenth century, both as part of a sophisticated circle of intellectuals and in his relationship with his patrons.

In his two periods in Venice(1494- 95 and 1505-07) he came in-
to direct contact with renaissance art, and disseminated the new modes and forms on his return to the north. The impact of this style is reflected in the work of Grünewald, Holbein the Younger and Altdörfer. Flanders developed independently in the highly and fantastical language of Hieronymus Bosch and in the folk paintings of Pieter Bruegel the Elder.

Following the Sack of Rome and the subsequent spread of Italian artists throughout Italy and Europe, the renaissance style sometimes combined with mannerist tendencies, reached the courts of Rudolph II in Prague, Francis I at Fontainebleau, Albert V in Munich, and Philip II in Spain, giving birth to a new "international manner", a language that became common to the whole of Europe.

12

12. Mathias Grünewald,
Isenheim Altarpiece, 1515.
Colmar, Musée
d'Unterlinden.

THE RENAISSANCE IN GERMANY

In the course of the sixteenth century German art assumed more importance on the European scene, not only because of the extraordinary talent of the German masters – Albrecht Dürer was described as "the first modern artist north of the Alps" – but also because their work was more widely circulated and understood through the spread of prints and engravings. The German painters, engravers and sculptors profited from the growth of a prosperous merchant class and their productions reflected the spiritual crisis caused by the movements of Luther and Calvin away from the Catholic Church in Rome. The impact of German Reformation was expressed in painting in a variety of modes: from the mood of dramatic religious upheaval present in Grünewald, to the immersion in the natural world proposed by Altdörfer, and in the portraiture of Cranach the Elder. Mathias Gothart Nithart, known as Grünewald, worked primarily for the Cardinal Archbishop and elector of Mainz Albert of Brandenburg, who was also the patron of Cranach and Dürer. He commissioned the *Meeting between St Erasmus and St Maurice*, for the collegiate church, the Halle an der Saale, in Saxony. The archbishop is portrayed as St Erasmus, the patron saint of sailors, and wears a chasuble embroidered in gold; opposite him stands St Maurice, the soldier saint with fine armour and white gloves. He is depicted as a Moor because of the popular etymology of the word 'Maurice' translated as "like a moor", and therefore black. This is a late work and the monumentality of the figures together with the rich coloring point

13

14

13. Mathias Grünewald, *Meeting between St Erasmus and St Maurice*, 1517-23. Monaco, Alte Pinakothek.

14. Lucas Cranach the Elder, *Crucifixion*, 1503. Munich, Alte Pinakothek.

to Grünewald's knowledge of Dürer. The fame of Lucas Cranach the Elder derives from his activity as a portraitist and court painter for the elector of Saxony, but also for his numerous mythological and allegorical paintings which echo, if only distantly, Italian models. Among his most extraordinary works is the 1503 *Crucifixion* in which Cranach places Christ at an angle to the right of the painting while the centre is occupied by the elongated and grieving figures of the Virgin and St John. After his conversion to Lutheranism Cranach painted a number of excellent portraits of the monk who triggered the Protestant Reformation. Together with Cranach, Albre-

cht Altdörfer was the main exponent of the so-called "Danubian school", encompassing a group of artists from Germany and Austria, in the valley of the Danube. The interest in landscape is derived from this school. It chose to emphasize the wild and mysterious element in nature and depicted it with colors derived from the Venetian tradition of Giorgione and Titian. This type of landscape, illuminated by intense shafts of light, characterizes the scenes in the *Polyptych of St Florian* and the visionary representation of the *Battle of Issus* between Alexander the Great and Darius, which offers a bird's-eye view into the mountainous far distance.

15

16

15-16. Albert Altdorfer,
Battle of Issus, **1529.**
Munich, Alte Pinakothek.

376

HIERONYMUS BOSCH AND THE FLEMISH RENAISSANCE

One of the major artists of the sixteenth century, Hieronymus Bosch, lived and worked exclusively in his native city, far from the great cultural centers and quite unaware of artistic developments there. His main interest was allegorical painting, in which he explores man's madness, excess and dishonesty (*Ship of Fools*, the *Haycart*, and the *Seven capital sins*). His creative and expressive powers are witnessed at their height in his triptych of the *Garden of Earthly* delights painted in about 1500 and in his *Last Judgment*. His unbridled imagination gave birth to complex compositions peopled with fantastical creations and loaded with allusions to alchemy and the bible.

He completely revitalized the modes of Flemish painting established in the fifteenth century, based on balance and harmony, with a modern and fifteenth-century sensibility, intent of reawakening man's spiritual conscience and reflecting his awareness of man's capacity to commit atrocities.

17

18

17. Hieronymus Bosch, *Ship of Fools*, 1490-1500. Paris, Louvre.

18. Hieronymus Bosch, *Last Judgement*, central panel of the tryptych. Bruges, Musée Groeninge.

GARDEN OF EARTHLY DELIGHTS
Hieronymus Bosch, 1503-04
Madrid, Prado

SUBJECT

The scene is the central panel from the triptych depicting the *Garden of Earthly delights*, the place where man gives himself up to the pleasures of the senses. Countless concentrated episodes are depicted in a broad landscaped garden presenting us with the scope of Bosch's fertile creative mind. The meaning of the painting is unclear, but one of the most widely accepted interpretations suggests that the *Garden of Earthly delights* is a satire on man's insatiable appetite for sensual pleasure.

In this light we can make sense of the figures frantically gathering strawberries and the fruit of the strawberry tree which are the symbols of the pleasures of the flesh.

Some of the groups are inspired by popular proverbs, such as the two lovers in a crystal ball who illustrate the saying, "Pleasure is as fragile as glass".

In the top level are men riding fantastical devices perhaps symbolizing man ensnared, or carried away, by vice.

COMPOSITION

The painting encompasses a wide area, where the figures are seen from on high, offering a crowded visual panorama. A sense of depth is created by the diminishing size of the figures as they recede into the background.

The centre of the composition, at the point where the two diagonals meet, is a fountain of youth, its circular form echoed in the ring of riders on a variety of real and imaginary beasts.

Crows, black figures, and young girls appear together in the Fountain of Youth.

Despite the random distribution of the groups, the painting has a central vertical axis, marked by the strange sphere in the lake dividing the scene into two equal parts.

THE SCHOOL OF FONTAINEBLEAU

Rosso Fiorentino, after he fled from Rome in 1527 following the sack of the city, stayed in Tuscany. He traveled through northern Italy before moving to France in 1530 where he was one of the leading artists in the school of Fontainebleau.

In 1528 the chateau of Fontainebleau, not far from Paris, became the chosen residence of the French king Francis I, who summoned a group of Italian artists to complete the decoration of the castle. Fontainebleau became one of the most creative and fascinating centers of International Mannerism, characterized by extreme intellectual and formal virtuosity. Rosso Fiorentino, who was designated the king's official painter in 1532, decorated the superb gallery for Francis I, with painted mythological subjects and landscapes enclosed in elegant stucco frames created from a rich repertory of female figures, festoons, garlands and architectural elements. Following his death 1540, he was succeeded by his assistant, the Bolognese artist Francesco Primaticcio, who decorated the Gallery of Ulysses and ballroom where he was assisted by another Emilian artist, Nicolò dell'Abate. We know their works, now nearly all destroyed, through a rich source of preparatory drawings. Other artists working in Fontainebleau at the time were the architect Sebastiano Serlio, appointed director of buildings for Francis I in 1541, and the sculptor Benvenuto Cellini, whose training as a goldsmith reached its fullest expression in his work for Francis I. For the Porte d'Or he made numerous statues including the *Nymph*, in the Louvre, and executed his first large works in bronze. His goldsmith's work included the magnificent salt, begun for Ippolito d'Este and finished for Francis I of France. Finely worked in gold and decorated in enamel, it is a work of extraordinary elegance. The base is adorned with two figures of Neptune and the Earth, reclining in elegant but artificial poses: they alluding to the sea and therefore to the salt destined to be contained within it.

19

19. Benvenuto Cellini,
***Nymph*, 1542-44. Paris,**
Louvre.

THE COURT OF RUDOLPH II OF PRAGUE

The spread of Mannerism in Bohemia from the mid-century was largely due to the Hapsburg patronage of Italian artists.

At the court of Rudolph II of Prague particular favor was enjoyed by the Lombard painter, Giuseppe Arcimboldi, who first emerged as an artist in Milan.

He arrived in Bohemia in 1562 and soon became the chosen painter of Maximilian and later of his successor Rudolph II. He is celebrated for his extravagant portraits and allegorical figures built out of fruit, fish and vegetables (*Water*, *Fire*, *Summer* and *Winter*).

These unusual productions were incredibly successful in their transformation of the northern genre of still-life into an amusing new form.

In the twentieth century, his work was seen as anticipating certain aspects of surrealism and enjoyed renewed popularity.

20. Giuseppe Arcimboldi,
***Summer*, 1573. Paris,**
Louvre.

ROME IN THE MID-SIXTEENTH CENTURY: THE PAPACY OF PAUL III FARNESE

The pontificate of Paul III Farnese (1534-49) coincided with a period of crisis for the Church in Rome, which was engaged not only in a program of internal reform to counter the advances made by Protestantism but also in defending her political power in the papal states in the final stages of the Franco-Spanish rivalry in Italy. Paul III Farnese, like his predecessors, sponsored ambitious artistic projects and chose Michelangelo to carry out a number of schemes which employed his skills as a painter, an architect and in urban development. Paul III's patronage attracted other artists, notably Tuscans, such as Giorgio Vasari, Francesco Salviati, Jacopino del Conte and Daniele da Volterra, who interpreted the second phase of Mannerism. Titian's arrival in the city in 1545, where he had been summoned to paint a portrait of the pope, created a tremendous impact as he was by then famous throughout Europe, especially as a portraitist.

21

21. Michelangelo,
Conversion of St Paul,
1542-45. Rome, Pauline Chapel.

22

23

MICHELANGELO THE PAINTER: THE *LAST JUDGEMENT* AND THE PAULINE CHAPEL

In 1534 Michelangelo left Florence to return to Rome, where Pope Paul III entrusted him with the painting of the *Last Judgment* in the Sistine Chapel. Having prepared the cartoons, Michelangelo completed the enormous fresco in just under five years from 1536 to 1541, returning to the chapel where, some twenty years earlier he had painted the ceiling. Michelangelo did away with the architectural compartments, typical of the Renaissance, he had adopted in the earlier scheme, to distribute more than four hundred figures in disconnected groups against an open sky without any perspective frame of reference. The massed bodies of the Damned and the Saved appear to be in orbit around the central figure of Christ, who, with his raised arm, orchestrates the dynamic movement of the whole compositionas it ascends to the right and descends to the left. The faces of those condemned to hell are full of dramatic tension while the Saved are assisted on their journey to heaven by the angels. The visionary quality of the scene accords well with the spiritually tense climate in the Church in those years and with Michelangelo's own desire to see a reform of the Church from within. He later painted the frescoes of the *Conversion of St Paul* for the Farnese pope and the *Crucifixion of St Peter* in the *Pauline Chapel*, where a predominantly desolate setting, is peopled with twisted and anguished groups of figures without any concessions made to the traditional rules of perspective.

22-23. Michelangelo, ***Last Judgement*** **and detail, 1536-41. Rome, Sistine Chapel.**

MICHELANGELO THE ARCHITECT

Michelangelo was also constantly engaged on Paul III's architectural projects and active in his attempts to revitalize the city of Rome. Following the death of Antonio da Sangallo the Younger in 1546 he was put in charge of supervising the building of St Peter's. The plan he put forward was essentially a revival of Bramante's original design because, as he is supposed to have remarked, "whoever moved away from Bramante, as Sangallo did, moved away from the truth". As an alternative to Sangallo's project, which was a compromise between the central plan proposed by Bramante and Raphael's longitudinal one, Michelangelo revived Bramante's central block, with the four large piers and the main arms of the cross, while choosing to eliminate all the minor articulation. He therefore created a very simple corpus, in which the Greek cross plan intersected the square one. In order to give a unified appearance to the exterior, Michelangelo articulated the walls with a single order of giant Corinthian pilasters, known as the "giant order". The vertical dynamism created by these elements culminates in the enormous hemispherical dome, and is continued by the giant ribs encircling the dome and terminating in the lantern. Michelangelo's visionary approach to urban planning is reflected in his rebuilding of Piazza del Campidoglio which Paul III had chosen as the ideal location for the statue of Marco Aurelius and as the civic centre of Rome. The piazza was conceived as a large trapezoidal space bound by the Palazzo dei Senatori, behind, approached by a staircase with a double ramp and flanked by buildings with a portico on either side. These palazzi were also faced with the giant order of Corinthian pilasters: the palazzo dei Conservatori, on the right, was started by Michelangelo in 1563 and finished five years later by Giacomo Della Porta, while the Palazzo Nuovo was not built by Carlo Rainaldi until the middle of the seventeenth century.

24

25

24. Michelangelo, St Peter's, view of the apse, from 1547. Rome.

25. Piazza del Campidoglio. Rome.

MICHELANGELO: THE LATE SCULPTURES

Michelangelo's last sculptures were not commissioned and are all left in an "unfinished" state. Michelangelo focused in these works on his contemplation of the death of Christ, choosing the theme of the Pietà. He chose to undermine any facile conception of beauty by concentrating of the spiritual dimension of the event. Between 1545 and 1555 he sculpted a Pietà with St Joseph of Arimathea and St Mary Magdalen for his own tomb in which the four figures are arranged in a pyramidal group around the figures of Christ. His last and most demanding piece was the *Pietà Rondanini*, which he was still working on in the days before his death.

26-27. Michelangelo,
***Pietà* and detail, 1545-55.**
Florence, Museo
dell'Opera del Duomo.

PIETÀ RONDANINI
Michelangelo, 1552-64
Milan, Castello Sforzesco

SUBJECT

In the inventory of works left in Michelangelo's studio at the time of his death in Rome in 1564 mention is made of "another statue begun of Christ with another figure above, joined together, roughly hewn and unfinished". In 1561 Michelangelo had given the block, which he was still working on, to his manservant Antonio del Francese, but he continued sculpting it until his death and it allows us a unique opportunity to follow the evolution of his tormented creative process.

The *Pietà*, called Rondanini after the family who owned it for centuries, in its spare plastic form, in its composition and dramatic power draws inspiration from medieval sculpture and in particular is reminiscent of the restrained *pathos* of certain northern gothic pieces.

COMPOSITION

The group reflects various stages of work: some parts of the figures are almost completely finished like the superb right arm of Christ,

while others show signs of reworking and reflect Michelangelo's change in approach. The Virgin's face, for example, shows an original version in the process of being remodeled,

while the body of Christ was dramatically altered to appear almost squashed against the body of his mother, molding them into a unified mass.

PAINTING DURING THE PONTIFICATE OF PAUL III FARNESE

In the 1530s the presence of Michelangelo and the patronage of Paul III attracted a new generation of Tuscan artists to Rome who became the protagonists of a new Roman school. As they moved between Florence and Rome, they were able to combine the achievements of Raphael with a repertory of forms taken from Michelangelo and from the first generation of Mannerists, creating a sophisticated, decorative language. The leading figures in this movement were Francesco Salviati and Giorgio Vasari, who came to Rome in 1531, where they were joined in 1535 by Jacopino del Conte and Daniele da Volterra. The decoration of the oratory of San Giovanni Decollato, belonging to a Florentine Confraternity, provides a perfect illustration of this new pictorial language, a confluence of the various ornamental elements of Mannerism. In 1538, Perin

del Vaga, after a long period in Genoa, also returned to Rome where, as an outstanding pupil of Raphael's, he gained important commissions: the most prestigious of all being for the decoration of the pope's private apartments in Castel Sant'Angelo. In the Sala Paolina he revealed his sophisticated and highly cultivated style, incorporating muscular figures into his *Scenes from the Life of Alexander the Great* and *Episodes from the Life of St Paul* (in honor of Paul III, whose baptismal name was Alessandro), set within a rich decorative framework. In the 1550s Salviati was employed on the decoration of a number of Roman palazzi: in Palazzo Sacchetti he painted *Scenes from the Life of David*, interpreted with a dazzling, inventive formal repertory combining imitation tapestries and low-reliefs. Daniele da Volterra reflected a stronger debt to Michelangelo and in his *Deposition* for Trinità dei Monti revealed the diverse components of his pictorial language, ranging from Rosso Fiorentino to the Roman manner, with an emphasis on the dramatic and monumental.

28

28. Francesco Salviati,
Visitation, 1538. Rome,
San Giovanni Decollato.

29. Jacopino del Conte,
Baptism of Christ, 1538.
Rome, San Giovanni
Decollato.

11. Venice in the second half of the sixteenth century

In the sixteenth century Venice enjoyed a long period of political stability together with all the advantages of a flourishing economy. Furthermore, after the peace of Cateau-Cambresis in 1559, marking the end of the Franco-Spanish rivalry, Venice and Tuscany were the only independent states in the peninsula. For these reasons a constant flow of artists was attracted to the city where the patrician oligarchy provided lavish patronage and where a program of urban renewal was under way. Among the most exciting projects was one for the reconstruction of Piazza San Marco by Jacopo Sansovino and for the rebuilding of the Rialto bridge. During this period the hold on the Venetian territories on the mainland was strengthened with the construction of fortifications by Michele Sanmicheli. One of the most original architects to appear was Andrea Palladio who was also an architectural theorist. After the rise to fame of Titian, Venetian painting continued to be celebrated in the work of Tintoretto, Veronese, and Bassano.

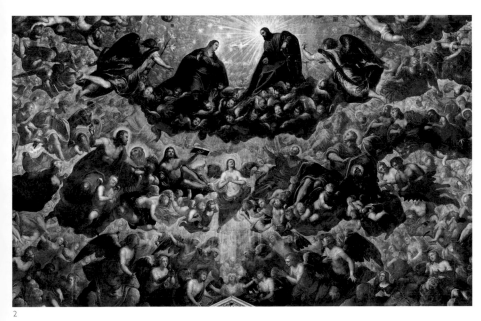

2

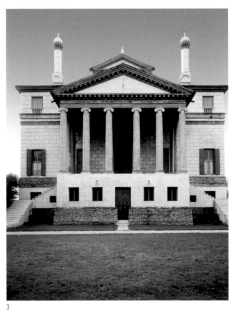

3

RENAISSANCE ART

1. Facing page: Bonifacio de' Pitati, *God the father and St Mark's square*, detail. Venice, Accademia.

2. Tintoretto, *Paradise*, detail, 1588-92. Venice, Ducal Palace.

3. Andrea Palladio, *Villa della Malcontenta*, facade, 1560. Mira.

TITIAN'S LATE WORKS: THE FREE HANDLING OF PAINT

In the late 1530s Titian abandoned the serene classicism of his earlier works in search of new formal modes. These matured noticeably after 1540 as he rejected the soft style of his youth in favor of a more plastic dynamism and illusionist virtuosity, evident in the *Biblical scenes* painted for the ceiling of the church of Santo Spirito a Isola, now in Santa Maria della Salute. In the *Crown of thorns* of the same period, Titian highlights the dramatic dimension also through the choice of a palette based on a dark ground with golden and red lights, giving the work an intense physical quality. In this stylistic transformation Titian's contact with the culture of central Italy was crucial. The writer Pietro Aretino, and of the painters, Giorgio Vasari and Francesco Salviati were all working in Venice at the time. At the end of the 1540s Titian reached the height of his career when he became official portrait painter to the Emperor Charles V and later court painter to his son Philip II. In his last phase from the 1560s, the handling of the paint was increasingly free, and Titian used color and bright patches of light increasingly to model form.

4

6

5

4. Titian, *Portrait of Pietro Aretino*, 1545. Florence, Pitti Palace, Palatine Gallery.

5. Titian, *Sacrifice of Isaac*, 1542-44. Venice, Santa Maria della Salute.

6. Titian, *Cain and Abel*, 1542-44. Venice, Santa Maria della Salute.

SPACE AND LIGHT IN THE FARNESE *DANAE*

The *Danae* in the Capodimonte Museum was painted for Ottavio Farnese in 1546, during Titian's stay in Rome. The subject of the picture (there is also a version by Correggio) is taken from the story of Danae, who was impregnated by Zeus in the guise of a shower of gold. The young woman lies naked, serenely awaiting her encounter with Zeus, in the presence of Cupid. The compositional structure is simplified, the naked body is warmed by glowing tones of brown, and the interpretation is highly sensual, and expressed in a free, chromatic language.

The work was much admired by Titian's contemporaries as Vasari records: "One day Michelangelo and Vasari went to see Titian in the Belvedere, and saw in a painting he had finished, a female nude, representing Danae, who was overlaid by Zeus in the form of a shower of gold and they praised him for it highly". Titian made a number of copies of this understandably successful work, including one for Philip II, now in Madrid.

7. Titian, *Portrait of Charles V on horseback*, 1548. Madrid, Prado.

8. Titian, *Deposition*, 1567. Madrid, Prado.

9. Titian, *The Crown of Thorns*, 1542-44. Paris, Louvre.

10

TITIAN: THE DRAMATIC INTENSITY OF THE LATE WORKS

In the 1560s, despite his advanced years, Titian was constantly engaged on projects for Philip II. In addition to a number of portraits, Titian also painted religious works and a series of mythological paintings which he himself described as "poesie". In both these genres we witness the steady break up of the painted surface into patches of color. The *Flaying of Marsyas* depicts the cruel death of the satyr who is flayed alive after his defeat by Apollo in a musical competition. To the right another satyr is seen carrying a bucket of water in an attempt to alleviate his companion's suffering.

The scene is closed in by a natural setting which offers no sense of depth or perspective glimpse of a wider landscape.

Titian large brushstrokes full of light are described by Vasari as "stains [...] which close up can not be seen and from a distance appear perfect".

11

10. Titian, *Danae*, 1546. Napoli, Capodimonte.

11. Titian, *Flaying of Marsyas*, 1570. Kromeriz, Museum Kromerizka.

MANNERISM IN VENICE

The first indications of the Mannerist mode reached Venice through Pordenone, who worked in the city between 1527 and 1528, in a monumental language full of plastic tension and daring illusionism.

The central Italian style had an even greater impact with the arrival of Giorgio Vasari and Francesco Salviati, who stayed in Venice between 1539 and 1543 and after Titian's journey to Rome in 1545. These ex-

changes brought about a gradual change in the artistic climate in Venice which affected both Titian's contemporaries and slightly younger artists, such as Paris Bordone and Bonifacio de' Pitati. With the arrival of Andrea Schiavone in 1535 forms derived from Parmigianini became known in the Veneto.

A remarkable interlude was the presence of Domenico Theotokopulos, known as El Greco, in Venice in 1566. He traveled to the city from his native Crete which was then under Venetian rule.

12

12. El Greco, *Last Supper*, about 1567. Bologna, Pinacoteca Nazionale.

THE CHIEF PAINTERS AFTER TITIAN: TINTORETTO, VERONESE AND JACOPO BASSANO

In the second half of the sixteenth century the supremacy of Venetian painting was undisputed. While Titian was the unquestionably the greatest painter, remarkable contributions were made by Tintoretto and Veronese while Jacopo Bassano, at work in the Venetian territories, gave a very personal interpretation to the artistic developments of the lagoon. Tintoretto and Veronese, were both stimulated by the stylistic innovations of central Italy but had different interests, and created new, distinctly Venetian, figurative modes of expression.

13

TINTORETTO: THEATRICAL EFFECTS

Jacopo Robusti, whose nickname Tintoretto derives from his father's profession as a dyer (*tintore*), trained in Venice in the 1530s, when the city began to have more contact with the stylistic developments in central Italy. Tintoretto, from his earliest works, reflects a lively interest in Tuscan-Roman art of the High Renaissance. He studied the paintings and sculpture of such masters as Vasari and Sansovino while they

were in Venice and became familiar with the sculpture of Michelangelo through prints and drawings of his work. Through these influences he developed an intensely plastic and monumental style, developed to theatrical effect with dramatic lighting and magnificent architectural settings. Witness his early *Miracle of St Mark*, exhibited to the public in the Scuola Grande, or Confraternity of St Mark, in 1548, a revolutionary composition, conceived as a stage set with architectural wings. Startling too was the lighting, which made further demands on the

14

398

13. Tintoretto, *Assumption*, 1583-87. Venice, Scuola Grande di San Rocco.

14. Tintoretto, *Crucifixion*, 1565. Venice, Scuola Grande di San Rocco.

emotional involvement of the spectator. In his later years Tintoretto also painted mythological and biblical subjects including the *Susanna and the Elders* comparable with some of the finest productions in the international mannerist vogue and more directly with Veronese.

In the 1560s, he painted extraordinarily original and daring works such as the *Finding of the Body of St Mark*, in which the light becomes the protagonist in the scene which opens a dramatic perspective view of the nave. The magnificent decoration of the Scuola di San Rocco, took Tintoretto more than twenty years and was done in stages: the

Scenes from the Passion were painted between 1564 and 1567, the *Scenes from the Old and New Testament* from 1575 to 1581, and the *Scenes from the Life of the Virgin and of the Infancy of Christ*, lastly, between 1582 and 1587.

In these scenes Tintoretto's dramatic language is at its height, the spatial construction built around the articulated distribution of figures and the diffused but slanting light.

The surface paint is a mass of brushstrokes creating a mesh of color and light which highlight the visionary quality of these pictures.

15

15. Tintoretto, *Finding of the body of St Mark*, 1562-66. Milano, Pinacoteca di Brera.

MIRACLE OF ST MARK
Tintoretto, 1548
Venice, Accademia

SUBJECT

The painting relates the miraculous recovery of the servant of a Provencal knight who had abandoned his master in order to worship the reliquary of St Mark.

The knight, furious with his servant, attempted to blind him and break his legs.

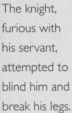

The intervention of St Mark left the servant unscathed from his master's attack and the saint is depicted, dramatically foreshortened, as he zooms out of the sky, radiating light.

The turbaned figures are Turks, the traditional rivals of Venice, and intended to symbolize the barbarian infidel.

The painting was the first of the canvases for the chapter room of the Scuola Grande di San Marco and was considered highly controversial at the time of its completion.

COMPOSITION

The Venetian public immediately expressed their enthusiasm for the work, especially for the dramatic *sotto in su* depiction of the saint, and for his depiction of the crowd who are quite unaware of the miraculous presence.

The onlookers are gathered into the form of an amphitheatre around the figure of the prisoner, who is turned naked on his back at the center of the scene.

Tintoretto uses rapid, energetic, brushstrokes, with violent chiaroscuro contrasting with superb chromatic combinations. The observer is compelled to participate in the action taking place, and becomes one of the baffled witnesses to the extraordinary event.

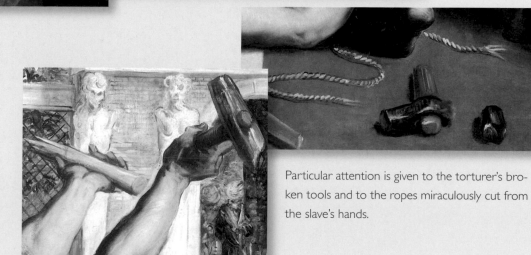

Particular attention is given to the torturer's broken tools and to the ropes miraculously cut from the slave's hands.

PAOLO VERONESE: OPULENCE AND COLOR

Paolo Caliari is known as Veronese after his native city of Verona, where he became aware of the wider cultural influences in the Po valley, especially of Giulio Romano in Mantua and of Correggio and Parmigianino in Parma. In 1553 he moved to Venice in order to decorate the Sala del Consiglio dei Dieci in the Ducal Palace. In the same year he embarked on a complex decorative cycle in the church of San Sebastiano, which he took thirty years to complete. His paintings were immediately successful: a bold architectural framework houses figures in the foreground depicted with broad patches of color which stand out against the luminous blue sky - witness the *Scenes from the life of Esther*. Although the daring illusionism recalls the work of Giulio Romano in Mantua, Veronese showed a distinctly individual flair in his use of color, characterized by the complete absence of chiaroscuro, by colored shadows and by the juxtaposition of complementary limpid tones. In the years that followed Veronese sought to create increasingly stately and measured classical compositions, a progress fully reflected in the decoration of Palladio's Villa Barbaro at Maser. This building offers the perfect combination of architecture and painting in which Veronese dissolves the physical walls by painting illusionist architecture opening onto landscapes, other buildings, and figures in front of illusionary doorways. Veronese was the favorite artist of many other aristocratic Venetian families apart from the Barbaro and he decorated their palazzi with sumptuous scenes whether treating secular or religious subjects. Several of his most celebrated late works incorporate monumental architectural settings directly inspired by the buildings of Palladio and Sansovino eminently suited to the refined secular world of Veronese's patrons. Among these are the numerous "suppers" which, although ostensibly related to the gospels, are really brilliant evocations of the social life of the Venetian nobility.

16

16. Paolo Veronese,
Giustiniana Barbaro and
her nurse with a puppy
looking over balcony,
about 1561. Maser,
Villa Barbaro.

17

18

19

17. Paolo Veronese, *Feast in the house of Levi*, 1573. Venice, Accademia.

18. Paolo Veronese, *Scenes from the Life of Esther, Esther crowned by Ahasuerus*, 1556. Venice, San Sebastiano.

19. Paolo Veronese, *Juno distributes her gifts on Venice*, 1553-54. Venice, Ducal Palace.

WEDDING FEAST AT CANA
Paolo Veronese, 1562-63
Paris, Louvre

This painting of the wedding feast at Cana, depicting a sumptuous and worldly banquet, provoked a severe critical reaction from the ecclesiastical authorities

The scene is set in a classical framework suggesting an enormous stage and reminiscent of Palladio:

the architecture serves to frame the elegant Venetian society of Veronese's world. Many of the figures can be identified: the musical quartet in the foreground, for example, portrays Bassano as the flautist; Titian, dressed in red, is on the double bass, Tintoretto plays the viola, and Veronese himself the cello. Christ sits isolated and dignified in the center of the composition, quite removed from the surrounding scene. The butchers hacking the meat above Christ's head prefigure the sacrifice of the Lamb.

The long balustrade divides the painting in half, separating land from sky, the eternal from the transitory. This painting, touching on both the sacred and profane, conveys a profound sense of disquiet, in the juxtaposition of, and inevitable comparison between, these two worlds.

Minute attention is given to the description of the jewelery, plate, and tableware. The animals too are carefully observed, from the parrot held by a dwarf on the left, to the cat on the opposite side, the two leashed greyhounds in the center, the tiny lapdog on the table to the right, with another looking down from the knee of the bridegroom, watched attentively by a hound.

COMPOSITION

Christ appears at the center, absorbed in his own thoughts, with his face fixed on the spectator. The vertical axis of the composition passes through him, dividing the lower half of the painting into two equal parts.

The apostles and religious figures are seated to the right while the left is crowded with the bride and groom and their guests.

The shape of the table is echoed in the balustrade with stairs sloping down on either side.

The banquet occupies the entire foreground and is closed in on both sides by columns supporting terraces with figures and a dog, all looking onto the scene below. The middle distance is also hemmed in by porticos with columns and peopled with figures intent on preparing the food.

There are further musicians and curious onlookers on the high balconies in the background.

The space in front of the table is also crowded: servants, jesters, musicians, all are depicted with scrupulous attention to detail.

JACOPO BASSANO AND RUSTIC GENRE PAINTING

Jacopo da Ponte, who is named Bassano after his birthplace, trained in the workshop of Bonifacio de' Pitati in Venice, but also devoted his attention to the works of Titian, Pordenone and the northern engravers. He returned to Bassano in 1540, and worked there for the rest of his life, originally showing an affinity with the Mannerists and then developing an individual style based on Venetian influences, characterized by an anti-monumental and anti-heroic tone, which remained constant in the rest of his production. From the Emilian Mannerists, Bassano adopted the elongated figures, softening the excessive intellectualism of the style with a richer palette, and employed natural settings in episodes taken from the Old and New Testaments. From the 1560s he worked increasingly on rustic scenes, with cycles of the seasons and of workers in the fields.

In his last works he became interested in the lighting effects associated with Tintoretto and he favored nocturnal scenes. His paintings, which were much admired in the seventeenth century with the popularity of genre scenes, were copied and disseminated in innumerable workshop versions.

20

21

22

20. Jacopo Bassano, *Adoration of the Magi.* Rome, Borghese Gallery.

21. Jacopo Bassano, *Crucifixion*, 1562-63. Treviso, Museo Civico.

22. Jacopo Bassano, *Two dogs*, 1555-60. Florence, Uffizi.

23. Facing page: Jacopo Bassano, *St Peter and St Paul*, about 1570. Modena, Galleria Estense.

THE ARCHITECTURE OF ANDREA PALLADIO

Andrea della Gondola, known as Palladio is the greatest Venetian architect of the sixteenth century. He was trained and later became most active in the Veneto, unlike Sansovino and Sanmicheli, who both spent their early years in Rome.

While still very young Palladio moved from Padua to Vicenza, where he worked as a stonemason. In about 1537, the humanist Gian Giorgio Trissino called on Palladio for assistance in building his villa at Cricoli, and introduced him to potential patrons in Venice having bestowed on him the classical name of Palladio. Palladio's study of the treatise by Sebastiano Serlio and his knowledge of the buildings of Michele Sanmicheli, Jacopo Sansovino, and Giulio Romano all contributed to the formation of his style. He traveled to Rome with Trissino in the 1540s, where he made a detailed study of the monuments of antiquity but also of those built more recently for the popes. The cultivated Venetian nobleman, Alvise Cornaro, directed Palladio's talents into devising practical housing solutions for the prosperous landowners engaged on reclaiming the land in the Venetian territories.

The commission to reface the Vicentine town hall, since known as the Basilica, definitely secured his hold on the Venetian aristocracy and for the rest of his life he was employed in designing their country villas. After the death of Trissino, his main patron was the learned prelate Daniele Barbaro, for whom Andrea illustrated an edition of the treatise *De architectura* by Vitruvius, and built the Villa Maser, also known as the Villa Barbaro. Among the prestigious projects executed in his later years for the city of Venice were the churches of San Giorgio Maggiore and the Redentore.

24

25

24. Paolo Veronese,
Portrait of Daniele Barbaro, 1560-70.
Florence, Pitti Palace, Palatine Gallery.

25. Vincenzo Catena,
Portrait of Gian Giorgio Trissino, about 1525.
Paris, Louvre.

26

27

PALLADIO IN VICENZA

In Vicenza, in 1546, Andrea Palladio received his first important public commission, to reface the Palazzo della Ragione, the city's town hall, and from then on known as the Basilica. The facade covered the existing two-storied gothic building, giving it the appearance of a renaissance building, but relating it harmoniously to the surrounding structures. Two superimposed rows of Serlian arches make up the facade; above these there rises a vast wooden covering like an upturned boat. There are a series of statues ranged along the balustrade at the top of the building, placed in relation to the columns below. These accentuate the rhythm created by the arches supported by smaller columns within the bays. His use of Roman architectural elements is especially evident in his adoption of arched windows, described as Serlian, and in the frieze of triglyphs and metopes separating the two storeys. His success in Vicenza soon earned him a number of commissions from the Venetian nobility for whom he built the Palazzo Chiericati and the Palazzo Valmarana.
His last project was the Teatro Olimpico in Vicenza.

28

413

26. Andrea Palladio,
Basilica, 1549.
Vicenza.

27. Andrea Palladio,
Palazzo Valmarana,
view of facade, 1565-66.
Vicenza.

28. Andrea Palladio,
Palazzo Chiericati, 1550.
Vicenza.

In the sixteenth century theater architecture developed in a number of exciting different ways. While, on the one hand, Palladio and the theatrical academies tackled the problem by studying the theatre designs of antiquity, temporary theaters, which were built for the court, were mainly concerned with scenography, the construction of the sets being considered far more important than the building itself.

There was far more interest in theatrical design and the spatial layout in lively intellectual centers and in places where the theatre represented a significant role in the community's social life.

I. View of the Roman Amphitheater, Verona.

II. TEATRO OLIMPICO, VICENZA

The theater was built for the Accademia Olimpica following Palladio's design and was completed after his death by Vincenzo Scamozzi. It opened on 3 March 1585 with a performance of *Oedipus Rex* by Sophocles, and was the first permanent theater in the Italian tradition. Palladio was inspired by classical models, both by the direct study of surviving monuments and by his reading of Vitruvius. The Olimpico brings together three important ideas: Palladio's reflection on the theaters of antiquity, his thoughts on perspective, and on stage design and illusionism. These are given extraordinary expression in the elaborate "facade", at the back of the stage, richly decorated with classical elements.

III. TEATRO OLIMPICO, SABBIONETA

Between 1588 and 1590 the architect, Vincenzo Scamozzi, built the Teatro Olimpico at Sabbioneta, a small city constructed by the duke of Mantua, Vespasiano Gonzaga, as the new Gonzaga capital.

This was the first free-standing theater, with no building attached to it on three sides so that its size and shape were not determined by pre-existing buildings.

In his design Scamozzi was inspired by the theories of Serlio: behind the classically – inspired semi-circular colonnade are walls with frescoes by the school of Veronese, and with landscapes and illusionist scenes of theatrical life.

THE VENETIAN CHURCHES: SAN GIORGIO MAGGIORE AND THE REDENTORE

In the 1560s Palladio built three religious buildings in Venice: the churches of the Zitelle, of San Giorgio Maggiore and of the Redentore.

The churches of San Giorgio Maggiore and of the Redentore are two of the most perfect attempts to reconcile classically-inspired Renaissance architecture with the liturgical and devotional requirements of a religious building. Both the facades are inspired by temple fronts, and their interlinked pediments, almost like a perspective section, reflect the structure of the church behind. The church of San Giorgio Maggiore is a long building with a nave and single aisles with a dome at its center above the crossing.

The church of the Redentore, built on the Giudecca in gratitude for the city's deliverance from the plague and the focus of a solemn procession every year, makes an impressive theatrical impact when seen from the water. The division into three sections satisfies the need for a nave with intercommunicating side chapels separated from the large apse by an exedra of columns.

The Redentore, together with the church of the Gesù in Rome and the church of San Fedele in Milan, represents a new model of religious architecture in accordance with the liturgical demands of the counter reformation.

29

30

29. San Giorgio Maggiore, interior, 1556. Venice.

30. Church of the Redentore, interior, 1577. Venice.

31

**31. Andrea Palladio,
San Giorgio Maggiore,
facade, 1556. Venice.**

**32. Andrea Palladio,
Church of the Redentore,
facade, 1577. Venice.**

Between 1530 and 1560 many families of the Venetian aristocracy, who had bought extensive estates in the Veneto with the wealth from their commercial activities, decided to build country properties where they could lead a relaxed and pleasant life while attending to the administration of their farms. Palladio build a number of villas for these landowners, many of which have survived: the Villa Barbaro at Maser with frescoes by Veronese and stucco work by Alessandro Vittoria, Villa Foscari at Gambarare, Villa Cornaro at Piombino Dese, the Rotonda at Vicenza, Villa Trissino at Meledo, Villa Emo at Fasolo, Villa Badoer at Fratta Polesine, Villa Pisani at Montagnana.

These Palladian villas bear extraordinary testimony to Palladio's superb inventiveness in his use of the classical language, so much admired by his patrons and the humanist circle in Venice, to create functional and wonderfully stylish buildings.

The structure of the buildings where classical architectural motives, such as pedimented temple fronts, are incorporated into complexes used as working farms.

33. Andrea Palladio, Villa della Malcontenta, facade, before 1560. Mira.

34. Andrea Palladio, Villa Barbaro, facade, 1555-59. Maser.

RENAISSANCE ART

**35. Andrea Palladio, Villa
Cornaro, facade, 1560-65.
Piombino Dese.**

LA ROTONDA
Andrea Palladio, 1570-72
Vicenza

SUBJECT

Andrea Palladio built the Villa Rotonda in a pleasant spot a short distance from Vicenza, as a pleasure palace for Paolo Almerico Capra, a worldly humanist and prelate. Mindful no doubt of the complex personality of his patron, Palladio devised a building with both sacred and secular resonance. It was inspired by religious architecture, evident in the use of the Greek cross plan but also by the temples built by the Romans on Greek models at Tivoli and Palestrina. The villa, presumably begun in 1570 and finished two years later, is not typical of Palladio's villa model and in his treatise he places it among his urban buildings. This, according to Palladio, was because of its proximity to the city but also because it was not, like the others, surrounded by "barchesse", the farm buildings attached to his other villas.

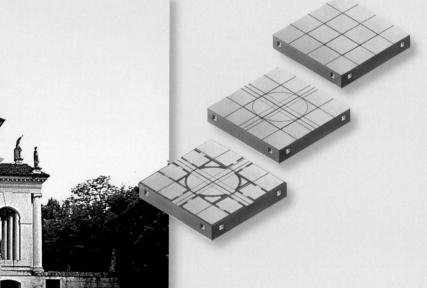

COMPOSITION

The building stands on a square base housing the kitchens and wine-cellars or as Palladio described them, "*rooms for the use and convenience of the family*". On this base Palladio laid out the whole scheme with logical determination.

The first grid was divided into 16 identical squares: over which were placed the north-south and east-west axes, with in the large circular hall, the Rotonda, at its center.

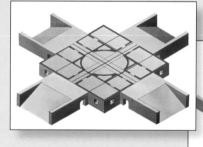

Four flights of steps descend from the extremities, as from a religious building, planned on a Greek cross.

Spatially the villa is divided into two distinct parts: the first, or public area, is made up of the four rooms at the entrances and by the great cylindrical drum of the central hall surmounted by the dome and lantern illuminating the space below. The four private apartments, each with one large rectangular and one smaller room, are hidden in the corners. The mass of the building is completed with the addition of the four temple fronts.

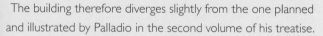

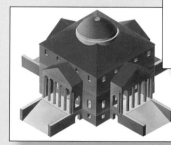

The building therefore diverges slightly from the one planned and illustrated by Palladio in the second volume of his treatise. The most striking difference is in the flattened cupola, originally planned as a much more prominent, semi-circular dome.

CHRONOLOGY

1401 · Competition for the north door of the Florentine baptistery. The contestants, including Filippo Brunelleschi, Lorenzo Ghiberti and Jacopo della Quercia, all make a panel depicting the *Sacrifice of Isaac*. Lorenzo Ghiberti wins.

1402-04 · Brunelleschi and Donatello visit Rome.

1404 · Venice takes possessions of the Visconti territories in the Veneto: Verona, Vicenza, Padua, Feltre and Belluno.

1406-07 · Jacopo della Quercia carves the *Tomb of Ilaria del Carretto* in Lucca.

1408 · Gentile da Fabriano in Venice.

1408-15 · Florence Cathedral facade : Nanni di Banco carves St Luke and Donatello *St John the Evangelist*, still in the gothic style.

1409 · The council di Pisa deposes Gregory XII and Benedict XIII and elects Pope Alexander V.

1409-19 · Jacopo della Quercia creates reliefs and statues in the round for the *Fonte Gaia*, the fountain in the centre of Siena.

1410-15 · Nanni di Banco executes the *Four Crowned Saints* for the niche on the church of Orsanmichele in Florence.

1411-13 · Donatello executes *St Mark* for the church of Orsanmichele in Florence.

1413-29 · The third phase of the Hundred Years War begun in 1337 is fought in France.

1414 · The humanist Poggio Bracciolini discovers Vitruvius's *De architectura* in the monastery at Montecassino.

1415-17 · The *Book of Hours* created by Jan van Eyck for the Duc de Berry marks the birth of naturalism in Flemish art.

1417 · Donatello's statue carves his *St George* for the church of Orsanmichele. Pioneering use of "a stiacciato", or very low relief in the panel below the statue depicting *St George and the dragon*.

1418 · In Florence Filippo Brunelleschi wins the competition to build the dome of the cathedral of Santa Maria del Fiore.

1419 · Filippo Brunelleschi works on the orphanage, the Ospedale degli Innocenti, in Florence.

1419-22 · Ghiberti's statue of *St Matthew* for the church of Orsanmichele.

1420 · The Master of Flémalle (Robert Campin) completes the *Entombment*.

1420-36 · Filippo Brunelleschi builds the dome of Florence cathedral.

1422 · Masaccio paints the *Triptych of the Madonna and saints* for the church of San Giovenale in Cascia (Arezzo)

1423-27 · Panels for the font in the baptistery of Siena executed by Donatello, Ghiberti and Jacopo della Quercia.

1424 · (about) Masaccio and Masolino paint the altarpiece *Sant'Anna Metterza*.

1424-27 · Frescoes in the Brancacci Chapel in the church of the Carmine in Florence by Masaccio and Masolino.

1425-27 · Tomb of the anti-pope John XXIII for the Florence baptistery by Donatello and Michelozzo.

1425-34 · Reliefs of Genesis and of *Childhood of Christ* for the door of San Petronio in Bologna by Jacopo della Quercia.

1425-52 · Ghiberti's *Doors of Paradise* for the baptistery of Florence.

1426 · Masaccio 's polyptych, now dismembered, for the church of the Carmine in Pisa.
· *Tomb of Niccolò Brenzoni*, by Pisanello and Nanni di Bartolo in the church of San Fermo in Verona.

1426-27 · Fresco of the *Trinity* by Masaccio in the church of Santa Maria Novella.

1427 · Tomb of Cardinal Brancacci in the church of Sant'Angelo a Nilo in Naples by Donatello and Michelozzo di Bartolomeo.

1428 · Brunelleschi designs the church of Santo Spirito in Florence.

1430 · In Florence Filippo Brunelleschi begins work on the Pazzi Chapel.
· Paolo Uccello paints one of the cloisters of Santa Maria Novella with late-gothic frescoes of scenes from *Genesis*.

1431-35 · Luca della Robbia's choir loft, *Cantoria*, for the cathedral of Florence.

1432 · Jan Van Eyck paints the Ghent altarpiece, the *Polyptych of the Mystical Lamb*.
· (about) Filippo Lippi paints the *Confirmation of the Carmelite Rule* for the Florentine church of the Carmine.

1433-38 · Donatello carves the second choir loft, *Cantoria*, for the cathedral of Florence.

1433-45 · The bronze doors are cast for the basilica of St Peter's by Filarete.

1434 · Van Eyck paints *The Arnolfini wedding*.
· Donatello's bronze statue of *David* now in the Bargello.

1435 · Rogier Van der Weyden paints the *Deposition*, now in the Prado.
· Leon Battista Alberti writes *De pictura*.
· (about) *Chancellor Rolin Madonna* by Jan Van Eyck, now in the Louvre
· (about) Fra Angelico paints the *Coronation of the Virgin*, now in the Uffizi.

1436	· Paolo Uccello's fresco of the *Equestrian Monument to Sir John Hawkwood* in Florence cathedral. · Fra Angelico paints the *Annalena altarpiece*. · Jan Van Eyck 's *Madonna of Canon Van der Paele* painted in Bruges · Wooden inlay in the Florence cathedral sacristy begun. · Francesco Squarcione opens his workshop in Padua: his pupils include Schiavone, Tura, and Mantegna.
1436-43	· Cosimo de' Medici commissions Michelozzo to rebuild the convent of San Marco. · Fra Angelico and assistants paint the frescoes in the convent.
1437	· Filippo Lippi 's Barbadori altarpiece for the church of Santo Spirito in Florence.
1438	· Pisanello, the most celebrated of the court painters in Northern Italy, completes the fresco of *St George and the princess* in the church of Santa Anastasia in Verona. · (about) Pisanello begins his activity as a medalist. Portrait medal of Byzantine emperor John Paleologus.
1438-42	· The Porta della Carta for the Ducal Palace in Venice by Giovanni and Bartolomeo Bon.
1439	· Jan Van Eyck paints the *Virgin of the fountain*.
1439-45	· Domenico Veneziano paints the frescoes (destroyed) for the church of Sant'Egidio in Florence.
1440	· Building of Palazzo Pitti begins.
1441-50	· Leon Battista Alberti writes *Descriptio urbis Romae*.
1442-44	· German painter Stephan Lochner executes *Adoration of the Magi* and the *Annunciation* for the altar of Cologne cathedral.
1443	· Luca della Robbia carves the tabernacle for the Chapel of the hospital of Santa Maria Nuova in Florence.
1443-45	· Leon Battista Alberti writes *De re aedificatoria*. · Michelozzo di Bartolomeo begins building Palazzo Medici in Florence. · Federico da Montefeltro succeeds his brother Oddone as duke of Urbino.
1445	· Domenico Veniceno paints altarpiece for the church of Santa Lucia de' Magnoli In Florence.
1445-50	· Donatello 's *Equestrian statue to Gattamelata* in Padua.
1446-50	· *Tomb of Leonardo Bruni* by Bernardo Rossellino in the church of Santa Croce, Florence. · High Altar in the basilica of Sant'Antonio in Padua by Donatello.
1447	· Ghiberti starts writing the *Commentaries*.
1448	· Fresco of the *Triumph of death* in Palazzo Schifani in Palermo (now the Galleria Nazionale della Sicilia).
1448-53	· Mantegna paints frescoes in the Ovetari Chapel in the church of the Eremitani in Padua.
1449-51	· Andrea del Castagno paints the cycle of *Famous men and women* for the villa at Legnaia, near Florence.
1449-53	· Fourth and final stage of the Hundred Years War, begun in 1337.
1450	· Leon Battista Alberti designs the Tempio Malatestiano in Rimini. · (about) Rogier Van der Weyden paints the *Deposition*, now in the Uffizi.
1450-60	· Leon Battista Alberti builds Palazzo Rucellai in Florence.
1452	· Piero della Francesca begins fresco cycle of the *Legend of the True Cross* in the church of San Francesco in Arezzo.
1453	· Mino da Fiesole carves portrait bust of *Piero de' Medici*. · Filippo Lippi begins frescoes of *Scenes from the life of St John the Baptist and from the life of St Stephen* in the cathedral of Prato.
1455	· (about) Enguerrand Charonton (or Quarton) paints *Coronation of the Virgin* for the hospice at Villeneuve-lès-Avignon. · First printed book in Europe - Gutenberg's *Bible*.
1455-58	· *Tomb of Carlo Marsuppini* in Santa Croce in Florence by Desiderio da Settignano.
1455-60	· (about) Bronze statue of *Judith and Holofernes* by Donatello. · (about) Filippo Lippi 's *Madonna and Child with two angels*, now in the Uffizi.
1456	· Fresco of *Monument to Niccolò da Tolentino* in Florence cathedral by Andrea del Castagno. · Leon Battista Alberti completes the facade of the church of Santa Maria Novella in Florence.
1456-60	· Andrea Mantegna paints the *San Zeno Altarpiece* in Verona.
1459	· Pius II Piccolomini commissions Bernardo Rossellino to design the new city of Pienza.
1459-60	· Benozzo Gozzoli paints the frescoes of *Journey of the Magi* in the Medici Chapel.
1460	· Piero della Francesca executes the *Flagellation* in Urbino.
1461	· In Ferrara Taddeo Crivelli, Franco de' Russi, Marco dell'Avogadro and Giorgio d'Alemagna complete the decoration of the *Borso d'Este Bible*.
1463	· (about) Piero della Francesca paints the fresco of the *Resurrection* in the Palazzo Communale of Borgo San Sepolcro (Arezzo).
1464-72	· Luciano Laurana builds the Ducal Palace in Urbino for Federico da Montefeltro.
1465	· (about) Giovanni Bellini paints the *Presentation in the Temple* in the Galleria Querini-Stampalia.

CHRONOLOGY

· Giovanni Bellini executes the *San Vincenzo Ferreri Altarpiece* for the church of Santi Giovanni e Paolo in Venice.
· Piero della Francesca paints *Portraits of Federico da Montefeltro and of Battista Sforza.*

1465-70
· (about) Antonello da Messina begins his career as a portraitist with his *Portrait of a man* in Cefalù.

1465-74
· Andrea Mantegna carries out the fresco decoration in the Bridal Chamber in the Ducal Palace in Mantua.

1466
· The first "nocturnal" painting in Italy: the *Dream of Constantine* frescoed by Piero della Francesca in his *Legend of the True Cross* cycle in the church of San Francesco in Arezzo.

1469-71
· Francesco del Cossa and Ercole de' Roberti assist in the decoration of Palazzo Schifanoia in Ferrara.

1470-73
· Giovanni Bellini paints the *Pesaro Altarpiece.*

1471
· The Flemish painter Justus of Ghent enters the service of Federico da Montefeltro, duke of Urbino.

1472-74
· Piero della Francesca paints the *Sacra conversazione* now in the Brera.

1473
· Martin Schongauer paints the *Virgin of the Rose-garden* for the church of San Martino a Colmar (Alsace).

1474-75
· The young Leonardo paints an angel and a landscape for the *Baptism of Christ* (Uffizi). while in Verrocchio's workshop.

1475
· Giovanni Bellini meets Antonello da Messina.

1477
· Melozzo da Forlì paints the fresco of *Sixtus IV appoints Platina to the Vatican Library.*
· The Spanish painter Pedro Berruguete arrives in Urbino

1449-53
· Quarta e ultima fase della Guerra dei Cent'anni iniziata nel 1337; formazione in Francia dello stato nazionale.

1477-89
· Francesco di Giorgio Martini in the service of Federico da Montefeltro in Urbino.
· The German painter and sculptor Veit Stoss carves the large wooden altarpiece for the church of Santa Maria in Cracow.

1478
· (about) Sandro Botticelli paints the *Primavera.*
· Andrea del Verrocchio carves the *Woman with a bunch of flowers.*

1479
· Gentile Bellini travels to Constantinopole to paint the *Portrait of Mohamed II.*

1480
· (about) Giuliano da Sangallo begins work on the villa at Poggio a Caiano for Lorenzo the Magnificent.
· The Tyrolean painter Michael Pacher completes the altar of St Wolfgang for the sanctuary of the same name in Salzburg.

1481
· Leonardo receives the commission for the *Adoration of the Magi* which is left unfinished when he moves to Milan.

1481-84
· Sixtus IV engages Perugino, Botticelli, Ghirlandaio, Cosimo Rosselli and others on the decoration of the walls of the Sistine Chapel.

1482
· Bramante directs the building of the church of Santa Maria presso San Satiro in Milan.
· Leonardo enters the service of the Sforza.

1482-86
· Ghirlandaio frescoes the Sassetti Chapel in the church of Santa Trinita, in Florence, with *Scenes from the life of St Francis.*

1483
· The *Adoration of the shepherds* by Hugo Van der Goes arrives in Florence from Ghent.
· Leonardo paints the *Virgin of the Rocks.*

1456
· Andrea del Castagno affresca il *Monumento a Niccolò da Tolentino* nel duomo di Firenze.
· Gutenberg stampa la *Bibbia*, prima opera tipografica d'Europa.
· (circa) A Firenze Leon Battista Alberti porta a termine la facciata di Santa Maria Novella.

1484-85
· Filippino Lippi completes the fresco cycle begun by Masolino and Masaccio in the church of the Carmine in Florence.

1485
· (about) Sandro Botticelli paints the *Birth of Venus.*
· Giuliano da Maiano builds the Porta Capuana in Naples.
· Henry VII, founder of Tudor dynasty, ascends throne of England.
· Niccolò dell'Arca makes the terracotta group of the *Lamentation* for Santa Maria della Vita in Bologna.

1486-90
· Domenico Ghirlandaio paints the frescoes in the choir of Santa Maria Novella in Florence of *Scenes from the life of the Virgin.*

1488
· Giovanni Bellini paints the *Frari Triptych.*

1488-90
· Michelangelo assists in the workshop of Ghirlandaio.

1489
· Benedetto da Maiano and Cronaca begin building Palazzo Strozzi in Florence.

1490-95
· Pinturicchio frescoes the Borgia apartment in the Vatican.

1491-92
· Michelangelo carves the *Battle of the Centaurs.*

1493
· Antonio Pollaiuolo makes the tomb of Sixtus IV in St Peter's.

1494
· Michelangelo carves the figures of St Petronius, St Procolus and of an angel for the *Arca of San Domenico* a Bologna.

1495
· Leonardo da Vinci begins his fresco of the *Last Supper* in the refectory of the church of Santa Maria delle Grazie in Milan.
· Botticelli recreates the painting described by the Greek writer Luciano: *Calumny.*
· Perugino paints *Apollo and Marsyas*, recently interpreted as *Apollo and Daphne.*

1496
· Michelangelo carves a *Cupid* which is then sold as a

classical statue and begins work on his *Bacchus*, now in the Bargello.

1497-98	· Luca Signorelli frescoes the cloister of Monte Oliveto Maggiore, near Siena.
1499	· Michelangelo receives the contract for the *Pietà* in St Peter's. · Andrea Mantegna paints the *Dead Christ*, now in the Brera (Milan)
1501	· Leonardo exhibits his cartoon of the *Virgin and Child with St Anne* in the cloister of Santissima Annunziata in Florence.
1501-04	· Michelangelo carves the *David* in Florence.
1502	· Donato Bramante begins the tempietto in the cloister of San Pietro in Montorio in Rome. · Mauro Codussi begins the Palazzo Vendramin-Calergi in Venice, the first private Renaissance palace in Venice.
1502-07	· Vittore Carpaccio paints the *Lives of the Dalmatian Saints*, *St George*, *St Jerome* and *St Tryphon* for the School of San Giorgio degli Schiavoni, in Venice.
1502-08	· In Siena Cathedral Pinturicchio paints the frescoes in the Chapel of San Giovanni Battista and the *Scenes from the life of Pius II* in the Piccolomini Library with the help of the young Raphael.
1503	· Sodoma is commissioned to paint a fresco cycle in the refectory of the monastery of Sant'Anna in Camprena (Pienza). · In Vienna Lucas Cranach paints the *Crucifixion*, now in the Alte Pinakothek (Munich).
1503-04	· In Bois-Le-Due Hieronymus Bosch paints the *Triptych of the Garden of Early delights*, his most famous work, now in the Prado (Madrid).
1503-05	· In Florence Leonardo paints the *Mona Lisa*, now in the Louvre (Paris).
1503-06	· In Florence Leonardo drew the cartoon for the *Battle of Anghiari*, for the fresco in the Great Council Hall of Palazzo Vecchio.
1503-09	· In Vigevano (Padua) the tapestry maker Benedetto da Milano wove the tapestries of the *Months* for Gian Giacomo Trivulzio, on cartoons by Bramantino.
1504	· Michelangelo, Leonardo and Raphael are all in Florence. · In Nuremburg Albrecht Dürer paints the *Adoration of the Magi*, now in the Uffizi (Florence). · Raphael executes the *Betrothal of the Virgin* for the Chapel Albizzini in the church of San Francesco in Città di Castello (Perugia), now in the Brera (Milan). · In Florence Michelangelo paints the Holy Family, known as *Doni Tondo*, now in the Uffizi.
1504-05	· Giorgione executes the *Castelfranco Altarpiece* for the church of San Liberale in Castelfranco Veneto.
1504-06	· In Florence Michelangelo draws the cartoon for the

Battle of Cascina, for the fresco in the Great Council Hall of Palazzo Vecchio.

1505	· Michelangelo receives the commission for the tomb of Julius II destined for the tribune of St Peter's. · Bramante designs the courtyard of the Belvedere in the Vatican for Julius II. · In Venice Giovanni Bellini paints the *San Zaccaria Altarpiece* for the church of the same name.
1505-06	· In Florence Raphael paints the *Madonna of the Goldfinch* (Uffizi) for the wedding of Lorenzo Nasi.
1506	· In Florence Raphael paints the *Portrait of Agnolo Doni* together with the *Portrait of Maddalena Strozzi*, his wife, now in the Uffizi. · In Treviso Lorenzo Lotto paints the *Penitent St Jerome* for Bishop Bernardo de' Rossi, now in the Louvre. · In Venice Dürer finishes the *Feast of the Rosary* the church of the German community, San Bartolomeo a Rialto, now in the National Gallery of Prague. · The statue of the *Laocoon* is discovered in the Domus Aurea in Rome. · Leonardo leaves Florence for Milan and Michelangelo is called to Rome to work for Pope Julius II.
1506-08	· Lorenzo Lotto paints the large *Recanati Polyptych* for the church of San Domenico there.
1506-14	· Bramante works on rebuilding St Peter's in the Vatican.
1506-26	· Michele Sanmicheli is head of the Cathedral works in Orvieto.
1507	· In Nuremburg Albrecht Dürer paints the panels of *Adam and Eve*, now in the Prado (Madrid).
1507-08	· Giorgione paints the frescoes on the German Exchange building on the Grand Canal in Venice, with the help of Titian.
1507-10	· In Venice Giorgione paints the *Tempesta*, now in the Accademia.
1508	· Sebastiano del Piombo paints the organ doors for the church of San Bartolomeo a Rialto in Venice, now in the Accademia.
1508-11	· Raphael paints the frescoes in the Stanza della Segnatura in the Vatican Palaces: the *Disputation on the Sacrament*, the *School of Athens*, *Parnassus and the Virtues*.
1508-12	· Michelangelo begins painting the ceiling of the Sistine Chapel in the Vatican.
1509	· Andrea del Sarto begins the frescoes of the *Scenes from the Life of St Filippo Benizzi* in the cloister of Santissima Annunziata in Florence. In 1514 he frescoes the scenes of the *Life of Mary*.
1509-11	· Baldassarre Peruzzi builds the Villa Farnesina in Rome for Agostino Chigi.
1511	· Sebastiano del Piombo assists in the decoration of the Villa Farnesina in Rome.

CHRONOLOGY

1511
· (about) In Venice Titian paints the *Fête Champêtre*, now in the Louvre (Paris).

1511-14
· Raphael frescoes the Stanza di Eliodoro in the Vatican Palaces.

1511-15
· Sebastiano del Piombo paints the *Death of Adonis*, now in the Uffizi (Florence).

1511-16
· Mathias Grünewald paints the large Isenheim altarpiece with three panels for the church of the hospital of St Anthony in Germany, now in the Unterlinden museum in Colmar.

1512
· In Florence Fra' Bartolomeo della Porta paints the *Mystic marriage of St Catherine*, now in Palatine gallery of the Pitti, which shows the influence of Raphael, Michelangelo and Leonardo.

1512
· (about) In Florence Jacopo Sansovino sculpts the *Bacchus*, now in the Bargello.

1513
· (about) Romanino executes the *Santa Giustina Altarpiece* for the church of the same name in Padua, now in the Museo Civico.
· Raphael paints the *Triumph of Galatea* in the loggia of the Farnesina in Rome.

1513-15
· In Rome Michelangelo carves the statues of the *Dying slave* and of the *Rebel slave*, now in the Louvre (Paris), and the figure of *Moses*, according to the second project devised for the *Funerary Monument to Julius II*.

1513-16
· Raphael directs the building of the Chapel Chigi in Santa Maria del Popolo in Rome.

1514
· In Rome Raphael paints the *Madonna della seggiola*, now in the Palatine gallery (Florence).
· Raphael begins the frescoes in the Stanza dell'Incendio in the Vatican Palaces, which are finished by his assistants.
· Dosso Dossi begins working at the d'Este court in Ferrara, where he paints mythological subjects and others inspired by Ariosto.
· Leo X entrusts Raphael with the direction of the building of St Peter's in the Vatican, first in collaboration with Giuliano da Sangallo, and then with Antonio da Sangallo the Younger.

1514-15
· Raphael writes his famous letter to Leo X, lamenting the state of the classical remains in the city.

1515
· In Venice Titian paints *Sacred and Profane Love*, now in the Borghese Gallery (Rome).
· In Siena Domenico Beccafumi paints the altarpiece of the *Stigmate of St Catherine*, now in the Pinacoteca.

1515-16
· In Rome Raphael draws the cartoons for the tapestries of the *Acts of the Apostles*, woven in Brussels by Pieter Van Aelst and destined for the walls of the Sistine Chapel in the Vatican.

1516
· Pontormo and Rosso Fiorentino work together on the decoration of the Chiostrino dei Voti in the Church of Santissima Annunziata in Florence.
· In Florence Michelangelo, is commissioned by Leo X, to design a facade for the church of San Lorenzo, but it is never built.
· The Spanish painter Alonso Berruguete works in Italy, where he paints his *Madonna and Child*, now in the Palazzo Vecchio (Florence).

1516-18
· Titian paints the *Assumption* for the church of Santa Maria Gloriosa dei Frari in Venice.

1485
· Giuliano da Maiano costruisce porta Capuana a Napoli.
· Regna in Inghilterra Enrico VII, capostipite della dinastia Tudor.
· (circa) Sandro Botticelli realizza la *Nascita di Venere*.
· (dopo) Niccolò dell'Arca modella il gruppo in terracotta del *Compianto sul Cristo morto* per Santa Maria della Vita a Bologna.

1517
· In Florence Andrea del Sarto paints his most celebrated work, the *Madonna of the Harpies*, now in the Uffizi.

1517-18
· Raphael designs the Villa Madama in Rome for Cardinal Giuliano de' Medici.

1517-24
· Gaudenzio Ferrari works on the decoration of the chapels in the sanctuary of the Sacro Monte di Varallo (Vercelli).

1518
· Pontormo paints la *Pucci Altarpiece* for the church of San Michele Visdomini in Florence.
· Rosso Fiorentino paints the *Madonna and Child with Saints*, now in the Uffizi (Florence).
· Pontormo paints the panels with Scenes from the Life of Joseph, commissioned by Pier Francesco Borgherini for his wedding chamber, now in the National Gallery (London).

1518-20
· In Rome Raphael paints the *Transfiguration* for Cardinal Giulio de' Medici, in the Vatican Picture gallery.

1519
· Correggio paints the ceiling of the mother superior's bedroom in the convent of San Paolo in Parma.

1519-34
· Michelangelo builds and decorates the New Sacristy in the church of San Lorenzo in Florence.

1520
· Giulio Romano takes over in Raphael's workshop: he paints the frescoes in the Sala di Costantino in the Vatican Palaces, assisted by other artists from Raphael's milieu.

1520-21
· Pontormo frescoes the Salone of the villa di Poggio a Caiano (Florence) with the lunette of *Vertumnus and Pomona*.

1520-22
· Correggio frescoes the spectacular *Vision of St John on Patmos* in the dome of the church of San Giovanni Evangelista in Parma.
· Titian paints the *Averoldi Polittico* for the church of Santi Nazzaro e Celso in Brescia.

1521
· Rosso Fiorentino paints the *Deposition* in Volterra, now in the Pinacoteca Comunale.

1521-24
· Romanino paints the *Raising of Lazarus* for the Chapel in the church of San Giovanni Evangelista in Brescia.

1523	· Rosso Fiorentino paints the *Betrothal of the Virgin* for the church di San Lorenzo in Florence and *Moses defending the daughters of Jethro*, now in the Uffizi (Florence).
1523-25	· (about) Pontormo paints the cycle of the *Scenes of the Passion* in the Certosa at Galluzzo (Florence).
1523-27	· Rosso Fiorentino moves to Rome. The most important work of this period is his *Dead Christ* (1525-26), in the Museum of Fine Arts (Boston).
1523-40	· Benvenuto Cellini in Rome.
1524	· In Trescore (Bergamo), Lorenzo Lotto frescoes the Suardi Oratory with *Scenes from the lives of St Bridget of Ireland, St Catherine of Siena and St Barbara*. · Parmigianino frescoes the bathroom of Paola Gonzaga in the Rocca di Fontanellato (Parma) with *Scenes from Diana and Actaeon*. · Lorenzo Lotto paints the *Mystic Marriage of St Catherine*, now in the Accademia Carrara in Bergamo.
1524-34	· In Florence Michelangelo works on the New Sacristy in San Lorenzo. · In Florence building proceeds on the Laurentian Library, designed by Michelangelo in the cloister of San Lorenzo in Florence.
1524-35	· Giulio Romano builds the Palazzo del Te in Mantua for Federico II Gonzaga.
1525	· *Prose della volgar lingua* by Pietro Bembo is published in Venice. · Mathias Grünewald paints for Cardinal Albert of Brandenburg the *Meeting between St Erasmus and St Maurice*, for the collegiate church of Halle an der Saale now in the Alte Pinakothek (Munich). · In Siena Domenico Beccafumi paints the *Fall of the Rebel Angels*, now in the Pinacoteca.
1526-28	· Pontormo paints one of the masterpieces of early Mannerism, the altarpiece with the *Deposition*, for the altar of the Capponi Chapel in Santa Felicita in Florence.
1527-28	· In Mantua Giulio Romano frescoes the Cupid and Psyche Room in the Palazzo Te.
1528-29	· Pontormo paints the large altarpiece of the *Visitation* for the church of San Michele in Carmignano.
1529	· In Wittenberg (Germany) Lucas Cranach the Elder paints the *Portraits of Luther and his wife Catherine*, now in the Uffizi (Florence). · In Ratisbon (Baveria) Albrecht Altdorfer executes the *Battle of Issus* for William IV of Bavaria, now in the Alte Pinakothek (Munich).
1529-32	· Gaudenzio Ferrari paints the fresco cycle of Episodes from the Life of the Magdalene and of the Virgin for the church of San Cristoforo a Vercelli.
1530	· In Bologna Titian paints a *Portrait of Charles V*, and begins his career as a portraitist at the Imperial court. · Rosso Fiorentino, after moving to France, becomes one of the leading painters of the "school of Fontainebleau".
	· Correggio paints la *Madonna della scodella*, now in the Galleria Nazionale di Parma.
1530-32	· Correggio paints the *Danae* for Federico Gonzaga, duke of Mantua, now in the Borghese Gallery (Rome).
1530-34	· Michelangelo carves the *Prisoners* (Accademia, Florence) for the monument of Julius II.
1531	· Francesco Salviati and Giorgio Vasari move to Rome the Sack by the Imperial troops, contributing to the reconstruction of the artistic milieu in the city.
1531-32	· Dosso Dossi executes a fresco of cycles frescoes in the castle del Buonconsiglio in Trento.
1533	· Jacopo Sansovino directs the building of the Palazzo Corner in Venice.
1533-34	· Dosso Dossi paints his *St Michael fighting with the devil*.
1534	· (about) Polidoro da Caravaggio paints the Way to Calvary for the church of Santissima Annunziata dei Catalani in Messina, now in Capodimonte (Naples). · Baccio Bandinelli sculpts the group of *Hercules and Caccus* which stands in Piazza della Signoria in Florence. · Rosso Fiorentino begins his decoration of the gallery in the chateau at Fontainebleau.
1534-37	· Gaudenzio Ferrari paints the dome of the sanctuary in Saronno (Varese) with the *Assumption of the Virgin*.
1534-40	· The *Madonna with the long neck*, now in the Uffizi (Florence), completes the stylistic development of Parmigianino after the Roman years.
1534-49	· Pontificate of Paul III Farnese.
1536	· Hans Holbein the Younger becomes the official English court painter. · Francis I takes arms against Spain for the control of Lombardy.
1536-41	· Michelangelo frescoes the wall behind the high altar in the Sistine Chapel with the *Last Judgment*.
1537-40	· In Venice Sebastiano Serlio publishes the first part of his architectural treatise: *Trattato di architettura*.
1537-45	· Jacopo Sansovino designs and starts work on the new Piazza San Marco in Venice.
1538	· Titian paints the *Venus of Urbino* for Guidobaldo della Rovere, duke of Urbino, now in the Uffizi (Florence).
1539-43	· Michelangelo begins his rebuilding of piazza del Campidoglio, which is finished after his death in 1564.
1540	· Francesco Primaticcio takes over from Rosso Fiorentino in the decoration of Fontainebleau, working in the Ulyssees Gallery and in the ball room.
1540-43	· Benvenuto Cellini makes the gold and enamel *Salt* for Francis I di France, originally begun for Ippolito d'Este, and which is now in the Kunsthistorisches Museum (Vienna).

CHRONOLOGY

1540-45
· Benvenuto Cellini works for Francis I in Fontainebleau.
· The Spanish painter and sculptor Alonso Berruguete, in the service of Charles V, carves the polychrome group of the *Transfiguration* for the cathedral of Toledo.

1540-46
· In the service of the Medici from 1539, Bronzino frescoes the private Chapel of Eleonora of Toledo in Palazzo Vecchio in Florence.

1542-45
· Michelangelo paints the frescoes of the *Conversion of St Paul* and the *Crucifixion of St Peter* in the Pauline Chapel in the Vatican.

1545-54
· Benvenuto Cellini executes the *Perseus*, which is placed in the Loggia dei Lanzi in Piazza della Signoria in Florence.

1545-54
· In Rome Titian paints the celebrated *Portrait of Paul III Farnese and his nephews Ottavio and Alessandro Farnese*, now in the Museo di Capodimonte (Naples).

1546-64
· Michelangelo directs the building of St Peter's in the Vatican.

1548
· Titian paints his *Equestrian portrait of Charles V*, now in the Prado (Madrid).
· Tintoretto paints his *Miracle of St Mark*, for the Confraternity, or Scuola Grande, of the Saint in Venice, now in the Accademia.

1550
· In Florence Vasari publishes the first edition of his Lives: *Vite de' più eccellenti Architetti, Pittori, et Scultori italiani, da Cimabue insino a' giorni nostri*.

1551
· In Antwerp, the Flemish painter Aersten paints the *Butcher*, and attests to the rising popularity of still-life.

1552-64
· Michelangelo executes the *Pietà Rondanini*, now in the Castello Sforzesco (Milan).

1553
· Veronese begins his decoration of three rooms in the Ducal Palace in Venice.

1555-59
· Andrea Palladio oversees the building of the Villa Barbaro at Maser (Treviso).

1556
· With the help of various painters Vasari began the decoration of the apartments in Palazzo Vecchio in Florence for the Grand-Duke Cosimo I.

1557
· After he travels in France and Italy, the first signed and dated paintings by Pieter Bruegel the Elder appear in Antwerp.

1560
· In Florence Vasari begins work on the Uffizi, and the building is finished some twenty years later.

1560-77
· Bartolomeo Ammannati trasforms Palazzo Pitti in Florence into the suburban villa of the Medici, and creates a large courtyard with the three orders at the back.

1561-70
· Veronese paints the illusionist frescoes at Villa Barbaro at Maser (Treviso) and Alessandro Vittoria works on the stucco decoration.

1562
· Pieter Bruegel the Elder paints the *Triumph of Death*, now in the Prado (Madrid).

1562-63
· Paolo Veronese paints the *Wedding feast at Cana* for the church of San Giorgio Maggiore in Venice, now in the Louvre (Paris).

1562-66
· Tintoretto paints *Finding the body of St Mark San Marco* for the Confraternity, or Scuola Grande, of the Saint in Venice, now in the Brera (Milan).

1563
· Building begins on the Palazzo dei Conservatori in Piazza del Campidoglio in Rome, o Michelangelo's design.
· Juan de Toledo begins building the Escorial, in Madrid, in the Renaissance style, is continued by Juan de Herrera in 1567.

1563-72
· Vasari supervises the decoration of the Salone dei Cinquecento in Palazzo Vecchio in Florence.

1563-75
· In Florence Bartolomeo Ammannati builds the *Neptune Fountain* in Piazza della Signoria.

1564
· (about) Giambologna executes the small bronze statue of *Mercury*, now in the Bargello (Florence).

1564-87
· Tintoretto paints the Scuola Grande of San Rocco in Venice: the decoration is carried out in several stages.

1565
· In Florence Vasari takes only five months to build the Vasari corridor connecting Palazzo Vecchio to Palazzo Pitti.

1567-76
· The Flemish artist Jan Van der Straet, known as Stradano, draws the cartoons for a series of tapestries depicting hunting scenes for the Villa Medici at Poggio a Caiano. (Florence).

1568
· In Brussels Pieter Bruegel the Elder paints *The Parable of the Blind*, now in the Galleria Nazionale di Capodimonte (Naples).

1570-72
· (about) Andrea Palladio plans and builds the Villa Rotonda, near Vicenza.

1570-75
· The studiolo of Francesco I de' Medici in Palazzo Vecchio in Florence is decorated by the major artists of the Medici court: Vasari, Giambologna, Stradano, Allori, Santi di Tito and others.

1573
· Veronese paints the *Feast in the house of Levi*, for the refectory of the monastery of Santi Giovanni e Paolo in Venice, now in the Accademia.
· Giorgio Vasari decorates his Florentine house and also produces the *Painter's studio*.

1574-80
· Giambologna carves the *Rape of the Sabines* for the Loggia dei Lanzi in Florence.

1575-80
· Paolo Veronese paints the *Finding of Moses* now in the Prado (Madrid).

1577
· Andrea Palladio begins building the Church of the Redentore on the island of the Giudecca in Venice.

1579-80	· Palladio designs and directs the building of the Teatro Olimpico in Vicenza, which is completed by Vincenzo Scamozzi.
1583-87	· Tintoretto paints the *Annunciation* for the lower room of the Scuola Grande di San Rocco in Venice.
1586-88	· El Greco paints the *Burial of the Count of Orgaz* for the church di San Tomé in Toledo.
1586-94	· Pellegrino Tibaldi assists in the decoration of the Escorial Palace in Madrid.

INDEX OF ARTISTS

The artists cited in this book are listed in alphabetical order. Normal numbers refer to citations in the text; italic numbers refer to illustrations; bold numbers refer to Masterpieces.

A

Agostino di Duccio 35, *141, 247*
Alberti, Leon Battista 32, *32,* 33, *33,* **34**, *36,* 37, 279, 284, 285
Altdorfer, Albrecht 374, 375, 376, *376*
Andrea del Castagno, Andrea di Bartolo di Simone detto 98, *98, 99, 148,* 152, *152,* 180
Andrea del Sarto *239,* **274**, 325, 366, 370
Antonello da Messina 162, *162,* 163, **164**, 179, 180, 188, *188,* 189, *189,* 331, 339
Arcimboldo, Giuseppe *369, 383, 383*
Aspertini, Amico 366

B

Barocci, Federico 278
Bassano, Jacopo, Jacopo da Ponte, 393, 398, 406, 410, *410*
Bellini, Giovanni, Giambellino 179, *179,* 180, *180,* 181, **182**, 184, *184,* 185, *185,* **186**, 188, 189, *189,* 327, 338, *338,* 339, *339,* 340, *340,* 341, 357, 359
Bellini, Jacopo 179, 183
Bellini, workshop 179
Benedetto da Maiano 37, *42,* 226
Bernini, Gian Lorenzo 319
Bertoldo di Giovanni 226, *226*
Bonifacio de Pitati *393,* 397, 410
Bordone, Paris 397
Bosch, Hieronymus 374, 377, *377,* **378**
Botticelli, Sandro Filipepi detto 160, *160,* 161, *193,* 194, 196, *196, 197,* **198**, 199, *202,* 203, 204, *204,* 205, *205,* 206, 210, 211
Bramante, Donato di Pascuccio di Antonio 152, 220, *220,* 273, 278, *278,* 279, *279,* 280, *281,* 282, *282,* 285, 286, 287, 293, 297, 315, 319, 321, 322, 323, *323,* 325, 386
Bruegel, Peter I 374
Brunelleschi, Filippo 15, 16, 18, *18, 19,* 20, *20, 21,* **22**, 24, 25, *25,* 32, 36, 38, *38,* 53, 54, 55, 57, 62, 81, 101, 174, 265, 284
Bugiardini, Giuliano *273*

C

Carpaccio, Vittore 359
Catena, Vincenzo *412*
Cellini, Benvenuto 254, 382, *382*
Christus, Petrus *101,* 118, *118*
Cima da Conegliano, Giovan Battista Cima 179
Cort, Cornelis 275
Cossa, Francesco del *171, 173*
Cranach, Lucas I, 366, *375,* 376
Cristofano dell'Altissimo 273
Cronaca, Simone del Pollaiolo detto 37

D

Dalmau, Luis *137*
Daniele da Volterra, Daniele Ricciarelli, 384, 390
De' Pasti, Matteo 34, 35
Della Porta, Giacomo 386
Della Quercia, Jacopo 63, 219
Della Robbia, Andrea 22
Della Robbia, Luca 22, 46, *46, 47, 47,* 48, 49, *50,* 51, 146, *146*
De' Roberti, Ercole 172, 173, *173*
Desiderio da Settignano 78, 79, *79,* 142, 146, *146*
Domenico Veneziano, Domenico di Bartolomeo 86
Donatello, Donato di Niccolò di Betto Bardi 15, 16, 17, *17,* 38, *38, 39,* 40, 41, *41,* 42, 46, 49, *50,* 54, 62, 62, 63, *63,* 65, 78, 135, *142, 143, 143,* 144, *145,* 214, 219, 226
Dondi, Ludovico *153*
Dosio, Giovanantonio *280*

D (cont.)

Dürer, Albrecht **274**, 358, *358,* 359, *359,* **360**, 364, *364,* 365, 366, *366,* 367, 370, 372, 374, 375, 376

E

El Greco, Domenikos Theotokopoulos, *397, 397*

F

Fra Angelico, Guido di Pietro 64, *64,* 68, *68, 69,* 70, 71, *71,* **72**, 76, 86, 112, *112,* 150, *150*
Ferrari, Gaudenzio 366
Filarete, Antonio Averulino (o Averlino) 284
Fontainebleau, school 369, 382
Fra Giocondo, Monsignori Giovanni 243, 323

G

Ghiberti, Lorenzo 20, 24, *24,* 46, 49, 63, 64, 65, *65,* 66, 67, 76, 78
Ghirlandaio, Domenico, Domenico Bigordi 132, *132, 148, 149,* 194, *195,* 211, 213, 217, *217, 218,* 219, 226
Giorgione, Giorgio da Castelfranco detto 180, 327, *327,* 328, *328,* 329, *329,* 330, 331, *331,* 332, *332, 333,* **334**, 335, 338, 339, 341, 342, 343, 346, 347, 355, 356, 357, 366, 376
Giotto 57, *57,* 219, *219,* 239
Gozzoli, Benozzo 76, 77, *77*
Grünewald, Matthias, Mathis Gothart Nithart 374, *374,* 375, *375*
Guadagnini 179

H

Holbein the Younger, Hans 374
Huguet, Jaime 404, 412

J

Jacopino del Conte 384, 390, *391*
Jules Romain 384, 390, 391
Juste de Gand (or Joost van Wassenhove) 111

L

Leonardo da Vinci *141,* 174, *174,* 175, 176, *176, 177, 177,* 193, 205, 212, *212,* 213, *213,* 214, 216, *216,* 220, *220,* 221, *221,* 222, 239, 240, *240,* 241, *241,* 242, *242,* 243, *243,* 244, 244, *245, 245,* 246, 254, 255, 256, *256,* 257, 258, 263, 273, 284, 285, 296, 321, 328, 329
Leonardo de Vinci, school *255*
Limbourg, brothers 124
Lippi, Filippino 56, 131, 194, 206, *206, 207*
Lippi, Filippo 76, 131, *150,* 206
Lorenzetto, Lorenzo Lotti 319
Lorenzo di Credi 205, 216
Lorenzo Monaco, Pietro di Giovanni 68
Lotto, Lorenzo 356, *365,* 366
Lucas de Leyden 370

M

Master of (Robert Campin) 112, 118, 121, *121,* 122, *122*
Mantegna, Andrea *15, 16, 17,* 26, *26,* **28**, 29, 135, 153, *153,* 154, *154, 155,* 156, 157, 173, 179, 180, 182, 184, 186, 359
Martini, Francesco di Giorgio 175, *175,* 284
Masaccio, Tommaso di ser Giovanni Cassai 15, 16, *17,* 54, *54,* 56, *56,* 57, *57,* **58**, 60, *60,* 61, 64, 68, 71, 84, 142, **219**, 226
Masolino da Panicale, Tommaso di Cristoforo Fini 56, 57, *57,* 60, *61*
Melozzo da Forlì, Melozzo degli Ambrosi 210, *210*
Memling, Hans 101, 118, *118, 124*
Metsys, Quentin *130*
Michelangelo Buonarroti 65, 193, 210, 212, 213, *213,* 219, *219,* 226, *226,* 228, *228,* 229, 230, *230,* **234**, 235, 239, *239,* 246, *246,* 247, *247,* 248, *248,* 249, *249,* **250**, 254, 257, *257,* 258, 259, 262, 264, *264,* 265, *265,* 266, 267, 270, *270,* 271, *271,* 272, 273, 277, *277,* 285, 286, 287, *287,* **288**, 290, *291, 292,* 293, 296, 312, 317, 321, 323, *323,* 324, 325, 346, 347, *384,* 385, *385,* 386, *386,* 387, *387,* **388**, 390, 395, 398
Michelozzo di Bartolomeo 36, *36,* 71, 76, *76, 144,* 194, 270, 284
Mino da Fiesole 78, *142,* 143, *143*

N

Nanni di Banco 46, 49
Niccolò dell'Arca, Niccolò da Bari 288

P

Palladio, Andrea, Andrea della Gondola 285, 393, *393*, 404,
406, 412, 413, *413*, 414, 415, *416*, *417*, 418, *418*, *419*, **420**,
421
Pacher, Michael 134, *134*, 135, *135*
Palma il Vecchio, Jacopo Negretti 356, *356*
Parmigianino, Francesco Mazzola 397, 404
Penni, Gian Francesco 309
Perin del Vaga, Pietro Bonaccorsi 390
Perugino, Pietro Vannucci 53, *149*, 168, *168*, *169*, 170, *170*,
194, 195, 205, 210, 211, 216, 258
Peruzzi, Baldassare 277, 285, 317, *317*, 321, *321*, 322, *322*,
323
Piero della Francesca 84, *84*, 85, 86, 87, *87*, 88, 89, **90**, 94,
139, 162, 168, 169, 173, 175, *175*, 179, 180, 188
Piero di Cosimo *193*, 194, *195*, 205, 211
Pinturicchio, Bernardino di Betto 210, 211, 258
Pisanello, Antonio Pisano *53*
Pisano, Andrea 24, 65
Pisano, Giovanni 219
Pisano, Nicola 228
Pollaiolo, Antonio Benci 210, 214, 219
Pontelli, Baccio 210, *210*
Pontormo, Jacopo Carucci 366, 370, *370*, *371*, 372, *372*
Pordenone, Giovanni Antonio de' Sacchis 397, 410
Primaticcio, Francesco Primaticcio 382

Q

Quarton, Enguerrand 139, *139*

R

Rainaldi, Carlo 386
Raffaellino del Colle 309
Raphael, Raffaello Sanzio 210, 239, *239*, 250, 258, *258*, *259*,
259, **260**, 262, *262*, 263, *263*, 272, **274**, 277, *277*, 285, 286,
293, *293*, 294, *294*, *295*, **296**, 300, *300*, 301, *301*, *302*, 303,
303, *304*, 305, *305*, **306**, 308, *308*, 309, *309*, *311*, *312*, 313,
313, 314, *314*, 315, *315*, *316*, 317, 319, 320, *320*, 321, 323,
324, 346, 386, 390
Raphael, school 311
Rosselli, Cosimo 211
Rossellino, Antonio 78, *78*, 79, 142, 143
Rossellino, Bernardo 78, *78*, 144, *145*, 146, *146*
Rosso Fiorentino, Giovanni Battista di Jacopo 370, 382,
390
Rubens, Peter Paul 255

S

Salviati, Francesco *369*, 384, 390, *390*, 394, 397
Sangallo, Antonio da, the Younger 321, 322, 323, 325, 386
Sangallo, Antonio da, the Older 285, 322, 325
Sangallo, Aristotile da 257
Sangallo, Giuliano da 37, 284, 285
Sanmicheli, Michele 285, 393, 412
Sano di Pietro 131
Sansovino, Andrea, Andrea Contucci 325
Sansovino, Jacopo, Jacopo Tatti 274, 321, 325, *325*, 393,
398, 404, 412
Santi, Giovanni 258
Scamozzi, Vincenzo 414
Schongauer, Martin *134*
Sebastiano del Piombo, Sebastiano Luciani 317, 321, 324,
324, 339, 356, *356*, 357, *357*
Serlio, Sebastiano 285, 382, 412, 414
Signorelli, Luca *193*, 194, 210, 211, *211*, 258
Sluter, Claus 130
Sodoma, Giovanni Antonio Bazzi 317, *318*
Squarcione, Francesco 26

Stoss, Veit 134, 136, *136*

T

Tiziano Vecellio 180, 273, **275**, 327, *327*, 332, 340, 341, *341*,
342, *342*, 343, *343*, **344**, 346, *346*, 347, *347*, 348, *348*, 349,
349, **350**, 354, *354*, 355, *355*, 356, 357, 366, 376, 384, 393,
394, *394*, 395, *395*, 396, *396*, 397, 398, 406, 410
Tintoretto, Jacopo Robusti 275, 393, *393*, 398, *398*, 399,
399, **400**, 406, 410
Tura, Cosmè *172*, 173

U

Uccello, Paolo, Paolo di Dono 53, 80, *80*, *81*, **82**, 219

V

Van der Goes, Hugo *110*, 111, *111*, 132, *132*, 133, *133*
Van der Weiden, Rogier *102*, 103, 112, *112*, *113*, **114**, 118,
120, 123, *123*, 125, 139
Van Eyck, Jan 101, *101*, *103*, 104, *104*, 105, *105*, **106**, 112,
118, 119, *119*, 121, 126, *126*, *127*, 130, 139
Van Heemskerck, Maarten *282*
Vasari, Giorgio 216, 239, 241, 243, 247, 257, 260, 272, 273,
274, **275**, 314, 329, 338, 369, 384, 390, 394, 395, 396, 397,
398
Veronese, Paolo Caliari 393, 398, 399, 404, *404*, 405, **406**,
412, 414, 418
Verrocchio, Andrea di Francesco di Cione 168, 169, 205,
212, 214, *214*, *215*, 216, *216*, 226
Vignole, Jacopo Barozzi 285
Vivarini, workshop 179